Religious Lead
in Conflic

Journal of the European Society of Women in Theological Research

Revista de la asociación europea de mujeres para la investigación teológica

Jahrbuch der Europäischen Gesellschaft für theologische Forschung von Frauen

Volume 29

ESWTR

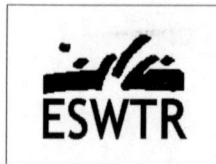

Bibliographical information and books for review in the Journal should be sent to:
Prof. Dr. Agnethe Siquans,
Universität Wien, Schenkenstraße 8-10, 1010 Wien, Austria

Articles for consideration for the Journal should be sent to:
Prof. Dr. Agnethe Siquans,
Universität Wien, Schenkenstraße 8-10, 1010 Wien, Austria

Religious Leadership of Women in Conflict and Crisis

Editors:
Agnethe Siquans, Anne-Claire Mulder,
Clara Carbonell Ortiz

PEETERS
LEUVEN – PARIS – BRISTOL, CT
2021

Journal of the European Society of Women
in Theological Research, 29

© 2021, Peeters Publishers, Leuven / Belgium
ISBN 978-90-429-4663-7
ISSN 1783-2454
eISSN 1783-2446
D/2021/0602/116
Cover design by Margret Omlin-Küchler

CONTENTS – INHALT – ÍNDICE

Journal of the European Society of Women in Theological Research 29 (2021) 1-8.
doi: 10.2143/ESWTR.29.0.3289658

Editorial

Theme: Religious Leadership of Women in Conflict and Crisis

The theme of the Journal of the ESWTR 2021 – "Religious Leadership of Women in Conflict and Crisis" – goes back to the ESWTR conference in Central and Eastern Europe in Lviv, Ukraine, in 2018. That conference dealt with the theme of the empowerment of women and with the ecumenical engagement with issues of peace and justice; a theme which originated in the situation of Ukraine, which has been a country of societal as well as military conflicts for many years now.

However, this situation of crisis is not limited to Ukraine. Conflicts and crises can be found all over the world: the corona crisis, the ecological crisis, the migration crisis, war, and terror. In many regions of the world, we find protracted tensions and conflicts due to poverty, racism, and violence against women. Churches and religious communities all over the world are affected by sexual and power abuse and inequality between the sexes.

At the same time, one can observe a growing engagement of women, precisely in these situations of conflict. Women take part in these movements, including religious ones, and with religious motivations. They thereby take up positions of leadership to explore new avenues, to search for creative approaches to deal with conflicts and to face new challenges. They take responsibility for others, take care for the community and for creation.

The contributions in this issue of the journal address this theme of religious leadership of women in conflict and crisis in very different manners. The text by *Oksana Kis* was first presented at the conference in Lviv. She looks back to the 1940s and 1950s when a substantial number of women were imprisoned in the Gulag on political grounds. In this situation, the women were left to their own devices, also in the performance of their religion. They organised and led liturgical meetings and feasts, always under the most difficult conditions. In this situation and in resistance to the Gulag-system, these women developed creativity, capacities to improvise, and leadership abilities.

Sytske Hofstee describes a historical example from the 16th and 17th centuries. When the Catholic Church in the Netherlands was repressed and official activities became impossible or dangerous, men and women offered resistance.

They worked together in secret to keep the religious and social life of Catholic people going. The author presents some of the women who took over different forms of leadership tasks in their historical, social, and religious contexts and offers an analysis of their labours.

Carol Dempsey OP presents the long history of female Dominicans in leadership positions in different domains of society over the world and in particular in the United States. She gives a retrospective of the beginning of the Order of the Dominicans and follows the traces of the engaged women from this Order and their versatile activities under ever-changing ecclesial and societal conditions into the present.

Friederike Eichhorn-Remmel explores the question: 'Is Mary suited for Rebellion?' She analyzes the contradictory constructions of Mary, which were broadcasted by different groups in the course of the debate around the (German) initiative 'Maria 2.0', as well as into their staging by the media and their effect. By referring back to the Magnificat in the Gospel of Luke, she is able to value and subsume these constructions critically.

Miscellanea

Elizabet Gurdus writes in her contribution about the ritual impurity of women in the tradition of the Russian-Orthodox Church, which marginalizes women and makes them invisible. She also explores the roots of the purity laws and the way they were (already) criticized in the texts of the Hebrew Bible and the New Testament. The traditional ritual purity prescriptions in the Russian-Orthodox Church are increasingly criticized from different sides, and a change is asked for.

Larissza Hrotkó presents Dvoyra Fogel, a Jewish writer who lived at the beginning of the 20th century in Lviv and Vienna. She was member of a movement which advocated the Yiddish language as an expression of Jewish identity. In this contribution, Hrotkó presents one of Fogel's poems in Yiddish as well as its stylistic formation.

Reviews

The last part of this journal is devoted to the review by Lene Sjørup of the first volume of the new series "ESWTR Studies in Religion". In this book 'The Wings of the Spirit', Julie Hopkins's occupies herself with the feminine symbolism in the early Christian, Syriac Pneumatology.

Agnethe Siquans is Professor for Old Testament Studies at the Faculty of Catholic Theology of the University of Vienna. agnethe.siquans@univie.ac.at

Clara Carbonell Ortiz is a PhD student at the University Complutense of Madrid. Her dissertation is devoted to the expression of sexual intercourse in the Hebrew Bible. clarcarb@ucm.es

Anne-Claire Mulder is associate professor for women's and Gender Studies in Theology and supervisor of the internships for the ministry at the Protestantse Theologische University, The Netherlands. acmulder@pthu.nl

Editorial

Tema: El liderazgo religioso de las mujeres en tiempos de conflicto y crisis

El tema de este número de la revista de ESWTR 2021, "El liderazgo religioso de las mujeres en tiempos de conflicto y crisis", se retrotrae a la conferencia de la ESWTR en Europa central y oriental en Lviv (Ucrania) en 2018. Dicha conferencia abordó el tema del empoderamiento de las mujeres y el involucramiento ecuménico en cuestiones de paz y justicia; un tema que se originó a partir de la situación en Ucrania, país que ha sufrido conflictos tanto sociales como militares en los últimos años. No obstante, esta situación de crisis no se limita a Ucrania. Los conflictos y crisis pueden encontrarse en todo el mundo: la crisis de la COVID-19, la crisis ecológica, la crisis de migración, las guerras y el terror. En muchas regiones del mundo, vemos tensiones y conflictos prolongados causados por la pobreza, el racismo y la violencia contra las mujeres. Las Iglesias y comunidades religiosas de todo el orbe se ven afectadas por el abuso sexual y de poder, así como por la desigualdad entre los sexos.

Al mismo tiempo, se puede observar un compromiso en aumento, por parte precisamente de las mujeres, en situaciones de conflicto. Las mujeres participan parte en movimientos, incluyendo aquellos religiosos. Adoptan, por ende, posiciones de liderazgo para explorar nuevos caminos y buscar aproximaciones creativas que aborden los conflictos y con las que enfrentarse a nuevos retos. Se responsabilizan de otros, cuidan de la comunidad y de la creación.

Las contribuciones a este número de la revista se ocupan del liderazgo religioso de las mujeres en tiempos de conflicto y crisis que se ha efectuado de formas muy diversas. El texto de *Oksana Kis* fue en primer lugar presentado en la conferencia de Lviv. En él, la autora retrocede hasta la década de los cuarenta y cincuenta, cuando un número sustancial de mujeres fueron encarceladas en el gulag por motivos políticos. En esta situación, las mujeres fueron abandonadas a sus propios recursos, también en lo que concernía a su actividad religiosa. Organizaron y dirigieron servicios litúrgicos y fiestas, siempre en las condiciones más difíciles. Así, y resistiendo al sistema del gulag, estas mujeres desarrollaron su creatividad, su capacidad de improvisación y sus habilidades de liderazgo.

Sytske Hofstee describe un ejemplo histórico de los siglos XVI y XVII. Cuando la Iglesia Católica de los Países Bajos fue reprimida y sus actividades oficiales se hicieron imposibles o peligrosas, hombres y mujeres ofrecieron resistencia. Trabajaron juntos en secreto para mantener la vida religiosa y social de la comunidad católica. La autora presenta a algunas de aquellas mujeres que asumieron distintas formas de liderazgo en sus contextos históricos, sociales y religiosos, y ofrece un análisis de su labor.

Carol Dempsey OP presenta la larga historia de las mujeres dominicas en posiciones de liderazgo para diversos ámbitos de la sociedad en todo el mundo y, en particular, en los Estados Unidos. La autora elabora una retrospectiva desde el presente hasta los inicios de la Orden de los Predicadores y sigue las huellas de las mujeres involucradas en dicha orden y sus versátiles actividades, todo ello bajo la evolución constante de las condiciones eclesiásticas y sociales.

Friederike Eichhorn-Remmel explora el siguiente interrogante: ¿está María hecha para la rebelión? La autora analiza las construcciones contradictorias de María que se transmitieron en el debate en torno a la iniciativa alemana "María 2.0.", así como su representación en los medios de comunicación y el efecto que ello tuvo. Retomando el Magníficat del Evangelio de san Lucas, la autora es capaz de evaluar y subsumir esas construcciones de manera crítica.

Miscelánea
Elizabet Gurdus se pregunta en su artículo acerca de la impureza ritual de las mujeres en la tradición de la Iglesia Ortodoxa Rusa, la cual margina a las mujeres y las invisibiliza. También explora las raíces de las leyes de pureza y

la manera en la que (ya) han sido criticadas en los textos de la Biblia Hebrea y el Nuevo Testamento. Las prescripciones de pureza ritual tradicional que hallamos en la Iglesia Ortodoxa Rusa están siendo cada vez más criticadas desde diversos ángulos, exigiéndose un cambio.

Larissza Hrotkó presenta a Dvoyra Fogel, una escritora judía que vivió al comienzo del siglo XX en Lviv y Viena. Fue miembro de un movimiento que defendió la lengua yiddish como expresión de la identidad judía. En esta contribución, Hrotkó presenta uno de los poemas de Fogel en yiddish, así como su formación estilística.

Reseñas
La última parte de esta revista está dedicada a la reseña del primer volumen de la nueva serie ESWTR Studies in Religion. La obra de Julie Hopkins, *The Wings of the Spirit* ('Las Alas del Espíritu') se ocupa del simbolismo femenino en la pneumatología siríaca temprano-cristiana.

Agnethe Siquans es catedrática de Antiguo Testamento en la Facultad de Teología Católica de la Universidad de Viena. agnethe.siquans@univie.ac.at

Clara Carbonell Ortiz es doctoranda en la Universidad Complutense de Madrid. Su tesis está dedicada al estudio de la expresión de las relaciones sexuales en la Biblia Hebrea. clarcarb@ucm.es

Anne-Claire Mulder es profesora asociada de Teología de las Mujeres y Estudios de Género y supervisora de las becas interinas para el ministerio en la Universidad Teológica Protestante (Países Bajos). acmulder@pthu.nl

Editorial

Thema: Religiöse Leitung von Frauen in Konflikt und Krise
Das Thema des Jahrbuchs der ESWTR 2021, „Religiöse Leitung von Frauen in Konflikt und Krise", geht auf die Zentral- und Osteuropäische Konferenz im Jahr 2018 in Lviv, Ukraine, zurück, die sich mit dem Engagement von

Frauen für Frieden und Gerechtigkeit in Konfliktsituationen beschäftigte. Die Ukraine ist seit Jahren ein Ort gesellschaftlicher, aber auch militärischer Konflikte. Konflikte und Krisen gibt es aber gegenwärtig in allen Teilen der Welt: die Coronakrise, die ökologische Krise, die Migrationskrise, Kriege und Terror. In vielen Gebieten der Welt finden wir lang andauernde Spannungen und Konflikte aufgrund von Armut, Rassismus und Gewalt gegen Frauen. Kirchen und religiöse Gemeinschaften in aller Welt sind durch Fälle von sexuellem Missbrauch, Machtmissbrauch und die Ungleichbehandlung der Geschlechter belastet.

Gleichzeitig ist zu beobachten, dass gerade in Konfliktsituation auch ein wachsendes Engagement von Frauen zu beobachten ist, auch im religiösen Bereich und mit religiöser Motivation. Frauen übernehmen dabei leitende Positionen, um neue Wege zu gehen und kreative Ansätze im Umgang mit Konflikten zu suchen. Sie übernehmen Verantwortung für andere, sie tragen Sorge für die Gemeinschaft und für die Schöpfung.

Die Beiträge in diesem Band beschäftigen sich mit ganz unterschiedlichen Aspekten dieses Themas. Der Artikel von *Oksana Kis* geht auf die Konferenz in Lviv zurück. Sie blickt in die 1940er und 1950er Jahre zurück, als zahlreiche Frauen in der Ukraine aus politischen Gründen im Gulag inhaftiert waren. Die Frauen waren in dieser Situation auch in der Ausübung ihrer Religion auf sich allein gestellt. So organisierten und leiteten sie liturgische Zusammenkünfte und Feiern – immer unter widrigsten Bedingungen. In dieser Situation entwickelten die Frauen Phantasie, Improvisationsvermögen und Leitungskompetenzen im Widerstand gegen die Unmenschlichkeit des Gulag-Systems.

Sytske Hofstee gibt Einblick in ein historisches Beispiel aus dem 16. und 17. Jahrhundert. Als die Katholische Kirche in Holland unterdrückt wurde und offizielle Aktivitäten unmöglich oder gefährlich waren, leisteten Männer und Frauen Widerstand. Sie arbeiteten im Geheimen daran, das religiöse und soziale Leben der Katholik*innen aufrecht zu erhalten. Einige dieser Frauen, die religiöse Leitungsaufgaben verschiedener Art übernahmen, werden in ihrem historischen, sozialen und religiösen Kontext vorgestellt und ihr Wirken analysiert.

Carol Dempsey OP präsentiert die lange Geschichte von Dominikanerinnen in Leitungspositionen in verschiedenen gesellschaftlichen Bereichen auf der ganzen Welt und besonders in den Vereinigten Staaten. Sie blickt auf die Anfänge des Dominikanerordens zurück und verfolgt die Spuren engagierter Frauen aus diesem Orden und ihre vielseitigen Aktivitäten unter sich immer wieder ändernden kirchlichen und gesellschaftlichen Bedingungen bis in die Gegenwart.

Friederike Eichhorn-Remmel geht der Frage nach: „Taugt Maria zur Revolte?" Sie wirft einen Blick auf die gegensätzlichen Konstruktionen von Maria, die von verschiedenen Gruppen im Zuge der Debatte um die deutsche Initiative „Maria 2.0" verbreitet wurden, ihre mediale Inszenierung und ihre Wirkung. Der Rückbezug auf das Magnifikat im Lukasevangelium hilft, diese Konstruktionen kritisch zu bewerten und einzuordnen.

Miscellanea

Elizabet Gurdus fragt in ihrem Beitrag nach der rituellen Unreinheit von Frauen in der Tradition der russisch-orthodoxen Kirche, die Frauen marginalisieren und unsichtbar machen. Sie geht auch den Wurzeln dieser Reinheitsgebote und ihrer Infragestellung in den Texten des Alten und Neuen Testaments nach. Die traditionellen rituellen Reinheitsvorschriften in der russisch-orthodoxen Kirche werden zunehmend von verschiedenen Seiten infrage gestellt und eine Änderung gefordert.

Larissza Hrotkó präsentiert Dvoyra Fogel, eine jüdische Schriftstellerin, die Anfang des 20. Jahrhunderts in Lviv und Wien lebte. Sie schloss sich einer Bewegung an, die die jiddische Sprache als Ausdruck der jüdischen Identität propagierte. Eines ihrer Gedichte in jiddischer Sprache und dessen stilistische Gestaltung stellt Hrotkó in diesem Beitrag näher vor.

Rezensionen

Den letzten Teil des Jahrbuchs widmen wir der Rezension des ersten Bandes der neuen Reihe „ESWTR Studies in Religion". Julie Hopkins befasst sich in ihrem Buch „The Wings of the Spirit" mit der femininen Symbolik in der frühchristlichen syrischen Pneumatologie.

Agnethe Siquans ist Professorin für Alttestamentliche Bibelwissenschaft an der katholisch-theologischen Fakultät der Universität Wien. agnethe.siquans@univie.ac.at

Clara Carbonell Ortiz ist Dissertantin an der Universität Complutense Madrid. Ihre Dissertation befasst sich mit dem Ausdruck von Geschlechtsverkehr im biblischen Hebräisch. clarcarb@ucm.es

Anne-Claire Mulder ist assoziierte Professorin für Frauen- und Genderstudien in der Theologie und Betreuerin des Praktikums für angehende Pfarrer*innen an der Protestantischen Theologischen Universität, Niederlande. acmulder@pthu.nl

Journal of the European Society of Women in Theological Research 29 (2021) 9-29.
doi: 10.2143/ESWTR.29.0.3289659

Oksana Kis

Faith as a Shield:
Ukrainian Women's Religious Practices in the Gulag

Abstract

In the 1940-50s thousands of Ukrainian women (especially from Western Ukraine) were sentenced to long-term imprisonment in the Gulag due to political accusations. The article examines personal narratives produced by the Ukrainian female Gulag survivors to explore the role of Christian faith and religious practices in the everyday life of imprisoned women in camps and prisons. Women's individual and group prayers, improvised all-women masses, hand-made crosses, rosaries, embroidered icons and memorabilia as well as celebrations of major Christian holidays in camps and prisons are considered women's nonviolent forms of resistance to the dehumanizing repressive regime.

Resumen

En la década de los cuarenta y cincuenta, miles de mujeres ucranianas, especialmente de la Ucrania occidental, fueron sentenciadas a largos períodos de encarcelamiento en el gulag por acusaciones políticas. Este artículo examina las narrativas personales producidas por las mujeres ucranianas que sobrevivieron al gulag para explorar el rol de la fe cristiana y las prácticas religiosas cotidianas de las encarceladas en campos y prisiones. Las oraciones individuales y grupales de mujeres, las misas femeninas improvisadas, los crucifijos hechos a mano, rosarios, iconos bordados y recuerdos, así como las celebraciones de las fiestas más importantes del cristianismo en los campos y las prisiones, fueron considerados como formas no violentas de resistencia femenina al régimen de represión deshumanizante.

Zusammenfassung

In den 1940er bis 1950er Jahren wurden tausende ukrainische Frauen (besonders aus der Westukraine) aufgrund politischer Anklagen zu langen Haftstrafen im Gulag verurteilt. Der Artikel untersucht persönliche Erzählungen von ukrainischen Frauen, die den Gulag überlebt haben, um die Rolle des christlichen Glaubens und religiöse Praktiken im Alltag der in Lagern und Gefängnissen inhaftierten Frauen zu erforschen. Persönliche und gemeinsame Gebete der Frauen, improvisierte rein weibliche Messen, handgemachte Kreuze, Rosenkränze, gestickte Symbole und Erinnerungsstücke sind ebenso wie die Feiern wichtiger christlicher Feste in Lagern und Gefängnissen als gewaltlose Formen des Widerstands der Frauen gegen das entmenschlichende repressive Regime zu verstehen.

Keywords: Ukrainian women, Gulag, Christian faith, religiosity, political prisoners, humanity.

In the late Stalinist period the Gulag, the Soviet penitentiary and repressive institution, came to its apotheosis. During the 1940s both the number of inmates and the number of Gulag personnel grew immensely and reached its peak in the early 1950s when about 2.5 million inmates served their sentences in the Gulag prisons and camps annually.[1] In the 1940s the demography of the Gulag population also changed substantially: the share of political prisoners, Ukrainians and women among the inmates rose simultaneously. During and after WWII the share of political prisoners skyrocketed from 18.6 percent in 1939 up to 60 percent in 1946.[2] By 1951 Ukrainians constituted one fifth of the Gulag population, and represented the second most numerous ethnic group of convicts.[3] At the same time the share of women increased drastically from 7.6 percent in 1941 to 30.6 in 1945.[4] All that makes research on the Ukrainian female political prisoners' experiences in the Gulag in the late Stalinist period legitimate and important.

The goal of the Gulag as a penal system was threefold: harsh punishment of the "enemies of the state" accompanied by a compulsory total re-education of the "renegades" combined with ultimate exploitation of the slave labor

---

[1] Galina Ivanova, *Istoriia GULAGa 1918-1958: sotsial'no-ekonomicheskii I politico-pravovoi aspekty* (Nauka: Moscow 2006), 317; Viktor Zemskov, "GULAG (istoriko-sotsiologicheskii aspekt)," in *Sotsiologicheskie issledovaniia*, no. 7 (1991), 3-16; Steven A. Barnes, *Death and Redemption: The Gulag and the Shaping of Soviet Society* (Princeton University Press: Princeton 2011), 47. It is hardly possible to establish an exact number of Gulag prisoners and victims, the Gulag scholars estimate up to 25-30 million of convicts and about six million dead in camps, colonies and prisons between 1929 and 1956: Golfo Alexopoulos, *Illness and Inhumanity in Stalin's Gulag* (Yale University Press: New Haven 2017), 53.

[2] Zemskov, "GULAG (istoriko-sotsiologicheskii aspekt)," 4; Barnes, *Death and Redemption*, 157-59.

[3] Zemskov, "GULAG (istoriko-sotsiologicheskii aspekt)," 3; Alexopoulos, *Illness and Inhumanity*, 53.

[4] Galina Ivanova, "GULAG: gosudarstvo v gosudarstve," in: Iurii Afanasiev (ed.), *Sovetskoe obshchestvo: vozniknovenie, razvitie, istoricheskii final* (RGGU: Moscow 1997), 209-72, here 216-17.

force. By exercising a total control over all the aspect of the prisoners lives and depriving them of virtually all rights and basic resources the regime aimed to subordinate prisoners, to destroy a convict's personality, to demolish his/her social identities and value system in order to turn them into a uniform faceless human mass of which new 'Soviet persons' were to be formed. Therefore besides a mere physical survival, the prisoners' major goal was to preserve their personalities from total disintegration.

Gender and religion in the Gulag Studies

The Gulag studies started to grow rapidly as a research field only after the collapse of the USSR when scholars were gradually granted access to previously classified archival documents and the former Gulag prisoners started to speak publicly about their experiences in camps and prisons. Fundamental research exploring the origins and evolution of this punitive institution, its structure and functioning, economy and demographics as well as the Gulag's political role in sustaining the Stalinist regime have been published in Russia and elsewhere.[5] Until recently the institutional history of the Gulag prevailed, while anthropological research of everyday life of prisoners remained marginal in the Gulag studies.

While women's experiences of imprisonment received relatively little attention from Gulag scholars, even those few anthropological studies have never discerned the Ukrainian female convicts as a particular group with specific characteristics which deserved a closer study.[6] What is more, in existing (relatively modest) scholarship on the gender particularities of women's experiences in the Gulag two themes prevail: scholars tend to focus on sexual violence against female prisoners and controversies of motherhood behind barbed wire.[7] Although both topics are legitimate, they reduce the wide variety of

---

[5] On the state of affairs in the Gulag studies see Wilson T. Bell, "Gulag Historiography: An Introduction," in: *Gulag Studies* 2-3 (2009-2010), 1-20; "New Directions in Gulag Studies: A Roundtable discussion," in: *Canadian Slavonic Papers/Revue Candaienne des Slavistes* 59 (3-4/2017), 376-395.

[6] Oksana Kis, "Zhinochyi dosvid GULAGu: stan doslidzhen' ta dzherel'ni resursy v ukrainskomu konteksti," in: *Ukrainskyi istorychnyi zhurnal* 3 (2016), 125-138.

[7] Olga Chesnokova, "Zhenskii opyt GULAGa v sovetskoi istorii 1930-1950 godov," in: Irina Chikalova (ed.), *Zhenshchiny v istorii: vozmozhnost' byt' uvidennymi* (BGPU: Minsk 2001), 189-193; Liubov Maksimova, "Materinstvo v lageriakh Gulaga," in: A. Pavlov (ed.), *Gendernaia teoriia i istoricheskoe znanie: materialy konferentsii* (Syktyvkar State University: Syktyvkar 2003), 271-277; Arsenii Roginskii and Aleksandr Daniel, "Arestu podlezhat zheny ...,"

women's experiences in camps and prisons to their sexual victimization and maternal functions, which is neither correct nor fair. There is much more about female prisoners' lives in captivity that is worth a scholarly inquiry.

Many former Gulag prisoners – both men and women – pondered in their memoirs on their own or their fellow inmates' Christian faith and religious practices as a significant aspect of their experiences of incarceration, but these topics remain generally overlooked in the Gulag studies. In her groundbreaking study on the Gulag, Ann Applebaum pointed out that religious practices have been prominent in men's Gulag memoirs: male survivors claimed that faith and prayers helped them to maintain their humanity.[8] The same applies to women's Gulag narratives. Many former inmates shared their memories of profoundly religious people (especially repressed priests, monks and nuns) they met in camps. Some studies show that the faithful people have demonstrated more steadfastness in the Gulag: Christians, Jews and Muslims used to hold on to their religious beliefs and perceived those ordeals as a probation of their faith, a spiritual challenge; so an aspiration to cope with it properly actually fed their endurance.[9] Nevertheless, the role and manifestations of religiosity among the general female Gulag population did not attract sufficient attention from scholars. Even the most thorough research on Polish women's experiences of imprisonment and exile in wartime USSR dedicated no more than 13 lines (out of 356 pages) to this issue.[10] In short, despite the general awareness of the great importance of religion for a great portion of prisoners, the Gulag scholarship has offered no comprehensive study on this subject yet.

---

in *Uznitsy "ALZHIRa": spisok zhenshchin zakliuchennykh Akmolinskigo i drygikh otdelenii Karlaga* (Zvenia: Moscow 2003), 6-30; Veronica Shapovalov, *Remembering the Darkness: Women in Soviet Prisons* (Rowman and Littlefield Publishers: New York 2001); Veronika Shapovalova, "Sestrenki, mamki, damki: tema nasiliia v zhenskikh lagernykh memuarakh," in: Marianna Muravyova and Natalia Pushkareva (eds.), *Bytovoe nasilie v istorii rossiiskoi povsednevnosti (XI-XXI vv.)* (European University Press: Saint-Petersburg 2012), 142-163. The only exception is Katherine Jolluck comprehensive research on the Polish women's lives in the Gulag camps and special settlements for exiles in the USSR during the WWII. Kathrine R. Jolluck, *Exile and Identity: Polish Women in the Soviet Union During World War II.* (University of Pittsburgh Press: Pittsburgh 2002). It is possible, however, that more studies of this kind exist in national languages.

[8]   Anne Applebaum, *Gulag: A History* (Doubleday: New York 2003), 383-384.

[9]   Leona Toker, *Return from the Archipelago: Narratives of Gulag Survivors* (Indiana University Press: Indianapolis 2000), 96.

[10] Jolluck, *Exile and Identity,* 134.

Ukrainian female politicals in the Gulag

During and after WWII the Gulag camps were flooded by Ukrainian women accused of real or alleged collaboration with the Ukrainian nationalist (anti-Soviet) underground from the newly incorporated Western Ukrainian regions. In the 1920-30s Eastern Galicia, Volynia, Bukovina and Trans-Carpathian were not under the Soviet rule and thus had not been exposed to the Bolshevik's policy of militant atheism. For female political prisoners from these territories Christian faith represented an inalienable part of their normal lives: women claimed that being a Christian constituted an important aspect of their social identity, so corresponding religious practices were integrated into their daily lives before their arrest. Those deeply religious women were not prepared to give up their faith even in the prisons and camps; moreover it turned out that their religiosity – albeit forbidden and punished – equipped female prisoners with a powerful tool to counteract despair and dehumanization in the Gulag.

This article explores the significance of Christian faith for Ukrainian women in the Gulag camps and prisons by examining a variety of religious practices they recall as common in detention.[11] It aims to show how – despite the strict prohibition of any manifestation of religiosity in camps and prisons –, individual and group prayers, varying items for individual spiritual usage, improvised liturgies and celebrations of major Christian holidays constituted an integral part of everyday life of this specific group of the Gulag detainees helping them to cope with inhuman conditions.

This article focuses on revealing meanings, manifestations and effects of religiosity among lay Ukrainian women convicted for various "political crimes," who continued to cherish and practice their Christian faith in captivity despite strict prohibitions and under threat of penalty.[12]

In this article I analyze a variety of first-hand accounts (memoirs, autobiographies, interviews, letters etc.) of the female Ukrainian survivors of the Gulag. Such recollections vary greatly, as they were produced and published by

---

[11] This study is a part of a wider research project, exploring various aspects of everyday lives of the Ukrainian female political prisoners in the Gulag camps and prisons in the 1940-50s. Oksana Kis, *Survival as Victory: Ukrainian Women in the Gulag*, trans. By Lidia Wolanskyj. Harvard Series in Ukrainian Studies (Academic Press: Boston 2020).

[12] There was a significant group of Gulag inmates persecuted and imprisoned precisely for their religious persuasions and activities (clergymen, monks and nuns), but exploring their specific experiences in captivity lies beyond the scope of this study. The exact number of those convicted specifically for religious reasons is unknown.

different people, at different times and under different circumstances. Most of them appeared after Ukraine gained its independence and the former political prisoners felt free to share their experiences of living through the Gulag.[13] Regardless of how versatile in genre, size, structure, detailing or rhetoric these women's stories are, taken together they complement, cross-verify and reinforce one another, allowing to reconstruct a complex picture of the everyday lives of Ukrainian women in the Gulag.

The source base of this study represents yet another methodological challenge: the majority of available personal testimonies (both written and oral) come from women who were imprisoned for their connections with the Ukrainian nationalist underground that operated mainly in the western part of Ukraine. There are virtually no memoirs of women sentenced for other "political crimes" (e.g., collaboration with the Nazi occupational regime) from other Ukrainian regions. Therefore, personal accounts used in this study cover experiences of a specific fraction of female Ukrainian Gulag prisoners only. Although the fates and views of many other former prisoners could be different, no relevant primary sources are available to explore them. Being aware of this limitation of my research, I still decided to explore the role of religiosity in women's daily lives in camps and prisons because this topic is present so prominently in their memoirs. I saw my task as revealing common patterns and characteristic traits in the experiences of Ukrainian women in captivity, identifying the issues that were significant to them, tracing popular religious activities and exploring the meaning of those spiritual experiences for their survival in the Gulag.

Although memoirs of male prisoners of the Gulag such as Aleksandr Solzhenitsyn, Varlam Shalamov, and Gustaw Herling-Grudziński are generally very informative and much better known, I make very little use of them in this study. This decision was driven by one of the key tenets of feminist approaches to women's histories: research into the past of women should rely primarily on the sources produced by women – their own testimonies of the events they lived through.[14] I share the position of Ronit Lentin, who

---

[13] For a detailed discussion on the primary sources used for this study, see: Kis, *Survival as Victory*, 45-57.

[14] Hilda Smith, "Feminism and the Methodology of Women's History," in: Berenice A. Carroll (ed.), *Liberating Women's History: Theoretical and Critical Essays* (University of Illinois Press: Chicago 1976), 372; Susan Geiger, "What's So Feminist about Women's Oral History?," *Journal of Women's History* 2 (1/1990), 170; Marjorie L. Devault, "Talking and

has researched women's experiences during the Holocaust and insisted: "Privileging women's lived experiences, I argue that we must consider women's own accounts of their lives as primary documents for interpreting their lives."[15] Such an approach makes it possible to better understand what the women themselves thought of their experiences, and to acknowledge their views of their own past. Women's personal narratives combined with the official Gulag documentation and statistics allow to reconstruct this aspect of women's experiences in order to understand what role it played in maintaining women's mental endurance and preserving their basic social identities in the confinement.

Personal and group prayers in camps and prisons
Former female prisoners constantly stress an exceptional role of the Christian faith which helped them to endure the tortures during interrogations, to keep loyalty to basic moral principles in the totally inhumane conditions of investigation and transit prisons, during transportation to and in the Gulag camps.

During the investigation by the NKVD[16] (before an interrogation and unavoidable tortures, waiting for the court session or expecting a verdict), on the transport towards the places of confinement, facing degradation and death in camps women turned in prayer to God and the Virgin Mary seeking their support and protection. "That night we did not sleep. Each of us whispered the most sincere prayer. We begged our Lord and the Virgin Mary for their custody, for protection. We needed that so much!"[17] "Perhaps I was saved by a prayer which I used to send daily to the Lord in the hope that He would help

---

Listening from Women's Standpoint: Feminist Strategies for Interviewing and Analysis," in: *Social Problems* 37 (1/1990), 96–116.

[15] Ronit Lentin, "Introduction: Engendering Genocides," in: Ronit Lentin (ed.), *Gender and Catastrophe* (Zed Books: London 1998), 5.

[16] Narodnyi Komissariat Vnutrennikh Del (People's Commissariat of Internal Affairs), the.agency charged with overseeing police work and the GULAG. The NKVD was formed in 1934 and dissolved in 1946.

[17] Anna Karwanska-Bailak, *Vo imia Tvoie (Merezhane zhyttiam)* (Ukrainskyi arkhiv: Warsaw 2000), 253, 267; Ivan Kryvutskyi (ed.), *V namysti z koliuchoho drotu: Spohady zhinok viazniv GULAGu uchasnyts' noryl's'koho povstannia 1953 roku* (Manuskrypt: Lviv 2009), 184; Halyna Hordasevych and Sofiia Voloshchak (eds.), *Neskorena Berehynia: zhertvy moskovs'ko-komunistychnoho teroru XX stolittia* (Piramida: Lviv 2002), 86-87, 137.

us to survive."[18] Anna Ivanytska recalls her prayers in the investigation prison where she had been exposed to violence at every interrogation session:

> But I prayed, I was going and praying. I prayed every time asking God to [help] keeping my silence and survive. I asked nothing but to keep silent (...) I repeated: My God, I did not plan that – You directed me to that path, so give me strength to endure! And that was the case, I endured everything, and not only me.[19]

Arrestees felt really feeble in front of the powerful Soviet repressive machinery, so they appealed to God as a supreme judge and protector.

> You can scream here – nobody will hear you, you can cry – nobody will have pity or help you. Only God Our Lord [will], so we prayed to Him asking for strength and health to endure all that and not to give up spiritually.[20]
> I kneeled and started praying passionately to God asking Him to (...) give us strength to endure everything.[21]
> At night we lied on plank beds and our blue lips rustled in prayers, we believed and prayed passionately.[22]

Many former prisoners describe their profound overwhelming need for prayer in confinement with virtually the same wordings. Women prisoners shared very similar experiences of sufferings, so it is rather natural that those prayers were similar: women asked for endurance and spiritual strength. In some cases, special 'prisoner's prayers' have been created and circulated in camps. Anna Kotsur authored one such prayer in a Taishet camp in 1952:

> God save us, and our families,
> Don't let us die in these hard times.
> Don't let us perish, we beg You, our Lord,
> And You, Our Lady,
> And you, all the Saints around God's throne.

---

[18] Hordasevych and Voloshchak (eds.), *Neskorena Berehynia*, 101.
[19] Interview with Anna Ivanytska, b. 1925, interviewer Taras Cholii, July 31 – August 1, 2009, transcript, Oral History Archive, Territory of Terror Memorial Museum. Fond 1, opys, 42-43; also Kryvutskyi (ed.), *V namysti*, 136; Dariia Korchak, *Pobachene i perezhyte: spohady polity'iaznia* (Ukrpol: Stryi 2016), 18-19.
[20] Hanna Pozniak (Skrypiuk), *Meni bulo 19: avtobiohrafichna rozpovid'* (Vydavnychyi dim Kyievo-Mohylianska Akademiia: Kyiv: 2001), 57.
[21] Hordasevych and Voloshchak (eds.), *Neskorena Berehynia*, 176.
[22] Oksana Meshko, *Ne vidstupliusia!* (Prava liudyny: Kharkiv 2005), 48.

We beg you, don't deny us a better destiny.
Protect our dearest homeland,
Have mercy over our people. [23]

Remarkably, this prayer is not only begging for alleviation of human suffering, but also asks for a better destiny for the homeland.

One may arguably speak of a real cult of Our Lady (Materi Bozhoi) among the Ukrainian female convicts: women unanimously perceived Our Lady to be their primary advocate, so they entrusted her all their grief and sought her help. Anastasia Zakydalska insisted: "There are good people in the world, but I was always under the custody of Our Lady. I feel so."[24]

Some women reported having prophetic dreams or visions with the Virgin Mary bringing good news (about family members, a recovery from a disease, a forthcoming discharge, etc.).[25] Kateryna Mandryk-Kyibida recalled her suicidal thoughts in a prison cell. As a good Christian, she felt remorse of having those sinful thoughts, but suddenly

> [t]he cell got illuminated [...] and the Virgin Mary showed up in the doorway. Her brightness dazzled me [...] Our Lady addressed me with a sweet kind voice: "Don't cry, my child, just pray, this is your fate, and believe that God will save you!" – and I felt relieved [...] and faith pervaded my soul: I will be free, whatever happens, and Our Lady will save me![26]

A story by Hanna Pozniak (Skrypiuk) is exemplary for the special role played by the Virgin Mary in preventing total despair among the imprisoned. She recalls the harshest period in her camp life:

> I stumbled and fell down, and when I was getting up I saw a small aluminum medallion featuring Our Lady Protectress. I took it and calmed down, and my pain lessened. I keep that medallion till the present day, because in every hard time we only could turn to Our Lady for help [...] It was better to pray and think, to dream,

---

[23] Anna Kotsur's hand-written prisoners prayer has been created in Taishet camp OLP-29 in 1952, the original belongs to the Archive of Lviv historical museum.

[24] Anastasiia Zakydalska, *Intyns'ki snihovii: dokumental'na povist', publitsystyka* (PP Ivaniuk V.P.: Lutsk 2014), 45.

[25] Interview with Anna Ivanytska, 59-60.

[26] Kateryna Mandryk-Kuibida, *Volia klyche nas do boiu* (Smoloskyp: Kyiv 2017), 267-8.

to build and to destroy our plans for the future, to recall the past. They could not take that away from us. That was the only pleasure in our lives.[27]

Women sincerely believed in her powerful protection and that belief helped them to continue hoping for survival: "For all that the Virgin Mary protects me and she won't let me die."[28]

Surprisingly, even the criminal convicts who served their sentences for robbery, murder, fraud, bribery and other felonies proved to be religious in their own way. Ivanna Mashchak's (Pshepiurska) story reveals an unexpected side to this criminal world after she witnessed one of those female *urka*[29] being shot in a fight by another criminal:

> The *blatnye*[30] immediately took her body back to their barrack. Strangely enough, these women, some of whom had been jailed more than once, wore crosses on their chests and somehow, in their own way, combined murder, theft, crime, and cursing – with faith in God. They dressed their murdered friend, obviously in stolen clothes, called on the "nuns," whom they ordered to pray over her the entire night... then came up to each of us and asked that we commemorate the soul of the dead woman.[31]

Beside an individual prayer as the most intimate communication with God, women have also prayed in groups, especially for their fellow girlfriends taken for interrogations while in the investigatory prisons. Thus having no other means to alleviate her suffering under torture, they tried to support her at least with a sincere common prayer. Maria Vahula, just as many others, describes such an episode: "We all prayed ardently, each of us and all together using beads made of bread. Besides an ordinary bead prayer, we also chanted a prayer to Our Lady of Unremitting Help."[32]

It was strictly prohibited for prisoners to have any personal items, especially those of religious usage (crosses, beads, prayer books, icons etc.). Those were taken away before transporting convicts to the places of confinement and constantly removed if found in camp barracks during regular searches. In the

---

[27] Pozniak (Skrypiuk), *Meni bulo 19*, 67.

[28] Mariia Vahula, *Moia doroha z domu cherez viaznytsi, laherni zony, zaslannia dodomu* (Ukrains'ki tekhnolohii 2006), 17.

[29] *Urka (pl. urki)* – jargon for a hardened, strict, violent, or inveterate criminal convict.

[30] *Blatnye* – jargon for common criminals, convicts belonging to and following the rules of a criminal subculture.

[31] Ivanna Mashchak, *Dorohamy mynuloho* (Klio: Kyiv 2019), 119.

[32] Vahula, *Moia doroha*, 18.

women's memoirs, however, one may find many references/ allusions to crosses and beads hand-made of dark bread. Maria Vahula explained:

> We prayed a lot on beads hand-made of bread. We kneaded crumbs by hand until it was a homogeneous mass and made beads of it. We pierced every granule with a needle (which despite the prohibition was carefully hidden in every cell), and then those beads were strung on a thread. We made crosses the same way.[33]

To make them women had to save a certain part of their scantly prisoner's bread ration, so obviously spiritual needs of those starving women were equal to (if not higher than) their need of food.

Beata Obertynska, a Polish writer, related an episode in a Zamarstyniv prison in Lviv (the story she heard from a Ukrainian woman called Olha in a Vorkuta camp):

> Many priests have been imprisoned in Zamarstyniv [prison]. Female detainees made some beads of bread. They knew that when they would be taken for a walk, male prisoners would be having a shower in the bathroom next to the hallway. Somehow one woman approached the [bathroom] window and asked a priest to bless the beads. A hand (which looked like a bloody mess) appeared in that window and crossed over those bread rosaries.[34]

A prayer book was a rarity in the confinement, but a personal (usually hand made, embroidered) icon was in possession of virtually each female convict.[35] They usually feature both Christian and national symbols as well as a few lines of a prayer for protection and help. Thus besides typical canonical images those personal icons included references to women's patriotic sentiments, yearning for freedom and justice, concerns for their family and kids left behind etc.[36]

---

[33] Vahula, *Moia doroha*, 18.
[34] Beata Obertynska, *W domu niewoli*, vol. 1-2 (Nakł. Oddziału Kultury i Prasy Korpusu A.P.: Warsaw 1946), 66.
[35] Former political prisoners have preserved numerous samples of those hand-made icons which are currently exhibited in the museums dedicated to Stalin's political repressions, for instance: Museum of the Ukrainian Nation Liberation Struggle in Lviv; the Local History Museum in Terebovlia, Ternopil oblast'; Memorial Museum of Political Prisoners in Buchach, Ternopil oblast; Historical Memorial Museum of Political Prisoners in Ternopil; Memorial Museum 'Lontsky prison" in Lviv etc.
[36] Svitlana Kocherhina, "Doli halyts'kyh politviazniv ta alehorychna symvolika v iikh tabirnykh vyrobakh," in: *Naukovi zapysky Lvivskoho instorychnoho muzeiu* 7 (1998), 283-295.

Women prisoners were quite aware of the risk that making, keeping and using religious items entailed: "They would penalize us for that, they would throw us into a punishment cell, they would deny us the right of correspondence. They confiscated beads and icons during the searches, took away prayer books. But they could not take away our prayer."[37] It seems that women's need to practice their faith was stronger than the fear of punishment they would be subjected to for transgressing camps rules and regulations.

Improvised liturgies

It appears that weekly liturgies were a common practice among Ukrainian female convicts. Notwithstanding prohibitions, women arranged improvised divine services on Sundays. Some women took the lead and initiated such activities because they understood how it could affect the exhausted convicts' presence of mind. Marta Hai explained:

> It was necessary to save the fellow girlfriends; it was necessary to find a way to strengthen their spirit. Christ! Faith! Nusia [Anna Kotsur] gathered us for prayer. Women conducted public prayer, the divine service. The guards prowled between barracks trying to catch those in prayer.[38]

It is also remarkable that there is no mention of conflicts or tensions among women of different Christian denominations; to the contrary women testify that their Christian identity and faith obtained some ecumenical features in camps and prisons so they felt some affinity with Christians of various denominations. Uliana Honchar-Bakai claimed: "During all the years of imprisonment there was God among us [...] We did not quarrel with each other on the basis of faith."[39]

Walli Schliess, a German woman who spent several years amongst Ukrainians in a camp, recalled those regular Sunday masses:

> Everyone hurried to finish [daily chores] by noon. Then we went for prayer, or, as we said, to the divine service... It was a secret [practice], so every Sunday we changed barracks and groups in order to avoid unwanted attention of the camp

---

[37] Walli Schliess, "Molytva v Vorkuti," in: *Our Life* 9 (1956), 7.

[38] Bohdan Hordasevych (ed.), *Nepokhytni: zbirnyk spohadiv* (Ridna shkola: Lviv 2005), 158.

[39] Iaroslav Lialka (ed.), *Litopys neskorenoi Ukrainy: dokumenty, materialy, spohady,* vol. 1 (Prosvita: Lviv 1993), 461.

administration to our meetings. We prayed quietly in front of a medallion or an icon that somebody managed to preserve.[40]

Women's memoirs testify that in many cases women and girls took over the roles of priest and deacon and thus conducted liturgies. Larysa Zadorozhan claimed: "We used to get together every Sunday to carry out a divine service. One of us who knew the mass served as a priest, and we sang as a choir. That helped us to endure all the hardships, it gave us strength."[41]

Anna Karwanska-Bailak recalled her cellmate Olia Halych: "She has got a nick-name 'ksiondz' [a priest] because when we all started a joint prayer aloud she used to lead it." She also mentioned another prisoner Anna Kozlovska "[w]ho was reading a divine service every Sunday. The majority of us took part in that unusual prison liturgy [...] Later Irynka Cheplia was reading the divine service."[42]

One cannot overestimate the role of such a mass for stiffening the spirit of those imprisoned women. Oksana Meshko (who became one of the most famous Soviet dissidents and human rights advocates in late Soviet times) put it very clearly: "A prayer and a divine service served for our spiritual recharge, it supplemented us with strength and energy."[43]

Stefania Chaban-Haval related her own experience in a camp located on the Taimyr peninsula in spring 1953.[44] Initially girls reconstructed a typical liturgy script together from what they remembered, they tried to recall all the details of divine service and thus follow the standard sequence of rites and prayers. At some point one prisoner managed to procure a little prayer book in a parcel from home, so since then it was used as a manual for conducting those improvised masses. Stefania performed the role of a priest on Easter when she conducted a morning mass in a crowded barrack. She preached about beloved families left behind, murdered and fallen fellow partisans and a homeland. The climax of her story is a moment when some representatives of a camp administration and guards suddenly entered the barrack. Stefania claimed that she did not lose courage, she continued chanting the prayer and ultimately those unbidden guests left the barrack in silence. Naturally, a woman who was only

[40] Walli Schliess, "Nedilia u Vorkuti," in: *Our Life* 8 (1956), 6-9, here 6.
[41] Halyna Datsiuk (ed.), *Usna zhinocha istoriia: povernennia* (Zhinochyi tsentr Spadshchyna: Kyiv 2003), 300; also: Hordasevych (ed.), *Nepokhytni*, 149.
[42] Anna Karwanska-Bailak, *Vo imia Tvoie*, 268, 305.
[43] Meshko, *Ne vidstupliusia*, 48.
[44] Kryvutskyi (ed.), *V namysti*, 15-19.

27 years then, was very proud of her courage and ability to challenge the regime.

Remarkably, despite the awareness of transgressing the church norms, the former Gulag prisoners speak of those experiences with pride and thrill. Those religious women consciously transgressed respective church norms prohibiting women from priesthood, but never regretted their misdemeanor, prioritizing their religious aspirations over formal church rules. Those experiences were both deeply spiritual and empowering.

Celebrations of major Christian holidays

Despite a total ban on any informal gathering in camps, virtually every former convict's memoir contains stories of celebrating major Christian holidays – Christmas and Easter – behind bars. Stefania Chaban-Haval recalled:

> All those years our "contingent" (that is how they called us there) kept our ances-
> tors' traditions which were strictly prohibited by the camps regime and persecuted
> by BUR[45] punishment or a penalty [food] portion. But those stubborn Banderites
> [a follower of Stepan Bandera][46] did not forget their [traditions] in the harshest
> conditions. They knew there will be punishment, but still on Christmas, on the
> Christmas Eve, at night after hard work they change their clothes for *vertep* [Ukrain-
> ian traditional Christmas performance based on the Biblical story of Christ birth]
> and go caroling so that even the barrack walls are trembling, they chant prayers and
> no punishment can stop them.[47]

For female prisoners such a holiday was a rare occasion for joy, a long-awaited feast which helped to fight depression and sorrow, as Orysia Mochulska informed: "We tried to never give up, to keep all our holidays – both religious and national, so we celebrated, we sang, and we caroled on Christmas and *shchedruvaly* [Ukrainian tradition of group singing] on the Epiphany day."[48]

Despite enormous hardships of everyday survival in camps, Ukrainian women waited eagerly for these holidays and prepared everything for a 'proper' celebration in advance. They did their best to stock up necessary

---

[45] BUR – abbreviation from *Barak Usilennogo Rezhima*. Enforced regimen barrack, a punishment block or a penalty cell used to totally isolate and punish prisoners for transgressing camp rules.

[46] Stepan Bandera, 1909-1959, one of the top leaders of the militant wing of the Organization of Ukrainian Nationalists. The term *banderite* was pejoratively and broadly used to designate Ukrainian nationalists in the USSR.

[47] Kryvutskyi (ed.), *V namysti*, 15.

[48] Kryvutskyi (ed.), *V namysti*, 151.

foodstuff and other accessories (substitute Easter eggs, pussy willow or fir branches, wheat grain for 'kutia' [traditional Ukrainian ritual meal made of cereals for Christmas eve] et cetera. In camps where each bite of bread was worth its weight in gold, female prisoners saved part of their daily bread ration to make a holiday meal of it. On the holiday a barrack or a cell had to be neat and decorated, the clothes had to be the best available and clean.

Women attempted to reconstruct all possible aspects of a traditional celebration, to keep at least their core elements. Thus for Christmas they prepared a substitute of a Christmas tree:

> We made a Christmas tree from a bush – a kind of a dwarf tree, because nothing else grows in Vorkuta. We decorated it with colored paper and cotton. We tried to make it a beautiful Christmas tree. And it was so.[49]
> After work the celebration began in the barrack. We dressed up in the best clothes we had. We made big tables [...] In the middle there was a big bowl with *kutia* – wheat grain sweetened with sugar. Then Christmas Eve began. One Ukrainian woman walked around with white bread cut into small pieces (it came in a parcel from home). Everyone took a bite and responded "Glory to Him" to the greeting "Jesus Christ was born!" Then everyone wished each other to be released in the near future and then we stood by the table for a prayer. [...] At the end we sang some carols and listened to a couple of speeches.[50]

Different Gulag survivors' memories of holiday preparations sound very similar.[51] Typically, women mention "sweets" as a mandatory treat on a holiday table: they made substitute "cakes" of ingredients available behind bars (sweetened bread or porridge, crumbled cookies, etc.).[52] Those "sweets" amplified an illusion of a real holiday and supported a festive atmosphere in

---

[49] Datsiuk (ed.), *Usna zhinocha istoriia*, 335.

[50] Walli Schliess, "Rizdvo u Vorkuti," in: *Our Life* 1 (1957), 4; also Vahula, *Moia doroha*, 29.

[51] Hanna Zaiachkivska-Mykhalchuk, *Zaruchnytsia imperiï (spohady polytv'iaznia)* (Lviv: PP Soroka, 2009), 160; Halyna Kokhanska, *Z Ukraïnoiu v sertsi: Spohady*, ed. Mykola Posivnich, Litopys UPA, ed. Petro I. Potichnyi, vol. 9 (Litopys UPA: Lviv 2008), 277-78; Karwanska-Bailak, *Vo imia Tvoie*, 286-87; Hordasevych and Voloshchak (eds.), *Neskorena Berehynia*, 75-76; Polina Benoni, *Taka nasha hirka pravda: spohady i rozdumy politviaznia* (Chortkiv 1994), 23; Pozniak (Skrypiuk), *Meni bulo 19*, 142; Interview with Olha Hodiak, b. 1925, interviewer Mariana Pyrih, August 27, 2009, transcript. Oral History Archive, Territory of Terror Memorial Museum, Fond 1, opys 1, 22-23; Interview with Dariia Husiak, b. 1924, interviewer Taras Cholii, June 1, 2009, transcript, Oral History Archive, Territory of Terror Memorial Museum, Fond 1, opys 1, 43.

[52] Hordasevych and Voloshchak (eds.), *Neskorena Berehynia*, 75, 139.

an environment alien to any joy. Stefania Chaban-Haval described the holiday preparation:

> Easter was coming. A few days before that holiday, all the people in the barrack did not eat their evening portion of bread [...] On Saturday we made "cakes" of porridge. We invented Easter bread from regular bread. Easter eggs were made of clay and colored with paint used for writing banners. We brought green tree branches, covered tables with whatever was available. All that "beauty" was put on the table, cheered up with green branches, and then everybody felt really in a holiday mood... It's Easter now. Everybody dressed up in whatever clothes people had from home, but everything was clean. The barrack was in order. We were ready for the liturgy.[53]

Hanna Zaiachkivska-Mykhalchuk told a story of her girlfriend Lina Petrashchuk, a daughter of a priest, who encouraged her female cellmates to pray and chant hymns, and even conducted a liturgy:

> Christmas was coming. The barrack is full of depressed female slaves. They lie down after hard work, and it seems impossible to raise them up. Lina [Petrashchuk] wakes up long before the reveille and starts the divine service. "God is among us!" [...] Then the Christmas carols [followed] which sound like church bells. And something happened to people: one by one they start raising their heads and get up, they cry and rejoice.[54]

For prisoners a holiday was a rare occasion to mentally return home and reunite with a native community: "I spent a holiday in a special mood. We prayed, I wished happy and joyful holidays to all, I spoke of Ukraine, of our family members who are waiting for us, of our customs. We caroled quietly."[55]

Another typical feature of stories about Christmas or Easter behind bars is a statement that Ukrainian women always invited all other inhabitants of their barrack or a prison cell to join a celebration regardless of their national or religious affiliation. Walli Schliess recalled her experience with Ukrainian women in a Vorkuta camp:

> Ukrainian female prisoners carefully prepared a celebration [...] they tried to engage each of us in that celebration. Their enthusiasm and desire were transmitted to

---

[53] Kryvutskyi (ed.), *V namysti*, 17.

[54] Hanna Zaiachkivska-Mykhalchuk, *Zaruchnytsia imperii (spohady politviaznia)* (PP Soroka: Lviv 2009), 76

[55] Hordasevych and Voloshchak (eds.), *Neskorena Berehynia*, 76.

prisoners of other nationalities and we all helped them [...] They involved everyone who lived in a barrack, no matter whether she was of the same faith or believed in God at all.[56]

Common fate and shared experiences of suffering have leveled to some extent possible tensions between representatives of various Christian denominations, women tried to show certain (rather reserved) respect and tolerance to each other's faith, especially in the context of a holiday. Anna Karwanska-Bailak recalled:

> There were Polish women sitting next to us by the festive table. We created our inner ethical code of behavior, our customs in a prison. One of its features implied that Polish women invited us to join on the Catholic Christmas day, and we invited them on our holiday. They did not conceal their delight with the richness of our tradition.[57]

Ievdokiia Kotelko (Kapko) writes in her memoirs about celebrating Easter in a camp, for which the Ukrainian women put together an improvised altar with an icon of the Blessed Virgin Mary.

> The crew of recidivists, though endlessly overbearing, nevertheless behaved respectfully toward the religious practices, including morning and evening prayers, of the Ukrainian women. And so, on Easter morning, the overseers tried to drive the Ukrainians out to work, but their forewoman, Sukhoruchka, herself a criminal, volunteered her crew to fulfill the quota instead of them: "These girls aren't going anywhere. My crew will go to unload. How can we leave the Mother of God all alone? . . . Girls, you sing, sing away, and pray for us."[58]

Sometimes even camp guards were imbued with a spirit of sacral moment and in defiance of strict instructions they allowed female convicts to pray and celebrate. Hanna Pozniak (Skrypiuk) informed of an occurrence in a camp in Kharkiv oblast' in spring 1947:

> On Easter day everyone got up early, before the reveille, on sunrise [...] We've got a prayer book and we started "conducting" a divine service. The guards came in but they said nothing, some of them even had tears in their eyes [...] They have not

---

[56] Schliess, "Rizdvo u Vorkuti," 4; also Vahula, *Moia doroha*, 29.
[57] Karwanska-Bailak, *Vo imia Tvoie*, 288.
[58] Dariia Poliuha, *Vse zh ne daremno!* (Lviv 2014), 78-80.

given us a day-off for Easter however, they sent us to the forest for work under supervision of a chief of the educational department. We said we wouldn't work on such a great holiday. We made a circle and started praying [...] He understood that he couldn't force us to work and said: "Okay, I won't tell anyone of this sabotage – go celebrate, but after the holiday you have to catch up the norm". We agreed. We appreciated his understanding.[59]

In some cases women speak of complete tolerance of camp administration towards their religious practices and celebrations. Halyna Shubska shared her experience in one of the Mordovia camps where they "[d]id not forbid women to conduct a liturgy accompanied by singing in a barrack every Sunday. We gathered in barracks to celebrate significant dates of our history. Guards pretended they did not see or hear anything."[60] Maria Yakovyshyn recalled one Christmas in a Vorkuta camp when Ukrainian women prepared everything and invited the camp administration to join the celebration.

We put everything we had on the table. And then an officer and a camp head entered [the barrack]. "What are you doing?" they asked. "It's our Christmas day' we replied [...] Everyone had got seated and invited the administration to sit with us. We prayed and then we sang a carol. They perceived that calmly, and left the barrack satisfied, they only commanded to keep quiet [...] We celebrated Easter in the same way later on.[61]

To celebrate major Christian holidays the Ukrainian women political prisoners secretly and openly transgressed several rules and regulations prohibiting those practices in the Gulag. They consciously took the risk of (sometimes quite severe) punishment, showed impressive courage, resourcefulness, solidarity and purposefulness in finding ways to satisfy their religious needs and revere national traditions. Preparations for a celebration filled a camp routine with a new meaning and mobilized the imprisoned women emotionally, it stimulated their interest in life in a broader sense. Aspiring to reconstruct the traditional way of celebrations as accurately as possible stimulated women's creative potential, strengthened their social ties, boosted their spirit. Daily life in a camp was notable for its monotony and uniform rhythm as each day was like a previous or a next one being filled with exhausting work on a verge of survival, hunger, diseases and total absence of information from outside the Gulag. Those

---

[59] Pozniak (Skrypiuk), *Meni bulo 19*, 45.
[60] Datsiuk (ed.), *Usna zhinocha istoriia*, 331; also Vahula, *Moia doroha*, 29.
[61] Datsiuk (ed.), *Usna zhinocha istoriia*, 235-36.

circumstances adversely affected women's mental state as they were losing a sense of time, interest towards others and even towards themselves leading to depressions, dull stupor and even suicidal thoughts. Nina Gagen-Torn, a famous scholar and a political prisoner, has described the typical emotional state of a convict: "A difference between a camp consciousness and a normal one is that a prisoner loses a reference point in time. Locked in a limited space s/he perceives time in a very limited way, too – in terms of days. After that an uncertainty follows."[62] The improvised Sunday liturgies and celebration of the major Christian holidays in fact helped women to regain a sense of time flow behind bars and thus helped to keep up the mental health of imprisoned women. That is why religious celebrations were of great importance.

Embroidered icons and memorabilia for kids and family

Embroidered icons featuring Jesus Christ and Our Lady played a very important role in the religious life in the women's camps. Embroidering obtained an unprecedented prevalence among the female convicts despite prohibition and penalties it entailed. Imprisoned women had neither free time nor necessary materials nor tools for embroidering, but still they produced enormous number of embroideries, including those of religious character. Women could relatively easily hide those patches during regular searches in barracks, so many camp icons survived and can be found in museum collections and private family archives in Ukraine today. Their aesthetic value is rather modest, their compliance with Church canons is often doubtful, but the role those primitive icons played in the maintenance of the Christian faith among women was enormous: for many it was the very last plot of their religious identity.

Besides icons, women embroidered small memorabilia addressed to their kids and families left behind. That fancywork often featured small kids under guardianship of an angel or the Virgin Mary whom a woman entrusted with tutelage of her children for the period of their mother's absence. The picture is accompanied by a few lines of prayer for the kids' safety and wellbeing. "Oh, Mother of God, I beg you to take my little daughter under your guardianship, don't leave her an orphan!" or "Oh, Maria, Mother of God, you're full of kindness, take my family under your powerful guardianship."[63]

---

[62] Nina Gagen-Torn, *Memoria* (Vozvrashchenie: Moskow 1994), 242.

[63] These inscriptions appear on the icons embroidered by Hanna Protskiv-Liven in the Chortkiv remand prison during her detention in 1948-1949 (memorabilia from Marianna Baidak's family archive).

Imprisoned mothers usually turned to the Virgin Mary asking her for maternal custody over their orphaned kids. Women use to send those embroidered items to family members to serve as a maternal blessing, a talisman to protect children against any evil.

Conclusions

Since the Gulag regime aimed to destroy the inmates' personalities, retaining a traditional value system on which fundamental social identities were based, remained a key task in the Gulag. Christian faith and corresponding religious practices played an essential role in pursuing that goal as they helped women to sustain a humanist worldview and basic moral principles, to stay connected to their native national culture and to cherish loyalty to traditional social norms. Performing traditional women's ritual roles before and during the holiday celebrations, women reproduced normative women's scripts and behaviors (they did what a normal Ukrainian woman is supposed to do) and thus revived, performed and strengthened their (endangered) gender identities.

The prevalence of religious motives in women's creative works testifies to a special role of Christian faith in women's lives behind bars. The Ukrainian female inmates' need to have usual religious activities and practices in camps (divine services and improvised liturgies) resulted in new spiritual and social experiences they acquired: they performed all-women's church rituals and thus obtained an unprecedented opportunity to try the roles of clergymen. Paradoxically, under the circumstances of virtually total deprivation of civil rights and a radical restraint of opportunities the aforementioned practices of group prayers and improvised liturgies provided Ukrainian women with completely new unique experiences of church service and religious leadership (pastorate). As a matter of fact, those women and girls have never had any chance to play a central/leading role in a Christian church ritual in their normal lives.[64] That new religious experience – although induced by circumstances – may be understood as a kind of emancipation: for the first time Ukrainian women did get access to a sphere and roles previously totally forbidden and closed for them.

Women's memories from the Gulag testify to an exceptional role of Christian faith, prayers and religious practices in keeping up the prisoners' presence of mind and their emotional stability, which increased the chances for survival

---

[64] A discussion of the (religious) leadership of women would need a different article and is therefore not further explored in this text.

in camps. Vanda Horchynska reflected on the role of religious practices for the female prisoners' feeling of being inwardly free even in captivity: "Despite the cruelty of the camp regime, despite unbearable living conditions, in defiance of all the prohibitions in a moral sense we continued to live a life of freedom, as we cherished the tradition of daily prayers, honoring the holidays."[65] Daria Korchak explicitly stated: "Christian faith boosted us with fortitude to keep a spiritual balance and strengthened our hope that we would return from captivity back to Ukraine anyway."[66]

As a matter of fact, Ukrainian female politicals used their Christian faith as a powerful instrument to counteract the dehumanizing Gulag regime. Women's religious practices in the camps helped inmates to sustain their core social identities (religious, national, gender); it stiffened their spirit and enabled them to cope more efficiently with extreme circumstances in terms of preserving (their) mental health; it helped them to maintain their respective value system and to retain a purpose of life; these practices structured a time flow, generated positive emotions, and promoted solidarity among the convicts etc. All that worked to increase their chance for survival. Those practices should be considered as forms of nonviolent resistance to a repressive system as they undermined its totality and showed its incapacity to control the female prisoners' minds.

Oksana Kis is a historian and an anthropologist, Ph.D. in History/Ethnology, a Leading Research Associate and head of the Department of Social Anthropology at the Institute of Ethnology, National Academy of Sciences of Ukraine. She authored two books (both in Ukrainian) *Women in the Traditional Ukrainian culture in the second half of the 19ᵗʰ and early 20ᵗʰ centuries* (Lviv, 2008, 2ⁿᵈ ed. 2012) and *Ukrainian Women in the GULAG: Survival Means Victory* (Lviv, 2017; 2ⁿᵈ ed. 2020). The later book (translated into English) is published in 2021 within the Harvard Series in Ukrainian Studies Ukrainian https://books.huri.harvard.edu/books/survival-as-victory. Dr. Kis is a co-founder and a president of the Ukrainian Association for Research in Women's History. email: kis@ucu.edu.ua Web: https://social-anthropology.org.ua/en/author/oksana-kis/
ORCID 0000-0002-8656-9374

---

[65] Bohdan Savka (ed.), *'A smert' ikh bezsmertiam zustrila': narysy, spohady, dokumenty pro uchast' zhinotstva Ternopillia v natsionalno-vyzvol'nii borot'bi OUN-UPA* (Dzhura: Ternopil 2003), 73-74.
[66] Korchak, *Pobachene i perezhyte*, 24.

Journal of the European Society of Women in Theological Research 29 (2021) 31-59.
doi: 10.2143/ESWTR.29.0.3289660

Sytske Hofstee

"Partners in Crime": Dissident Male and Female Religious Leaders of the Clandestine Catholic Church in the Dutch Republic (1570-1800)[1]

Abstract

During the early modern period, over 5,000 spiritual virgins were active in Catholic communities in the Republic of the Seven United Netherlands. This paper explores the religious leadership of early modern Catholic women during the crisis period of the Catholic Church in the Dutch Republic. The paradigm of the "priest-assistant" appears to be dominant in church historical studies, and therefore little attention has been paid to leadership positions of these Catholic (semi-religious) women. The paradigm emphasizes the domestic or serving function of spiritual virgins and ignores the motivations of early modern women themselves, in particular their choice of becoming "bride of Christ". Spiritual unity was the ultimate goal, as they put their lives in the service of Christ and, in the situation of the Republic, at the service of the oppressed and crisis-ridden Catholic faith community.

In this article, I elaborate the concept of religious leadership in relation to Catholicism and give an outline of both female and male religious leadership in the aforementioned period within the Dutch context. This context was defined by the unusual mix of, on the one hand prohibition and persecution and, on the other hand, toleration of Catholics by the authorities, a mix that affected the practices of Catholic leadership. I use the double-voice agency concept to understand forbidden voices of female, as well as male Catholics in a framework of dissimulation. Finally, I present a number of leadership examples from the province of Friesland to demonstrate that spiritual virgins and lay women in different settings have led Catholic faith communities in various innovative ways and ensured the survival of Catholicism in times of crisis and conflict.

Resumen

Durante la Edad Moderna, alrededor de cinco mil vírgenes espirituales estuvieron activas en las comunidades católicas de la República de los Siete Países Bajos Unidos. Este artículo explora el liderazgo religioso de las mujeres católicas de este período

---

[1] This article is based on my PhD research, which is ongoing at the time of writing.

Sytske Hofstee
"Partners in Crime" : Dissident Male and Female Religious Leaders of the Clandestine Catholic
Church in the Dutch Republic (1570-1800)

durante la crisis de la Iglesia Católica en los Países Bajos. El paradigma del "sacerdote-asistente" aparece como dominante en los estudios eclesiásticos históricos y, por ello, se ha prestado poca atención a las posiciones de liderazgo de estas mujeres católicas (semirreligiosas). El paradigma enfatiza la función doméstica o servicial de las vírgenes espirituales e ignora las motivaciones de dichas mujeres, en particular su elección de convertirse en "esposas de Cristo". La unidad espiritual era la meta final, pues pusieron sus vidas al servicio de Cristo y, en lo que respecta a la República, al servicio de aquella comunidad de fe católica oprimida y arrasada por la crisis.

En este artículo, elaboro el concepto de "liderazgo religioso" en relación con el catolicismo y delineo tanto el liderazo femenino como el masculino en el período mencionado para el contexto neerlandés. Dicho contexto estaba definido por la mezcla insual entre, por un lado, la prohibición y la persecución y, por otro, la tolerancia hacia los católicos por parte de las autoridades; mezcla que afectó a las prácticas de liderazgo religioso. Uso el concepto de la "agencia de doble voz" para entender las voces prohibidas de las mujeres así como de los hombres católicos en un marco de disimulo. Finalmente, presento un número de ejemplos sobre el liderazgo en la provincia de Friesland para demostrar que las vírgenes espirituales y las mujeres laicas de diferentes escenarios dirigieron comunidades de fe católicas de diversas e innovadoras maneras, y aseguraron la supervivencia del catolicismo en tiempos de crisis y conflicto.

Zusammenfassung

In der frühen Neuzeit waren über 5.000 spirituelle Jungfrauen in den katholischen Gemeinden in der Republik der sieben vereinigten Niederlande aktiv. Dieser Beitrag untersucht die religiöse Leitung von frühneuzeitlichen katholischen Frauen während der Krisenzeit der katholischen Kirche in der holländischen Republik. In kirchenhistorischen Studien scheint das Modell der „Priester-Assistentinnen" dominant zu sein. Daher fanden Leitungspositionen dieser katholischen (semi-klerikalen) Frauen wenig Aufmerksamkeit. Das Modell betont die häuslichen und dienenden Funktionen der spirituellen Jungfrauen und ignoriert die Motivationen dieser frühneuzeitlichen Frauen selbst, besonders ihre Entscheidung, „Braut Christi" zu werden. Spirituelle Einheit war das letzte Ziel, wenn sie ihr Leben in den Dienst Christi stellten und, in der Situation der Republik, in den Dienst der unterdrückten und krisengeschüttelten katholischen Glaubensgemeinschaft.

In diesem Artikel führe ich das Konzept religiöser Leitung in Beziehung zum Katholizismus aus und präsentiere eine Skizze sowohl weiblicher als auch männlicher religiöser Leitung in der zuvor genannten Zeit im holländischen Kontext. Dieser Kontext war definiert durch eine ungewöhnliche Mischung des Verbots und der Verfolgung einerseits und Toleranz gegenüber Katholik*innen durch die Autoritäten andererseits, eine Mischung, die sich auf die Praxis katholischer Leitung auswirkte. Ich verwende das Konzept der *double-voice agency* (Handlungsmacht der doppelten Stimme), um die verbotenen Stimmen weiblicher sowie männlicher Katholiken in einem Kontext der

Sytske Hofstee
"Partners in Crime": Dissident Male and Female Religious Leaders of the Clandestine Catholic
Church in the Dutch Republic (1570-1800)

Verstellung zu verstehen. Zuletzt präsentiere ich einige Beispiele von Leitung aus der Provinz Friesland, um zu zeigen, dass spirituelle Jungfrauen und weibliche Laien in unterschiedlichen Situationen katholische Glaubensgemeinschaften in verschiedenen innovativen Weisen geleitet und das Überleben des Katholizismus in Zeiten von Krise und Konflikt sichergestellt haben.

Keywords: Early modern period, Dutch Republic, semi-religious women, female and male Catholic leadership, religious authority, dissimulation.

Introduction

After the breakdown caused by the Reformation, the organization of the Catholic Church was a great challenge for early modern Dutch Catholics, top-down as well as bottom-up. To explore the effect of this situation on leadership (positions), four questions are central to this paper. What was Catholic female and male religious leadership and what did this leadership mean for the Dutch Catholic Church in crisis? What positions of religious leadership were possible for early modern women and how did they establish religious authority?

In answering these questions, I will discuss, firstly, the crisis situation of the Dutch Catholic Church and the vacuum of associated leadership; a vacuum that was dealt with by three categories of Catholics – spiritual virgins, priests, and lay women and men – in three closely intertwined domains: virgins' assembly, mission station, and poor relief.[2] Secondly, I observe male and female Catholic leaders, focusing on female religious leaders in relation to male leaders, with special attention to the practice of cooperation between priests and spiritual mothers and virgins. The restricted length of this article does not permit a full overview of all aspects of early modern female religious leadership. In addition, the scarce primary source material used for the Frisian examples in the last paragraph, provides few leads for an in-depth leadership analysis of the women studied. However, it is important to situate early modern female religious leadership and thus depict a context for the possibilities and constraints for Frisian women to wield religious authority. Preceding the paragraphs on Catholic leadership, a brief introduction will be given to the phenomenon of semi-religious women in the Dutch Republic and other western European countries, followed by an overview of the four Frisian women who were studied. The last section of the introduction contains a short outline

---

[2] See for an explanation of "mission station" note 10.

Sytske Hofstee
"Partners in Crime" : Dissident Male and Female Religious Leaders of the Clandestine Catholic
Church in the Dutch Republic (1570-1800)

of Dutch early modern church history, with an emphasis on the Catholic denomination.[3]

Dutch "spiritual virgins" were referred to by a variety of names, such as "spiritual daughters", "spiritual widows", and "spiritual damsels". The common Dutch term is "klopzuster", often abbreviated to "klop". Like their medieval predecessors such as Beguines, Tertiaries and Sisters of the Common Life, they held a semi-religious state.[4] This meant living a religious life outside the walls of the monastery. Early modern spiritual women took a vow and lived often by a third order virgin-rule. They provided for their own livelihood (wealthy spiritual virgins lived off their rental income) and performed tasks in all areas and hierarchical levels of the clandestine Catholic Church.

The appearance of spiritual virgins and third order members was not uncommon in Western Europe.[5] In the Dutch Republic, the phenomenon had a different character due to the context of the clandestine Catholic Church. Whereas in countries and regions with a legal Catholic context spiritual virgins (including spiritual mothers) functioned in a strongly male-dominated public Catholic atmosphere, Dutch spiritual virgins and mothers operated the mission stations in collaboration with priests and male church administrators, in a tolerated but

---

[3] Jonathan Israel, *The Dutch Republic: Its Rise, Greatness, and Fall, 1477-1806* (Oxford University Press: Oxford et al. 1998). Joris van Eijnatten and Fred van Lieburg, *Niederländische Religionsgeschichte* (Vandenhoeck & Ruprecht: Göttingen 2011). Lodewijk Rogier, *Geschiedenis van het Katholicisme in Noord-Nederland in de 16de en 17de eeuw* (Urbi et Orbi: Amsterdam 1947). Pontianus Polman O.F.M., *Katholiek Nederland in de achttiende eeuw, deel 1: De Hollandse Zending 1700-1727, deel 2: De Hollandse Zending 1727-1795, deel 3: Buiten de Hollandse Zending 1700-1795* (Paul Brand: Hilversum 1968). Harmen Oldenhof, *In en om de schuilkerkjes van Noordelijk Westergo* (Koninklijke van Gorcum: Assen 1967).

[4] A continuity of this "semi-religious" phenomenon can be observed from the early Christian virgins on.
Marit Monteiro, "Ick ben gekomen inde werelt om vuur te brenghen: Inspiratie, ambitie en strategie van katholieke geestelijke maagden in de vroegmoderne tijd," in: Annelies van Heijst and Marjet Derks (eds.), *Terra Incognita. Historisch onderzoek naar katholicisme en vrouwelijkheid* (Kok Agora: Kampen 1994), 57-87, here 62. For this continuity see also Anneke Mulder-Bakker, *Verborgen Vrouwen. Kluizenaressen in de middeleeuwse stad* (Uitgeverij Verloren: Hilversum 2007).

[5] Monteiro, "Ick ben gekomen inde werelt"," 63. Examples of studies of semi-religious women in Western Europe: Anne Conrad, *Zwischen Kloster und Welt: Ursulinen und Jesuitinnen in der Katholischen Reformbewegung des 16./17. Jahrhunderts* (Von Zabern: Mainz 1991); Elisabeth Rapley, *The Dévotes: Women and Church in Seventeenth Century France* (McGill University Press: Montreal 1990). Alison Weber (ed.), *Devout Laywomen in the Early Modern World* (Routledge: London 2016).

Sytske Hofstee
"Partners in Crime" : Dissident Male and Female Religious Leaders of the Clandestine Catholic
Church in the Dutch Republic (1570-1800)

illegal private context. Operating in this clandestine sphere had its consequences for Catholic worship, leadership positions, apostolate, pastoral care, catechesis, and poor relief.

Among the four Frisian early modern Catholic women that are retrieved from the archives and examined with the leadership concept are two spiritual virgins. The first is the 17th century Maria Clara van Wytsma, lady of the family castle, honourably buried as Jesuitess among Jesuit priests in the Catholic church on the Frisian island of Ameland. The other one is city lady Geliana Petronella van der Lely, living at the turn of the 18th century, who used her two traditional costumes for performance in public space: a spiritual virgin's robe and a damsel robe. The other subjects of study are two devout lay women, who "operated", so to speak, in the periphery of the spiritual virgin-definition. Their activities have also been of great importance to the survival of the Catholic community and are therefore included in my research. The 17th century businesswoman and noblewoman, His van Emingha, was a linchpin in the Catholic networks in Friesland and beyond.[6] Last but not least, there is 18th century countrywoman Baukje (Barbara) Bouwes Faber, who marked three of her hundreds of donations to the clandestine church community with her own coat of arms. The choice for these four women is based on the available material. Nearly all scarce sources concerning Frisian spiritual virgins contain indirect data. Despite the relatively high numbers of Frisian virgins, no ego documents in the form of autobiographies, memoirs, diaries and personal correspondence have been found so far.[7]

In the Republic of the Seven United Netherlands, there was no such thing as a state church. Between approximately 1570 and 1595 – that is after the Reformation, the political reaction to Spanish rule and the treaty of the Union of Utrecht in 1579 – society in the different regions of the Dutch Republic became

---

[6] A salient detail about His van Emingha is the fact that she was, together with a couple (lawyer Albert van Loo and his wife Neeltie Rommerts), the buyer of part of the estate of "Uylenburgh" in Rijperkerk. In a mortgage act dating from 1637, her name is mentioned with that of Rembrandt van Rijn (1606-1669), son-in-law of the owner, Rombertus van Uylenburgh. Tresoar Leeuwarden: 13-38, inventory number 0090.

[7] The resources used for the first three examples are mainly will documents and messages for buying and selling; the fourth example is based on several church cashbooks. Van Emingha is mentioned in the biographies of her daughters written by spiritual mother Catharina Jans Oly (1585-1651). Joke Spaans, *De Levens der Maechden. Het verhaal van een religieuze vrouwengemeenschap in de eerste helft van de zeventiende eeuw* (Uitgeverij Verloren: Hilversum 2021), CD-ROM, Bijlage III, 215r-224v.

Sytske Hofstee
"Partners in Crime" : Dissident Male and Female Religious Leaders of the Clandestine Catholic
Church in the Dutch Republic (1570-1800)

religiously pluralistic.[8] This treaty contained the crucial principle of freedom of
conscience including more or less freedom of religion. However, the Reformed
Church became the privileged church, which meant that only this church community and its church buildings were permitted in the public domain. All other
church communities, including Catholic, Mennonite and Lutheran churches,
were tolerated but had to organize and maintain themselves in the private
domain.[9] A centuries-long period of crisis began for the Catholic Church, which
had previously been dominant in the Dutch area. The political decision-making
at regional level maintained an official ban on all kinds of Catholic matters,
from Catholic worship and the hierarchical administrative structure, to priests,
monasteries and monastics, including semi-religious Beguines. As a result, the
northern Netherlands were designated a mission area by the *Curia* in Rome.
Institutionally speaking, this meant there were no longer parishes with a vicarage, but "staties" or "mission stations" instead.[10] The remaining scattered
Catholic adherents organized themselves into Catholic assemblies and assemblies of spiritual virgins (as explained below). Together these organizations
formed the mission stations, since the 19th century referred to as "hidden
churches". The period of illegality lasted until French rule between 1795 and
1806, also called the "Batavian Republic". Particularly during the 17th century,
but also from time to time in the 18th century, Catholics were confronted with

---

[8] The actual year of the Reformation differs per province and city: Holland in 1572, Amsterdam
1578, Friesland 1580, Utrecht 1586, and Groningen 1594.

[9] This policy of toleration differed for each region. Holland and Utrecht were the most liberal
regions, while Friesland was one of the provinces with a strict policy towards Catholics. See
for the Frisian regulation regarding Catholics, Joke Spaans, *Armenzorg in Friesland 1500-
1800: Publieke zorg en particuliere liefdadigheid in zes Friese steden* (Uitgeverij Verloren:
Hilversum and Leeuwarden 1997), 280-281.

[10] In (Roman Catholic) historiography, *statie* is interpreted as a "parish and/or parish church"
during suppression of Catholicism in early modern times. This definition needs some nuance
because the characteristics of a parish (church) are partly incorrectly linked to an early modern
statie. A parish consists of a church building, a vicarage and a priest. An early modern *statie*
or "(mission)station" initially did not have a church building, nor a vicarage or its own priest.
The sources of income for maintaining a church (organization) were also lacking for a *statie*.
The clandestine Catholic community used all kinds of alternative financial sources. Catholic
vicarages did not exist at all in the first decades after the Reformation. Houses of spiritual
virgins often served as vicarages. A priest was an itinerant and had no permanent place of
residence. The term *statie* indicates simultaneously Catholic communities and church buildings
and covers a very diverse world of organization(s) and buildings. An overview of the implica-
tions of the different organizational models for leadership positions is beyond the scope of this
paper. I will use "mission station" in referring to the Dutch word *statie*.

Sytske Hofstee
"Partners in Crime": Dissident Male and Female Religious Leaders of the Clandestine Catholic
Church in the Dutch Republic (1570-1800)

a frequent absence of priests, which meant lack of male leadership. My research concentrates on the province of Friesland, where the lack of priests was quite serious. During this period there were moreover hardly any priests of Frisian descent in this area.[11] In contrast, about 500 Frisian women were active as spiritual virgins in the "Frisian Mission".[12] The deficit in priests for the mission stations in the Frisian area was mostly resolved by priests from the southern Netherlands and other areas of the Republic.

Finally, there is one more observation that needs to be made with regard to the social position of the marginalized Catholic people in the Republic. Lay Catholics, in comparison with Protestant civilians, were treated as second-class citizens throughout this period. For Catholic men it was difficult, if not impossible, to secure the attractive, prestigious, and exclusively male positions in the administrative and academic field.[13]

Catholic leadership in times of conflict and crisis

The main feature of Christian leadership, both male and female, is the spiritual element of "gifts of the Spirit".[14] Thus leadership and its fulfilment are based on an authority derived from God.[15] A second important feature of Catholic leadership is "chastity", called "celibacy" primarily for men and under the condition of a priest ordination. For women (nuns and semi-religious women) and monks it was referred to as "virginity", with the condition of taking a vow and entering a (monastic) community. In the early church, virginity or chastity became an important concept, especially with regard to speaking with authority.[16] The study of Kathleen Coyne Kelly shows that the concept of chastity has a long tradition and therefore is extremely complex and diverse. This complexity is illustrated by some definitions of chastity from the early

---

[11] For instance, I counted between five and ten Frisian male Jesuits between 1580 and 1800. The number of Frisian female Jesuits in this period presumably exceeds the amount of 100.

[12] Sytske Hofstee, "Geestelijke maagden ofwel 'klopkes' in Friesland. Oriëntatie en inventarisatie", in: *It Beaken*, jaargang 76, 2014, 34-54, here 53. For the earlier mentioned number of 5,000 spiritual virgins in the Republic, see Marit Monteiro, *Geestelijke maagden: Leven tussen klooster en wereld in Noord-Nederland* (Uitgeverij Verloren: Hilversum 1996), 54.

[13] Lodewijk Rogier, *Geschiedenis van het Katholicisme*, 740.

[14] Rosemary Radford Ruether and Eleanor McLaughlin (eds.), *Women of Spirit: Female Leadership in the Jewish and Christian Traditions* (Wipf and Stock Publishers: Eugene 1998), 19-21.

[15] Monteiro, "Inspiratie, ambitie en strategie," 79.

[16] Kathleen Coyne Kelly, *Performing Virginity and Testing Chastity in the Middle Ages* (Routledge: London 2000), 1-17.

Sytske Hofstee
*"Partners in Crime" : Dissident Male and Female Religious Leaders of the Clandestine Catholic
Church in the Dutch Republic (1570-1800)*

Christian period: besides "sexual virgin" and "spiritual virgin" we find also "monogamous marriage fidelity" as reference to chastity. In the distinction between the two concepts of virginity and chastity – both used interchangeably and sometimes overlapping –, chastity is seen as a spiritual quality and virginity rather as a physical technical fact. Spiritual chastity was rated higher.[17]

Basically, there are two overlapping formats of Catholic leadership: religious-administrative and spiritual. Religious leaders operate mainly within an established ecclesiastical order. Spiritual leadership is rather charismatic and can also take shape outside the usual authority and institutional frameworks.[18] As far as female Catholic leadership is concerned, both leadership styles include an underlying concept of "spiritual motherhood" (see below). With regard to religious authority or authoritative speaking, female Christian leaders claim and/or derive their religious authority from charisma rather than from office.[19] Within the Roman Catholic Church, women and men are assigned different positions of authority. The Catholic Church did not provide institutions for female religious leadership outside the walls of the monasteries.[20] Beguinages and sister convents of the Modern Devotion were an exception. Institutional positions of authority are derived from functions, automatically linking function and the allocation of authority. Women were excluded from both ecclesiastical and academic positions. In this way a formal theological speaking role was not available for them. In order to be heard, medieval and early modern women were forced to claim religious speaking roles in alternative ways.[21] One way was to turn to the spiritual leadership traditions of mystical and visionary women.[22] These medieval predecessors presented themselves as "mouthpieces of God" through a mystical lifestyle, representing the embodiment of spiritual values.[23]

But early modern women could also draw from a pool of other examples of female leadership. Since early Christianity, religious women had been acting

---

[17] Kelly, *Performing Virginity*, 1-17.
[18] A distinction based on the use of leadership descriptions by De Baar, Monteiro and Ruether in the mentioned studies.
[19] Ruether and McLaughlin, *Women of Spirit*, 19.
[20] Mirjam de Baar, "Ik moet spreken: Het spiritueel leiderschap van Antoinette Bourignon," in: Annelies van Heijst and Marjet Derks (eds.), *Terra Incognita: Historisch onderzoek naar katholicisme en vrouwelijkheid* (Kok Agora: Kampen 1994), 87-108, here 108.
[21] De Baar, "Ik moet spreken," 101.
[22] De Baar, "Ik moet spreken," 108.
[23] De Baar, "Ik moet spreken," 108.

Sytske Hofstee
"Partners in Crime": Dissident Male and Female Religious Leaders of the Clandestine Catholic
Church in the Dutch Republic (1570-1800)

as spiritual virgins, hermits, prophetesses, visionaries, abbesses and grand mistresses. Behind these female variants of religious and spiritual leadership lies the concept of "spiritual motherhood", dating from the early Middle Ages.[24] This model underlies the leadership of an abbess or prioress of a monastery, or a grand mistress of a beguinage, and, also in the early modern period, a spiritual mother of a virgins' assembly.[25] Being a spiritual mother heading a community of women was the highest form of female authority. A grand mistress, for example, had great decision-making power over the earthly and spiritual welfare of Beguines and was responsible for the material survival of the court.[26] In addition to administrative and organizational tasks, an abbess, grand mistress, or spiritual mother was engaged in the spiritual guidance of novices. This was her core task. She also supervised observance of the daily order and rules of life and acted as a spiritual counsellor for young novices.[27]

During the clandestine church period this female leadership concept knew many examples in the form of spiritual mothers of the widespread spiritual virgins-associations.[28] Joke Spaans argues that spiritual mothers radiated authority not only because of their exemplary piety and seniority in the meetings of the virgins, but also because of their noble or patrician descent. An important condition for becoming an early modern semi-religious spiritual mother was that a male authority figure was involved in the association. A priest also functioned as a spiritual guide and had assigned the leadership (sometimes by request) to a spiritual mother.[29]

After this brief introduction to Catholic leadership and women leaders, I zoom in on what it meant to lead a religious community during oppression. How did leadership work in the Catholic Church in the early modern northern

---

[24] Mirjam de Baar, *"Ik moet spreken": Het spiritueel leiderschap van Antoinette Bourignon (1616-1680)* (Walburg Pers: Zutphen 2004), 438.

[25] Monteiro, *Geestelijke maagden*, 294.

[26] Monika Triest, Guido van Poucke and Cecile Vanooteghem, *Grote Madammen: Het Sint-Elisabethbegijnhof en Sint-Amandsberg* (Uitgeverij Averbode N.V.: Averbode 2011), 29. This book is written from the perspective of female leadership.

[27] De Baar, *Antoinette Bourignon (1616-1680)*, 437-440.

[28] Spaans, *De Levens der Maechden*, 77-83.

[29] De Baar, *Antoinette Bourignon (1616-1680)*, 439. The various additional complex gender, social and authority aspects of a relationship between a male priest as a confessor and a spiritual virgin cannot be discussed in this paper. An extensive study on this topic is the work of Jodi Bilinkoff, *Related Lives: Confessors and their Female Penitents, 1450-1750* (Cornell University Press: Ithaca and London 2005). See also Monteiro, *Geestelijke Maagden*, 175-187 and 293-314.

Netherlands, in this church, which was a dissident and therefore clandestine organization that found itself in a long-term situation of deep crisis, due to the prohibition of Catholicism by worldly authorities? To interpret the "negotiating practices" of both Catholic male and female leaders as to wielding authority in the forbidden and hidden context, I will use the concept of "double-voiced agency". The double-voice concept originates from anthropology and was further developed within the study of literature, theology and gender studies. It is used within these disciplines to provide insight into the dynamics of female voices in a dominant male discourse.[30] The concept can be used in different settings to clarify hidden voices and it is of help in deconstructing androcentric history.[31] Fokkelien van Dijk-Hemmes has used the double-voice concept to detect women's voices as silenced by patriarchal dominance in biblical texts.[32] Annelies van Heijst, Marjet Derks and Kristien Suenens use this concept in a frame of social interaction, to reconstruct the subservient voices of women in (authority) relationships between nuns and priests. Kristien Suenens can be credited with adding "agency" to the concept in her recent dissertation.[33] Within the notion of agency, I include the closely related term of "practices". The concept of double-voiced agency expresses the ambiguity between ways of being both integrated into the prevailing culture and separated from it: between assent and contradiction at the same time.[34] In addition to masculine normativity, I distinguish two other dominant discourses: the dominant Protestant discourse inside the Republic and the dominant normative Catholic discourse outside the Republic.

Further, I will link forbidden Catholic voices, female as well as male, to the associated "dissimulative practices" of dissident Catholic women and men. Like Perez Zagorin I do not use the term "dissimulation" in a negative

---

[30] Annelies van Heijst and Marjet Derks, "Godsvrucht en gender: naar een geschiedschrijving in meervoud," in: Annelies van Heijst and Marjet Derks (eds.), *Terra Incognita: Historisch onderzoek naar katholicisme en vrouwelijkheid* (Kok Agora: Kampen 1994), 7-39, here 26-29. See also Fokkelien van Dijk-Hemmes, Jonneke Bekkenkamp and others (eds.), *The Double Voice of Her Desire: Texts* (Deo Publishing: Leiderdorp 2004).

[31] Van Heijst and Derks, "Godsvrucht en gender," 28.

[32] Fokkelien van Dijk-Hemmes, *De dubbele stem van haar verlangen: Teksten van Fokkelien van Dijk-Hemmes. Verzameld en ingeleid door Jonneke Bekkenkamp en Freda Dröes* (Meinema: Zoetermeer 1995).

[33] Kristien Suenens, *"Too robust to be saint": Female congregation founders in 19th-century Belgium: double-voiced agency, religious entrepreneurship and gender tension* (Leuven University Press: Leuven 2018).

[34] Van Heijst and Derks, "Godsvrucht en gender," 26 and 30.

Sytske Hofstee
"Partners in Crime": Dissident Male and Female Religious Leaders of the Clandestine Catholic
Church in the Dutch Republic (1570-1800)

judgmental way, but in an indicative way. According to Zagorin, dissimulation was an important part of religious, intellectual, and social life in early modern Europe.[35] In daily life early modern Europeans had to cope with severe social sensitivities and political and theological doctrines. Following Zagorin, I see "dissimulation" as an umbrella term for a wide range of power strategies used by a minority in relation to an authority. I will use the concept of double-voiced agency in a broader setting, not only in texts or within one particular community, but in multiple dissident Catholic groups in early modern society. Therefore, I employ a definition of religious dissimulation in which double-voiced agency counts as a dissimulative strategy according to which a minority (group or individual) makes simultaneously use of adhesion and resistance practices or tactics or both while negotiating with an authority. These tactics can be expressed by word – spoken and written – and act. For instance, the tactic of "crypto-Catholicism" (double identity) is a quite well-known dissimulative strategy, mostly performed by elite Catholic men. The examples of "double-voiced practices" of the clergy described below are individual tactics in writing. "Double-voiced practices" of spiritual virgins are mainly "tactical" acts, on the individual as well as collective level.[36]

Male Catholic leaders in a clandestine context

During the period of crisis, which lasted for over two centuries, Catholic communities were entangled in constant minor and major conflicts with local authorities. Priests and gatherings of believers in particular as well as spiritual virgins were targets of persecution on a regular and random basis. Catholic dissidents often paid a high price for the tolerated illegality. The price ranged from seizure and destruction of liturgical vessels to heavy fines or blackmail charges imposed by authorities of cities and municipalities.[37] To compensate

---

[35] Zagorin distinguishes, among others, religious, political, and intellectual dissimulation. Perez Zagorin, *Ways of lying: Dissimulation, Persecution, and Conformity in Early Modern Europe* (Harvard University Press: London 1990), 1-15.

[36] Because of the limited space of this article, reverse examples of gendered double-voice practices, masculine tactical and feminine written ones, unfortunately have to be left out.

[37] Unlike in England, priests and members of dissident religious groups were not punished with the death penalty by law. Still, Dutch Catholics suffered some casualties, for instance the "19 Martyrs of Gorkum" in 1572, who were killed in Den Brielle. Caroline Lenarduzzi's dissertation provides a nuanced picture of the experience of Dutch Catholic dissidents in this matter. Caroline Lenarduzzi, *Katholiek in de Republiek: De belevingswereld van een religieuze minderheid 1570-1750* (Uitgeverij Vantilt: Nijmegen 2019).

Sytske Hofstee
"Partners in Crime" : Dissident Male and Female Religious Leaders of the Clandestine Catholic
Church in the Dutch Republic (1570-1800)

for this, devoted Catholic believers were willing to donate large amounts of money with spiritual virgins being often the largest donors.[38]

The circumstances under which a priest had to administer the sacraments were often harsh, although the situation differed by region. In the first decades after the revolution of the Reformation – and in Friesland for almost the entire 17th century –, priests usually served the Eucharist at night, in different houses at remote places. Priests found themselves in an isolated position in society. For a number of apostolic vicars this even applied literally, as they were lodged in women's monasteries just outside the national borders of the Republic.[39] In the Protestant-oriented society clergy lacked any social status. Within Catholic communities a priest was held in high esteem. Priests were of high symbolic value for the oppressed Catholic faith community, while spiritual virgins were of high symbolic value to the dissident Catholic institute.[40]

In their isolation, priests found new ways to assert their religious authority. Quite a few priests were engaged in the writing of books and song texts. There seems to be a correlation, moreover, between writing priests and large spiritual virgins' communities.[41] In addition to the special "virgin books", a literary genre distinguished by Pontianus Polman, the enormous amount of Catholic

---

[38] Apostolic vicar Johannes van Neercassel (1625-1686) noted that spiritual virgins were attractive to the mission because of their financial strength. Earlier his predecessor, Philippus Rovenius (1573-1651), wrote about the spiritual virgins' contribution to the Dutch Mission as being, next to spiritually benefiting, also materially convenient. Elisja Schulte van Kessel, *Geest en Vlees in godsdienst en wetenschap* (Staatsuitgeverij: Den Haag 1980), 105. For examples of generosity by spiritual virgins, see: Eugenie Theissing, *Klopjes en Kwezels* (Dekker & Van de Vegt N.V.: Nijmegen 1935), 53, 128-131, 138-141. Imelda van der Linden, "Laveren tussen hemel en aarde: Over klopjes in de zeventiende en achttiende eeuw," in: *Tidinge van die Goude*, jaargang 27, Nr. 1, 2009, 19-32, here 29, note 66.

[39] For example, the community of the monastery of "Maria Vlucht" in Glane, founded in 1665 by former nuns from Almelo, and the Franciscan sisters of the Saint Elisabeth Convent in the city of Huissen.

[40] From the circle of the apostolic vicars comes the characterization of spiritual virgins as "dat edele sieraad van de missie" or "that precious jewel of the mission". Gian Ackermans, *Herders en huurlingen, Bisschoppen en priesters in de Republiek (1663-1705)* (Prometheus/Bert Bakker: Amsterdam 2003), 144.

[41] Stalpart van de Wiele (1579-1630), seminar priest in Delft, and the Jesuit Johannes van Sambeeck (1601-1666), working in Harderwijk, collaborated with choirs of spiritual virgins for their songbooks. Natascha Veldhorst, *Zingend door het leven: Het Nederlandse liedboek in de Gouden Eeuw* (Amsterdam University Press: Amsterdam 2009), 53. Two priests of virgins' assemblies in the city of Utrecht have contributed books to the virgins' genre. Monteiro, *Geestelijke Maagden*, Bijlage III, 364.

Sytske Hofstee
"Partners in Crime" : Dissident Male and Female Religious Leaders of the Clandestine Catholic
Church in the Dutch Republic (1570-1800)

books produced by priests in the 17th century included books in a range of fields: asceticism and mysticism, apology and polemics, homiletics, liturgy, hagiography, dogmatics, morality, and catechesis.[42] As far as Catholic spiritual songs are concerned, a spiritual virgin song genre can also be distinguished.[43]

A remarkable Catholic response to the dominant Protestant discourse is the practice of the highest leadership of the mission in the Republic.[44] Only a few examples can be discussed here, such as the case of an apostolic vicar and his "double-voiced agency" towards the *Curia* in Rome and Brussels. Apostolic vicar Sasbout Vosmeer (1548-1614) asked the Pope for permission to deploy lay people at religious gatherings during the frequent periods of a priest's absence, thus paving the way for laity preaching and leading in prayer and

---

[42] Monteiro, *Geestelijke maagden*, 122-133, here 124, note 3.
My hypothesis of the intensive book production in the 17th century is based on research I conducted in 2018 on the book collection of one of the many so-called Jesuit libraries in the Republic. The Jesuit book collection of Leeuwarden (capital of Friesland) contains over 1,100 titles from the early modern period. The table, based on the dating of the editions, clearly shows the peak of Catholic book production during the 17th century.

period	number of titles	percentage	total
1580-1600	53	5%	
1600-1650	557	49%	
1650-1700	329	28%	
1600-1700	886	77%	
1700-1800	208	18%	
1580-1800		100%	1147

Research is needed to see whether this outcome can be compared with other early modern Jesuit libraries and also if this table can be connected to a booklist made by Rudolf van Dijk. Between 1971 and 1974 Van Dijk worked on a project entitled "Spiritual life in the Netherlands under the Apostolic Vicars". He registered 2,100 manuscripts (15th-18th century) from 150 libraries in The Netherlands, Belgium and West Germany. Rudolf van Dijk, *Twaalf hoofd-stukken over het ontstaan, de bloei en de doorwerking van de Moderne Devotie* (Uitgeverij Verloren: Hilversum 2012), 10.

[43] Veldhorst, *Zingend door het leven*, 53. Charles van Leeuwen concludes the same. Charles van Leeuwen, *Hemelse Voorbeelden: De Heiligenliederen van Stalpart van de Wiele (1579-1630)* (SUN Uitgeverij: Nijmegen 2001), 330.

[44] Since all bishops and other Catholic officials were banned in the Republic, the illegal church organized itself nationally with an "apostolic vicar" as a kind of bishop, and regionally with "archpriests" as heads of a province.

song. In practice, though, mainly spiritual virgins performed these tasks.[45] In another discussion between Vosmeer and the nuncio, the question whether spiritual virgins (choirs) were permitted to sing during mass also reflects double-voiced argumentation. Nuncio Guido Bentvoglio (1579-1644) wrote to Vosmeer about complaints he had received from clergy, concerning the important role of spiritual virgins during the Eucharist and the fact that they sang the Divinum Officium.[46] He had also heard of semi-religious women accompanying confessors on their missionary journeys to sing mass. Vosmeer replied: "The presence of spiritual virgins on the altar was not to be welcomed, but the situation in the Republic, where a priest was not always available, allowed no other choice." He added, "[that] in Catholic lands religious women also acted as acolytes (altar servers)".[47] In fact, traditional Catholic rules were under such great pressure in the Dutch Republic that it was actually impossible to observe them in many situations. On the one hand, double-voiced agency used by a male leader shows discrepancy with normative Catholic practices, usually carried out by men. On the other hand, this discrepancy clarifies the urgency of the involvement of semi-religious women in the mission.

Spiritual virgins in a clandestine context

To further position the Frisian women religious leaders, who will be discussed further below, the focus in this section will be on individuals or groups of spiritual virgins who were closely connected to the clergy in the Republic. In this paragraph I will pay attention to types of "double-voice practices" by spiritual virgins, mainly within a dominant Protestant discourse. I will give a description of leadership positions and of some collective dissimulation practices of spiritual virgins and of their female spiritual leaders.

The Reformation was followed by a period of transition for religious and semi-religious women. Monasteries were closed, sometimes reused as universities and for other public functions, and even destroyed, as was often the case in Friesland. However, according to my research the remaining population of the communities of nuns, third order members and Beguines were in a number of cases at the root of the formation of mission stations. For instance, a group of Dominican sisters in Leeuwarden, the capital city of the province of

---

[45] Spaans, *Levens der Maechden*, 47.

[46] Lenarduzzi, *Katholiek in de Republiek*, 219. Although Lenarduzzi pays ample attention to spiritual virgins, she describes their activities, in my opinion, from a priest-assistant perspective.

[47] Lenarduzzi, *Katholiek in de Republiek*, 219.

Sytske Hofstee
"Partners in Crime" : Dissident Male and Female Religious Leaders of the Clandestine Catholic
Church in the Dutch Republic (1570-1800)

Friesland, "transformed" to the semi-religious state. Their former monastery buildings became the basis for three mission stations. The buildings, which were under their ownership, housed both a Dominican and a Franciscan illegal church for at least two centuries. Examples of semi-religious women's communities elsewhere which became the starting point of a mission, are found throughout the Republic: the well-known virgins' assembly in Haarlem, the beguinages in Delft, Haarlem and Amsterdam, an elite boarding school by spiritual virgins in Culemborg (Gelderland), and also the so-called *hofjes* or "women's courtyards"; for instance the "Sint Andrieshof " in Amsterdam.[48] The collective and social infrastructure of groups of semi-religious women was used by apostolic vicars and priests for hiding, administrative work, as a base, and so forth.[49] The mission centres of the Dutch Mission (Haarlem, Delft, Utrecht, Oldenzaal and Leeuwarden) appear to coincide with large virgin associations in those cities.[50]

The persecution of spiritual virgins was not, for various reasons, as extensive as that of the priests. Yet the virgins faced opposition by administrative measures and *plakkaten* or public notices, directed specifically at them. Also, like priests, some virgins were not safeguarded from banishment and penalties, though to a lesser extent. From about 1640 onwards, specifically designed notices against spiritual virgins appeared so as to undermine their economic, social and cultural activities in support of the clandestine church community.[51] This legislation concerned the social (cohabitation), cultural (education), and economic activities (bequeathing to priests) of spiritual virgins. Spiritual virgins attuned their semi-religious way of life and their associated activities very precisely to the limits of the possibilities permitted by the authorities. For example, the special laws that prohibited them from living together were

---

[48] The school in Culemborg was ruled by spiritual virgins and founded in 1626, and the associated mission station was founded in 1628. Theissing, *Klopjes en Kwezels*, 152. A few houses of the Andrieshofje were donated in 1623 by a grandparent of Catharina Jans Oly and converted into a church, which was served by a younger brother of Oly. Els Kloek, *1001 Vrouwen uit de Nederlandse Geschiedenis* (Uitgeverij Vantilt: Nijmegen 2013), 290-292.

[49] Conclusion based on the study of Gian Ackermans, *Herders en huurlingen*. Another example is Ael Gerrets, the grandmother of Catharina Jans Oly, whose house functioned as a refuge for the leaders of the Mission. Spaans, *Levens der Maechden*, 148.

[50] Conclusion based on my own research and the mentioning by Ackermans of mission centres. Ackermans, *Herders en huurlingen*, 14.

[51] The virgin association in Haarlem was targeted by the authorities as early as the year 1590. Theissing, *Klopjes en Kwezels,* 186-192.

Sytske Hofstee
"Partners in Crime" : Dissident Male and Female Religious Leaders of the Clandestine Catholic
Church in the Dutch Republic (1570-1800)

circumvented by living with family members – semi-religious sisters, mothers, nieces and aunts –, or in poor houses and sometimes *en masse* in courtyards (*hofjes*).[52] Another dissimulative "strategy" was the use of uniform sober and shabby clothing, which carried out a double message. The uniformity made them recognizable as virgins, while their dressing as poor people made them unpunishable.[53] The double set of clothing of Geliana van der Lely, the virgin's robe and damsel robe mentioned earlier, can probably also be interpreted as strategic. The outfits suggest a double identity and may have been used by her for reasons of dissimulation in the power play with authorities.

The ban on Catholic education provided by spiritual virgins was circumvented by operating in a decentralized manner and without statutes, instead of centrally and officially. Acting this way prevented control by authorities.[54] Religious education took place regularly under the cover of "handicraft training". This dissimulative undercover strategy can be understood using the concept of "frontstage- and backstage conduct" of Erving Goffman.[55] A tolerated women's collective in public space – like a women poorhouse – served as a frontstage for all sorts of clandestine backstage activity, for example an assembly of spiritual virgins or Beguines. The virgin association in Haarlem (frontstage) even offered protection to women who followed the Order of Saint Clare (backstage),[56] an extremely risky venture because of the very strict prohibition of nuns and the difficult illegal conditions for implementation of a contemplative life. Another example of dissimulation is a bobbin lace school or a general girl school serving as a cover of a (boarding)school for Catholic education. All these practices can be seen as female variants of dissimulative practices, including double-voice agency in a dominant Protestant discourse.[57]

---

[52] Conclusion regarding poor housing based on Lenarduzzi's description. Lenarduzzi, *Katholiek in de Republiek*, 25.

[53] Lenarduzzi, *Katholiek in de Republiek*, 150-155.

[54] Spaans, *Levens der Maechden*, 44-46.

[55] I follow Willem Frijhoff who uses this concept for analysing social interaction of Catholic dissidents in public space. Willem Frijhoff, *Embodied Belief: Ten Essays on Religious Culture in Dutch History* (Uitgeverij Verloren: Hilversum 2002), 39-66, here 52.

[56] Spaans, *Levens der Maechden*, 11, 47, 75-77, 91. In line with "hidden church", the term "hidden monastery" is appropriate here. To what extent the Order of Saint Clare was followed elsewhere in the Republic is unknown.

[57] The double-voice agency concept can be seen as a further elaboration of the practices of dissidents who were confronted with the situation of the *omgangsoecumene* or "interconfessional conviviality", mentioned by Willem Frijhoff. The concept of "social ecumenism" mainly concerns the everyday coexistence of residents in the religiously plural society of the Republic.

Sytske Hofstee
"Partners in Crime" : Dissident Male and Female Religious Leaders of the Clandestine Catholic
Church in the Dutch Republic (1570-1800)

Finally, a few last remarks on the social position of semi-religious women in society and within the dissident Catholic community. In contrast to frequent absence of priests, spiritual virgins represented the presence of a permanent Catholic spirituality in the Republic throughout the period of crisis. From a lay perspective, their presence was the constant factor in the lives of Catholic dissidents. Institutionally speaking they embodied the Catholic church and the guarantee of its continuity over the centuries. The social position of spiritual virgins can be called ambiguous, or – in other words – it implies a double-voiced character. Unlike priests, spiritual virgins had a "double" recognition in society caused by their "dual position". On the one hand, most semi-religious women carried out recognized functions in society as workers, shop-keepers, nurses, teachers, and so on, thus earning their own livelihood. On the other hand, they held various positions, and performed all kinds of tasks in the clandestine church. The virgins also were (frontstage) "the eyes and ears, hands and feet" of the isolated priest (backstage) in society. In addition to social appreciation and esteem from the local population, spiritual virgins possessed high status and esteem because of their spiritual authority within the Catholic community. Local authorities were ambivalent about this dual position of virgins and their assemblies. Although the educational and social "undercover strategies" performed by the virgins for Catholic purposes presented the authorities with enforcement problems, their philanthropic work could not be punished.

Female Catholic leaders in the Province of Friesland

In the previous section the leadership position of spiritual mothers has been described more or less indirectly. Their decision-making power in the power play of negotiation with secular and ecclesiastical authorities has remained somewhat underexposed. Here, I will focus on female religious leaders in the northern province of the Republic called Friesland, a region in which the phenomenon of spiritual virgins has not been studied before. The results of the case studies of my dissertation about the support of dissident church communities in Friesland by early modern semi-religious and laywomen show that women took the lead in various areas concerning the Catholic Church. The

---

Willem Frijhoff, *Embodied Belief*, 39-66. See also with regard to religious coexistence in the Republic and the debate on the various views and interpretations of the alleged or mythical "Dutch tolerance", the introduction of Lenarduzzi's dissertation. Lenarduzzi, *Katholiek in de Republiek*, 12-13.

Sytske Hofstee
"Partners in Crime" : Dissident Male and Female Religious Leaders of the Clandestine Catholic
Church in the Dutch Republic (1570-1800)

four women studied were active in the domains of virgins' assembly, mission station, and poor relief. Choosing these four women, I include diversity in time, place, Catholic signature, spiritual and marital state, and social origin. The investigated women came from towns as well as rural villages; two are spiritual virgins (a Jesuitess and a Dominican *tertiaris*) and two are lay widows who were members of a secular mission station. Their social backgrounds range from nobility and patrician to farm-owners. Their financial position differs considerably, but their marital status is the same, namely that of an unmarried woman, since legally the widow state is equal to the civil unmarried state. The two noble ladies that are investigated managed their family castle, including associated lands and leasehold properties. Lady His van Emingha and freehold farmer Baukje Faber were also active on the local credit market. Van Emingha in particular had lent considerable sums and invested in real estate. Towards the end of her life patrician Geliana van der Lely was given the management of a number of farms and rental properties. All of the women had governance over tenants and servants. An unexpected additional similarity between the women is the fact that they were the last survivors of their family or extended family. Van Emingha survived one infant and four adult children; Faber survived three young daughters. Van Wytsma was the last survivor of her family of nineteen, Van der Lely the last of a family of four members.

The first example concerns Lady His van Sythiema-van Emingha (1580-1660). She had four children and became a widow at a young age.[58] Both of her daughters were housed as schoolgirls at the renowned spiritual virgin association in Haarlem in the province of Holland, where they later entered as spiritual virgins.[59] Van Emingha visited the Haarlem community quite regularly for a spiritual retreat.[60] Shortly after being widowed, Van Emingha moved to Leeuwarden. Here she purchased a house for herself in 1619 as well as the former Catholic women's poorhouse in 1623, in order to secure this form of care in a hostile Protestant surrounding.[61] Van Emingha probably had

---

[58] Her husband Haring Harings van Sythiema died in 1612.
[59] Nothing is known about the education or careers of the sons.
[60] Spaans, *Levens der Maechden*, CD-ROM, Bijlage III, 217 verso.
[61] The residential house and another house in the same street, purchased in 1622, might have been the basis for the founding of the secular mission station in Leeuwarden. This mission station was, until the selling of the church building in 1811, located in the same street (Bontepapesteeg). Wietse B. van der Velde, "(Oud)-Katholieken in Leeuwarden: De Cleresieparochie in de Noteboom," in: Tjebbe de Jong (eds.), *Van Vitus tot Titus. 500 jaar katholiek leven in Leeuwarden* (Titus Brandsma Parochie: Leeuwarden 2009), 85.

Sytske Hofstee
"Partners in Crime": Dissident Male and Female Religious Leaders of the Clandestine Catholic
Church in the Dutch Republic (1570-1800)

Picture 1: His van Emingha (1580-1660) in 1603
(Collection Fries Museum, Leeuwarden | restored with support of the Wassenbergh-
Clarijs-Fontein Stichting 2018)

a position as a guardian in the clandestine organization of Catholic poor relief. The "Van Emingha poorhouse" presumably remained after her death, as the location of the house has been destined for Catholic poor relief throughout the centuries.[62] Over time, private care for the poor by female guardians will be transformed into a more institutionalized form of care, solely run by male guardians.[63]

---

[62] A cadastral map from 1832 shows on roughly the same location the Catholic poorhouse.

[63] A list of only male Catholic guardians of the poorhouse dating from 1674, has been preserved. "Naamlijst de Heeren Voogden vanden Roomsch Katholijken Armenstaat te Leeuwarden," Historisch Centrum Leeuwarden. The list was composed in 1853. See also the notification of a poorhouse founded in 1783, called "Broodkamer" and situated in the Speelmanstraat. Hans Jorna, "Statiekerken in Leeuwarden," in: Tjebbe de Jong (eds.), *Van Vitus tot Titus*, 33-49, here 40.

Sytske Hofstee
"Partners in Crime" : Dissident Male and Female Religious Leaders of the Clandestine Catholic
Church in the Dutch Republic (1570-1800)

In 1638, Van Emingha was in charge of the renovation and expansion of the church of the secular mission station in Haarlem called "De Hoeck" or "Sint Bernardus".[64] This supervising responsibility, traditionally performed by the spiritual mother of a convent, appears to have been outsourced to Van Emingha. The reasons for this are unknown but might be connected with her authority position as a widowed noble lady, apparently without possessing the (formal) spiritual state. As a dissident and fervent Catholic, His van Emingha embodies in a certain way the four hallmarks of early modern female religious authority: piety, "informal" chastity (her widowed state), seniority, and the noble status.

Maria Clara van Wytsma (1617-c. 1686) was a noblewoman too, and a second cousin to Van Emingha. She became Jesuitess, following the example of the early modern female Jesuit movement. A Spanish lady – Elisabeth Rosella, who was a contemporary of Ignatius de Loyola (1491-1556), – had founded a female counterpart to the Jesuit order in the same time, which had spread widely in Italy, Germany, France, and the southern and northern Netherlands.[65] Van Wytsma founded a Jesuit mission station, in the mid-17th century, in the family castle inhabited by her, situated close to the city of Dokkum.[66] Possibly one or two unmarried sisters of Maria Clara took part in the (preparations of) dissident activities.[67] Van Wytsma facilitated the Jesuit priest and the local religious community, offering them hospitality and shelter. She also made the private chapel accessible to local Catholics. According to her preserved codicil, nearly all the silver liturgical supplies for the Eucharist were owned by Van Wytsma.[68] This codicil contains successively a rather complete list of church goods for celebrating the Eucharist, the surety of these liturgical objects at the time of her death, a lifelong yearly financial compensation for her priest-brother and the name of an executor and a witness. The enumeration

---

[64] Spaans, *Levens der Maechden*, CD-ROM, Bijlage III, 217 verso.

[65] Merry Wiesner, "Women's Response to the Reformation," in: Ronnie Po-chia Hsia (ed.), *The German People and the Reformation* (Cornell University Press: Ithaca and London 1988), 148-171, here 159.

[66] Paul Begheyn, *Gids voor de geschiedenis van de jezuïeten in Nederland 1540-1850* (Valkhof Pers; Nederlands Instituut voor Jezuïeten Studies; Institutum historicum Societatis Iesu: Nijmegen, Amsterdam and Rome 2006).

[67] Her older sister Thecla van Wytsma (1614-1653) died shortly before the mission years 1654-1657, which were registered by the Jesuits. Nothing is known about the youngest sister, Eelck van Wytsma (born 1623).

[68] Rijksarchief Beveren in Belgium – Inventaris van het archief van de Nederduitse provincie der jezuïeten (provincia Belgica, vervolgens provincia Flandro-Belgica): Inventory number 3073.

Sytske Hofstee
"Partners in Crime" : Dissident Male and Female Religious Leaders of the Clandestine Catholic
Church in the Dutch Republic (1570-1800)

of the church goods is divided into three parts, indicated by Van Wytsma: "all my silverware belonging to the church" (namely a silver gilt chalice and two silver ampoules with a silver dish), "all my ecclesiastical ornaments none excepted" and "all other jewellery belonging to the church" (a statue of Our Lady, a large crucifix inlaid with mother-of-pearl, a red velvet missal with silver fittings, and a large breviary with gilded sides).

Unfortunately, the sources do not provide data on her share in catechetical practices and other activities such as administrative affairs and girls' education.[69] Van Wytsma scores on all features of female religious leadership. It is unknown why the foundation of the mission station was only temporary. However, connections in female networks show that the founding initiative of Maria Clara van Wytsma was followed up in the early 18th century by the foundation of a Jesuit mission station by the noble Van Ockinga-sisters.[70]

The third example of Frisian female leaders is patrician daughter Geliana van der Lely (c. 1675-1730). She descended from a famous Leeuwarden family of silversmiths and lawyers. Van der Lely became a Dominican *tertiaris* in 1710 and was most likely in charge of the purchase of an organ for the church community. At first sight this seems a strange thing, for how can a young novice be qualified for such a role? The testamentary gift in 1694 of Fockien Jans Rinia (c. 1660-1705), a laywoman, to Van der Lely for "the purchase of a new organ", is the only evidence so far that she might have held position of leadership. The circumstances of this gift may be better understood by means of reports in manuscripts about music making and liturgical celebrations of spiritual virgins elsewhere.[71] The donation was not addressed to the priest nor to a male board member (the donor's husband was a church administrator), but explicitly to Van der Lely. The latter was presumably involved in musical activities during worship service. Before the Reformation, male choirs used to perform church music and clerics performed

---

[69] Education was the core activity of Jesuitess or Jesuitin women. For examples in the southern Netherlands see the study of M. de Vroede, *Kwezels en Zusters* (Paleis der Academiën: Brussels 1994), 90-95 and Marit Monteiro, *Geestelijke maagden*. The study of Haruko Ward gives insight into the activities of Japanese Jesuitesses in the same period. Haruko Nawata Ward, *Women Religious Leaders in Japan's Christian Century, 1549-1650* (Routledge: Oxon and New York 2009/2016).

[70] Spinster Sophia Amelia van Ockinga (1651-1730) and widow Helena Maria van Ockinga (ca. 1653-1718) on the "Ockinga-castle" in Burgwerd, Friesland. Begheyn, *Jezuïetengids*, 18.

[71] Lenarduzzi's chapter "Catholic soundscapes" extensively covers the song culture of Catholics and spiritual virgins in particular. Lenarduzzi, *Katholiek in de Republiek,* 211-245.

Picture 2: "Kloppenkoor" or choir of spiritual virgins in 1634 on the title page of the songbook "Gvlde-iaers feest-dagen" by Jan Baptist Stalpart van der Wiele (Collection Koninklijke Bibliotheek Den Haag (original from Tresoar Leeuwarden))

Gregorian chants in the Catholic liturgy. After the Reformation, in Dutch Catholic ecclesiastical communities spiritual virgins were often responsible for the liturgical chant, as altar servers and in special "choirs of virgins".[72]

---

[72] The pioneering role of semi-religious women in early modern Catholic church music becomes evident in various notes in the manuscripts of Catharina Jans Oly. Spaans, *Levens der Maechden*, 91-93.

Sytske Hofstee
"Partners in Crime" : Dissident Male and Female Religious Leaders of the Clandestine Catholic
Church in the Dutch Republic (1570-1800)

Spiritual virgins assisted in the accompaniment of high masses, funerals, praises and other church ceremonies, both vocally and instrumentally, as violinists and organists.[73] It is therefore quite plausible that Van der Lely, of patrician descent, was in charge of musical affairs performed by virgins of the Dominican mission station, possibly even as conductor of a spiritual virgin choir.[74] Geliana van der Lely lacks seniority concerning the female leadership features.

Finally, there is the example of the 18th century farmer Baukje Bouwes Faber (1700-1781). Cash books of the mission station "Roodhuis" in the countryside northwest of the city of Sneek, contain a remarkable amount of (sometimes) very large donations of Faber.[75] Over a period of 65 years and at various stages of her life (single, married, and widowed), she donated almost 300 non-anonymous financial or material gifts in excess of 5,000 guilders. Before marriage, Faber had been a member of the virgins' community of the rural community of Roodhuis. Even during her unmarried state, Faber's many donations – gifts to the poor as well as gifts to the clandestine church – are striking. After the death of her husband in 1761, she donated thousands of guilders, which made her the founder of the new church building.[76]

Faber can be seen as theologically decisive in the design of the main altar. She donated a complete altar full of biblical symbolism, including four life-size statues depicting Faith, Hope, and the apostles Peter and Paul. The story of the Last Supper and the imagination of God and the Holy Spirit were also central to the vision of the patroness. Remarkable, furthermore, is the gift of a large coat of arms of Faber's family and the motto *Largiter et Hilariter* (generously and cheerfully). This coat of arms hung from the church's attic above the main altar, a practice that might be regarded as innovative in the Catholic memorial cult of that time. The shield and motto were, on the one hand, a reminder of the patroness and, on the other hand, an inspiring, powerful message and appeal to contemporaries as well as future generations of

---

[73] Rogier, *Geschiedenis van het Katholicisme*, part II, 716.

[74] This assumption is supported by a document of a fundraising campaign in Leeuwarden, by some Jesuitesses for the purchase of an organ, some decades later in the nearby Jesuit mission station. Here women were also active in the organization, along with a few men, and functioned as choir members and instrumentalists as well. Historisch Centrum Leeuwarden, St. Bonifaciusparochie, inventory number 15.

[75] Tresoar Leeuwarden: 273-08, inventory numbers 03, 04, 05, 07 and 64-73.

[76] Baukje Bouwes married in 1728 to Sibe Minnes Faber (1704-1761), an old Catholic carpenter from Leeuwarden.

Picture 3: Coat of Arms of Baukje Bouwes Faber dating from 1765, in the parish church of Roodhuis (picture by Sytske Hofstee 2016)

churchgoers.[77] Today the coat of arms still hangs in the sacristy of the village church.

Naturally, Baukje Faber consulted the priest about these purchases.[78] The fact of her seniority and her donorship, in contrast to the young and not financially contributing priest, will have given Faber the lead in the business of altar design. At the time of the altar purchase, Faber was aged over 60 and had been dedicating her whole life to the clandestine church and Catholic community. She was active in the mission for years and was the well-known and greatest

---

[77] It is not known to what extent her inheritance influenced the giving behaviour of parish members. However, it is striking that during a large money-raising campaign in 2013, intended for the restoration of the church foundation, an amount of one million euros was raised by the small community, mainly by married farmer couples. Unpublished interview with custodian Mr. K. Andringa, 18 July, 2016.

[78] Such as the election of Peter and Paul over, for example, the missionaries Boniface and Willibrord.

patroness of the community. Priest Johannes van Rijswijk (1733-1806) was only 30 years of age at the time and for the first time active in the ministry. Baukje Faber's example meets all female leadership characteristics, even though she seems to act in the periphery as a devout lay woman and a spiritual virgin. It is possible, however, that she took up her vows as a spiritual widow sometime after the death of her husband. The case of Baukje Bouwes Faber adds an extraordinary aspect to the female religious leadership formats. Faber's extremely generous practice of gift giving could be interpreted as a way of inspiring leadership to an oppressed religious community. The authoritative speaking position of Faber seems to have taken the form of donating to a specific ecclesiastical cause. Gifts for the high altar were highly ranked, symbolically placing the donor in the centre of the Most Holy. This highest attainable and most honourable purpose of donating was achieved by Faber.[79]

Although these examples of female leadership positions unfortunately need much reconstruction, due to scarce resources, the data do give proof of it. As for the examples, Geliana van der Lely possibly displayed organizational leadership in the field of church music and liturgy. Her case also shows the involvement of lay women in financial and material matters of a mission station. The founders Maria Clara van Wytsma and Baukje Bouwes Faber constitute a clear counterbalance to the prevailing image in historiography of solely priestly founders of mission stations. The example of His van Emingha provides evidence of female management of a "private" form of poor relief. The dissident context of this "clandestine poor relief" allows it to be labelled as a dissimulative practice. Van Emingha might have used her poorhouse as a frontstage cover for her Catholic oriented activities. The terms "private" and "institutional" poor relief may be used interchangeably here, because of the dissident position and connected dissimulative practices. Early modern institutional care meant (mostly Protestant) government controlled social care, which was just not an option for Van Emingha. For this reason, it may be better to refer to Van Emingha's Catholic social care as "semi-institutional poor relief". Until now, it has been mainly male-dominated management

---

[79] This symbolic practice performed by Faber is in line with a conclusion in Rene Lugtigheid's research into the transformation of 18th century donated damsels' dresses into priestly robes. In this way, the donors, like their female medieval predecessors, most probably demanded a role in the Eucharist celebration in a symbolic sense. Rene Lugtigheid, *Van aardse stof tot hemelse lof* (Uitgeverij Verloren: Hilversum 2021), 185-187.

which has been studied in the field of sociological studies of principally institutionalized poor relief.

Leadership possibilities of women were closely linked to the process of institutionalization of the Catholic Church in the Republic. In general, after about the year 1700 the persecution of Catholics decreased, whence the self-awareness of the Catholics grew. During this process, Catholic men were given more room to act, which forced women to the background and made them return to former, smaller roles.[80] The three domains discussed above show some difference in the changes for women's leadership possibilities within an increasing discourse of Catholic normative male dominance within the Republic. The example of His van Emingha shows how already during the 17th century poor relief was influenced by institutionalization (eliminating women guardians), seemingly earlier then the banning of women from the domain of the mission station and the disappearance of virgins' assemblies. Concerning church music, besides local differences, during the 19th century church choirs became closed to women, and secondly, spiritual virgin's choirs were banned.[81] In Friesland spiritual virgins' assemblies seem to have disappeared before the year 1800, whereas assemblies in Holland and Utrecht remained until 1900, or like in the province of Overijssel, until the 20th century.

Concluding remarks

In the centuries following the Reformation, the Catholic Church in the Republic faced a unique situation in terms of leadership, gender and associated authority relationships. Normative Catholicism with its prescribed, mainly male leadership positions no longer existed in the religiously pluralistic society of the Republic. Crisis and conflict were not the sole determinants of the positions and activities of early modern female and male religious leaders. Public opinion had also been shifting. Figuratively speaking, Catholic church walls had been demolished, whereas Protestant walls had not or barely been resurrected in the first decades after the religious and political upheavals of both the Reformation and the ending of the Dutch Revolt of Eighty Years' War

---

[80] Institutional leadership reverts to the patriarchal pattern, eliminating women. This development is also characteristic of many Christian renewal movements. Ruether and McLaughlin, *Women of Spirit*, 21-22.

[81] Aloysius Kat, *De geschiedenis der kerkmuziek in de Nederlanden sedert de Hervorming* (N.V. Gooi & Sticht: Hilversum 1939), 171-176.

Sytske Hofstee
*"Partners in Crime" : Dissident Male and Female Religious Leaders of the Clandestine Catholic
Church in the Dutch Republic (1570-1800)*

(1568-1648) by the treaty of the Peace of Münster (1648). For early modern citizens of most layers of society, a choice for a certain religion was more or less open. At the level of Catholic leadership, a vacuum had emerged with new opportunities for (semi-religious) women and religious pioneers. This vacuum provided room for female initiative in the domains of faith, education and (pastoral) care. Paradoxically, the prevailing gender-based expectations, that is to say, the conventional view that "women are not leaders" turned out to be advantageous to Catholic (semi-religious) women. This adage made them unsuitable in the eyes of worldly administrators, at least during the first decades after the Reformation, and placed them beyond suspicion. The commitment and leadership of (semi-religious) women, based on ancient formats and personal ambitions for leadership, had therefore unexpectedly strong positive results and became strategic for the Dutch Mission. Conditions – and thereby the possibilities for female leadership – differed within various Catholic groups, local circumstances and periods. Early modern Jesuits for instance, were more liberal towards female leadership, as is evident in the case of Maria Clara of Wytsma, who could independently start, and possibly lead, a mission station for both men and women. Her noble, wealthy, influential and spiritual position enabled this. Such a progressive approach among Jesuit spiritual virgins is confirmed by Haruko Ward's research on Jesuitesses in early modern Japan. Ward categorized the Japanese Jesuitesses as leading "nuns, women catechists and sisters".[82] Semi-religious women of these categories showed leadership on spiritual, educational, and diaconal levels.

How can the authoritative speaking position of these four women be interpreted? Unfortunately, the first three examples provide too little material to reach a well-founded conclusion. However, it becomes clear that religious and spiritual leadership is possible by setting up one's own mission station. Furthermore, spiritual leadership may also be expressed through influential gift giving of spiritual and theologically significant valuables. The examples also show that financial assets play an important role in the possibilities of exercising leadership authority by women. Characteristics such as descent, wealth, spiritual state, and gift giving capacity transcended the early modern hierarchical social order, and the gender positions or roles prevailing at the time. A noble, senior, spiritual virgin or female layperson with many material and also immaterial gifts, could occupy the top of the hierarchical ecclesiastical

---

[82] Cf. Ward, *Women Religious Leaders,* Kindle-edition, 29 (of 405).

Sytske Hofstee
*"Partners in Crime" : Dissident Male and Female Religious Leaders of the Clandestine Catholic
Church in the Dutch Republic (1570-1800)*

pyramid, on a higher position than a non-noble and not-donating priest. The examples of the four women reveal early modern configurations of female religious leadership. The leadership shown by Baukje Faber, her religious speaking position based on theologically significant donations, is an until now unknown configuration. Furthermore, Faber "spoke" by means of her "chiselled word" in public sacred space.

All four examples raise the question, to what extent the female leaders were cooperating with the clergy. The impression rises that they have not been appointed – as was the requirement for a spiritual mother – as leaders by the clergy. They seem to have assumed or claimed leadership by themselves, while on the other hand, their social surroundings, including the isolated priest, will have awarded them religious authority too.

As for the religious authority of men, the gender perspective shows a difference in the possibilities of leadership by men and women in the context of Catholic prohibition. Priests did not necessarily have to contribute money to the Catholic community for possessing an authoritative position, whereas the examples show that for most women their leadership position was linked to a strong financial and economic position. However, for becoming a priest, a good financial and economic background was of importance for a young man. The specific limitations, with regard to Catholic male leadership caused by the long-lasting crisis and conflict situation of the Catholic Church in the Republic have not yet been a subject of investigation nor has the interpretation of a male version of double-voiced agency within a dominant discourse.

The concept of female religious leadership approaches women as religious leaders, rather than as women in solely submissive positions. This allows the activities and practices of female agents to be appreciated at their right value and more equal to those of male agents. The gender perspective and the concepts of religious leadership and double-voice agency help to better understand the intertwining of early modern male and female dissident leadership positions and dissimulative practices. This framework provides keys for understanding the resilience of Catholic culture in an ongoing time of religious crisis and conflict.

This paper shows how dissident Catholic female and male leaders have been cooperating as "partners in crime" within the gender conventions of the time. They were active within an illegal setting and under difficult clandestine conditions brought on by the worldly authorities in the Dutch Republic. Semi-religious women and laywomen collaborated in controversial positions and roles with priests and church board laymen. These observations imply a switch

Sytske Hofstee
"Partners in Crime" : Dissident Male and Female Religious Leaders of the Clandestine Catholic
Church in the Dutch Republic (1570-1800)

of the priest-assistant paradigm to a "cooperative paradigm", based on collaboration between priests and spiritual virgins within authority relationships at the time.[83] In this way, a new light can be shed on the early modern history of the Catholic Church in the Republic.

The new configurations of female leadership demonstrated in this paper raise new questions, for instance, with regard to the speaking position of female singers and spiritual virgins' choirs. Can religious singing be understood as an authoritative practice? How wide can a definition of religious authority be determined? What are the processes of appropriation of authoritative speaking by women and men from different social strata? And how do the processes of granting authoritative speaking, bottom-up and top-down, unfold in different contexts, and in particular in times of crisis and conflict? Questions like these, brought up by this paper about women and men in historical times, are equally relevant in our modern global society, facing several crises and conflicts worldwide. Planet Earth, is urgently in need for inclusive and cooperative leadership.

Sytske Hofstee is a PhD-candidate at the Faculty of Humanities of Leiden University, The Netherlands. With her research she reconstructs the contribution of Frisian Catholic women to the survival of the Dutch Catholic Church during the early modern era and excavates the as yet unexplored territory of the work of spiritual virgins in the region of Friesland.

---

[83] The studies of 19th century religious women's communities by Eijt, Van Heijst and Suenens demonstrate this mindset. Jose Eijt, *Religieuze vrouwen: bruid, moeder, zuster: Geschiedenis van twee Nederlandse zustercongregaties, 1820-1940* (Uitgeverij Verloren: Hilversum 1995). Annelies van Heijst, *Liefdewerk: Een herwaardering van de caritas bij de Arme Zusters van het Goddelijk Kind, sinds 1852* (Uitgeverij Verloren: Hilversum 2002). Suenens, *Too robust to be saint.*

Journal of the European Society of Women in Theological Research 29 (2021) 61-83.
doi: 10.2143/ESWTR.29.0.3289661

Carol J. Dempsey

Dominican Women Afire: Global Leaders and Trailblazers, Past and Present

Abstract

Since the 12th century, women of the Order of Preachers (Dominicans) have assumed prominent leadership roles in the Catholic Church and the world. Like Catherine of Siena, OP, Dominican women speak truth to power. Immigrants to the United States from Germany and France, Dominican women for decades have assumed leadership positions in such areas as education, politics, economics, health care, and ecology. They work untiringly to dismantle and transform unjust structures, systems, and attitudes to create a more just church and world. With little or no formal training in business and finance, many women founded and built many high schools, colleges, and universities that continue to thrive today. This essay offers a brief understanding of "leadership" as it relates to women in the Order of Preachers. Next, the essay presents a brief history of the life and movement of the Dominican women pioneers who came to "the new world." Their courageous spirit and exercise of leadership continue to inspire and ground Dominican women leaders today. The essay then showcases some of the work being accomplished by United States Dominican women leaders, most notably throughout the twentieth century and into this twenty-first century. Lastly, the essay considers the present and future challenges facing Dominican women today. These challenges need to be addressed creatively and substantively if the innovative, creative, intellectual, progressive, and practical aspect of the Dominican charism is to continue long into the future.

Resumen

Desde el siglo XII, las mujeres de la Orden de los Predicadores (dominicos) han asumido roles de prominente liderazgo en la Iglesia Católica y en el mundo. Como Catalina de Siena, OP, las mujeres dominicas enfrentan al poder con la verdad. Inmigrantes en los Estados Unidos procedentes de Alemania y Francia, las mujeres dominicas llevan décadas asumiendo posiciones de liderazgo en areas como la educación, la política, la economía, la salud y la ecología. Trabajan de forma incansable para desmantelar y transformar estructuras, sistemas y actitudes injustas para crear una Iglesia y un mundo más justos. Con poco o nada de educación formal en negocios y finanzas, muchas mujeres han fundado y construídos varios institutos, facultades y universidades que continúan prosperando a día de hoy. Este ensayo ofrece una breve comprensión del "liderazgo" tal y como este se relaciona con las mujeres de la Orden de los Predicadores. A continuación, el ensayo presenta una breve historia de la vida y el movimiento de las dominicas pioneras que vinieron al "Nuevo Mundo". Su valiente espíritu y su ejercicio del liderazgo continúan inspirando y fundamentando a las líderes dominicas de hoy en día. Este artículo muestra algunos de los trabajos llevados a cabo en los Estados Unidos por parte de mujeres dominicas líderes, especialmente durante el siglo XX y hasta el siglo XXI. Por ultimo, el ensayo considera los retos presentes y futuros que enfrentan las mujeres dominicas en la actualidad. Estos retos necesitan ser abordados de manera creativa y sustancial si es que el aspecto innovador, creativo, intelectual, progresivo y práctico del carisma dominico ha de continuar en el futuro.

Zusammenfassung

Seit dem zwölften Jahrhundert übernahmen Frauen im Predigerorden (Dominikaner) bedeutende Leitungspositionen in der Katholischen Kirche und in der Welt. Wie Katharina von Siena OP sprechen Dominikanerinnen offen zu Machthabern. Als Immigrantinnen in die Vereinigten Staaten aus Deutschland und Frankreich haben Dominikanerinnen seit Jahrzehnten Leitungspositionen in Bereichen wie Bildung, Politik, Wirtschaft, Gesundheitswesen und Ökologie übernommen. Unermüdlich arbeiten sie, um ungerechte Strukturen, Systeme und Haltungen abzubauen und zu verändern, um eine gerechtere Kirche und Welt zu schaffen. Mit wenig oder keiner formalen Ausbildung im Bereich Unternehmensführung und Finanzen gründeten viele Frauen Highschools, Colleges und Universitäten, die sie aufbauten und die bis heute weiter gedeihen. Dieser Aufsatz bietet eine kurze Erklärung von „Leitung", insofern sie die Frauen im Dominikanerorden betrifft. Dann präsentiert der Beitrag eine kurze Geschichte des Lebens und der Bewegung der dominikanischen Pionierinnen, die in die „neue Welt" kamen. Ihr mutiger Geist und ihre Ausübung von Leitung inspirieren und bereiten weiterhin den Boden für leitende Dominikanerinnen heute. Der Aufsatz zeigt sodann einiges von der Arbeit, die leitende Dominikanerinnen in den Vereinigten Staaten durchgeführt haben, besonders während des 20. und bis ins 21. Jahrhundert. Zuletzt bedenkt der Aufsatz gegenwärtige und zukünftige Herausforderungen, mit denen Dominikanerinnen heute konfrontiert sind. Diese Herausforderungen müssen kreativ und substantiell angesprochen werden, wenn der innovative, kreative, intellektuelle, progressive und praktische Aspekt des dominikanischen Charismas weit in die Zukunft weiterbestehen soll.

Keywords: Order of Preachers, Dominicans, charism, mission, women religious, leaders.

The term "leadership" means different things to different people in different circumstances and in different parts of the world. When I think of leadership in relationship to those women religious who are members of the worldwide Order of Preachers, also known as Dominicans, I think of leadership that is visionary, creative, innovative, and on the forefronts of the theological disciplines that have been historically associated with the male members of the Order, i.e., Thomas Aquinas, Albert the Great. For Dominicans, leadership is first and foremost collaborative and related to the charism and mission of the Order which is to praise, to bless, to preach. This charism and mission, sustained by prayer, study, and community, enables Dominican women to respond to the "call" to be spirit-filled leaders who are prophetic and on the frontiers of justice, who respond to the needs and signs of the times, who create new pathways that lead to the dynamic transformation of church and world, and who view all life through a contemplative lens and gaze. To be a leader and member of the Dominican Order is to be a trailblazer and a pioneer, forever speaking truth to power, and often living on the margins while being marginalized by a male dominated Catholic institutional church. Leadership for Dominican women also involves embracing certain positions of power not for the sake of having power "over" to dominate or to mandate but to work for systemic, structural, and attitudinal changes needed to create a more just world that has peace as its abiding goal. Thus, according to this understanding of leadership, many Dominican women in the United States can be seen as "leaders."

Dominican women of the twenty-first century are accomplished leaders in the areas of education, church, economics, ecology, health care, law, and all areas of justice that include human trafficking, immigration, race, gender, class, among others. They are preachers, teachers, professors, authors, editors, doctors, nurses, lawyers, corporate executives, contemplatives, mystics, artists, poets, musicians, activists, social workers, United Nations NGO representatives, counselors, psychologists, lobbyists, pastoral ministers, administrators, archdiocesan chancellors, founders of congregations, hospitals, grade schools, high schools, colleges, universities, alternative schools, skilled nursing care facilities, spirituality centers, educational ecological farms, and housing complexes for senior citizens. They are prioresses of congregations, theologians, biblical scholars, presidents and vice-presidents of professional societies, colleges, universities, theological schools, and presidents of religious sisters' leadership conferences worldwide. They serve on corporate boards nationally and internationally, and they are no strangers to adversity and the perils of war, experienced most recently by Iraqi

Dominican Sisters whose home was bombed during the Iraq conflict.[1] Dominican women embrace and live out the legacy of their women leaders who have gone before them, of whom the most notable is Catherine of Siena, saint and Doctor of the Church. Catherine went from hospitals, prisons, scaffolds, to papal palaces, in an effort to address, both formally and informally, the systemic injustices of her day. Not formally educated, Catherine wrote *The Dialogue*,[2] a spiritual classic that captures her tenacity and courage, her determination and forthrightness which were but a few of her stellar qualities that continue to inspire women today.[3] The evolution of Dominican women as leaders, especially in the United States, happened not only because of their own tenacity, courage, and vision but also because of the example and spirit of the founder of the Order, Dominic de Guzman, who established the women Dominicans as monastic contemplative nuns before he founded the male Dominican friars.

Dominic de Guzman (1170-1221),[4] born into Spanish nobility and well educated, lived in an age of tremendous change and upheaval characterized by a major shift in culture. An agrarian lifestyle, deeply rooted in the land and supported by a weakening feudal system, quickly gave way to a new emerging urban and commercial pattern of life. The changing times presented several challenges. People had to re-think their beliefs, clarify their convictions, and identify their roots. A once stable institution, the Church

---

[1] The women religious in these professions have either been in leadership positions, have broken new ground, or are making new inroads. While these professions may seem commonplace now for most people, they are not for women religious. Moving into these areas of leadership has been a long and arduous journey for them. They have had to get educated and experienced and move out of the "cloister" physically and attitudinally.

[2] See Catherine of Siena, *The Dialogue*. Translation and Introduction by Suzanne Noffke, OP (Paulist Press: New York, NY 1980).

[3] For other works on the life of Catherine of Siena, see Mary Catherine Hilkert, *Speaking with Authority: Catherine of Siena and the Voices of Women Today*, The Madeleva Lecture Series (Paulist Press: Mahwah, NJ 2001); Susanne Noffke, *Catherine of Siena: Vision through a Distant Eye* (The Liturgical Press: Collegeville, MN 1996); Mary O'Driscoll, OP, *Catherine of Siena: Passion for the Truth, Compassion for Humanity* (New City Press: New Rochelle, NY 1993); Catherine M. Meade, CSJ, *My Name Is Fire: Saint Catherine of Siena* (Alba House: Staten Island, NY 1991).

[4] For a concise yet comprehensive biography on the life of St. Dominic, see Guy Bedouelle, OP, *Saint Dominic: The Grace of the Word*, translated by Sister Mary Thomas Noble, OP (Ignatius Press: San Francisco, CA 1987); Simon Tugwell, OP, *The Way of the Preacher* (Templegate Publishers: Springfield, IL 1979); Marie-Dominique Poinsenet, *Saint Dominic*, translated by John Chapin (Macmillian Company: New York, NY 1963).

found itself in a precarious position of needing to articulate its Christian heritage and attest to the relevance of a Christian lifestyle and values. In the midst of these winds of change, Dominic was on fire with the gospel. He longed to preach it, and he dreamed of creating a dynamic lifestyle that would give witness to a simple life and provide an environment that would form, ground, and nurture contemplative apostles. Choosing not to embrace a life of economic privilege and social status, he followed his dream and in 1216 in France, he started a mendicant Order known today as the Order of Preachers, otherwise called the Dominicans. The primary mission of the Order then and now is to proclaim the word of God through preaching, grounded in contemplation, study, and a life lived in common. Dominic wanted the members to be well educated and steeped in the study of theology and Scripture. Always the lifestyle was to be flexible and open to dispensation and judicious change. Dominicans are meant to be itinerant, forming community in relation to mission.[5]

Today, Dominicans refer to their members as the "Dominican Family,"[6] and presently, this Order is the only one in the Catholic Church that maintains a sense of unity among its different members which consist of cloistered contemplative Nuns in monasteries, Sisters fully engaged in mission and ministry throughout the world, priests and brothers called Friars, and a whole host of laity known as "Third Order Dominicans" for those connected to the Friars, and "Associates" for those connected to the women's congregations of Sisters. As the women's congregations become smaller and their members age and

---

[5] For a history of the Order and a discussion of its charism and spirituality, see Benedict Ashley, OP, *The Dominicans* (The Liturgical Press: Collegeville, MN 1990); William A. Hinnebusch, OP, *The Dominicans: A Short History* (Alba House: New York 1975; Id., *Dominican Spirituality: Principles and Practice* (Thomist Press: Washington, D.C. 1965); and M.-H. Vicaire, *Saint Dominic and His Times*, translated by Kathleen Pond (Alt Publishing Company: Green Bay, WI 1964); Father Humbert Clerissac, OP, *The Spirit of Saint Dominic*, edited by Father Bernard Delany, OP (Burns Oates & Washbourne LTD: London 1939); Anselm M. Townsend, OP (ed.), *Dominican Spirituality* (Bruce Publishing Company: Milwaukee, WI 1934); and Very Rev. J. B. O'Connor, OP, *Saint Dominic and the Order of Preachers* (The Holy Name Bureau: New York, NY 1916). For a study on the renewal of the Order post-Vatican II, see Valentine Walgrave, OP, *Dominican Self-Appraisal in the Light of the Council* (The Priory Press: Chicago, IL 1968).

[6] For a comprehensive biographical study of notable Dominicans from the fifteenth to the twentieth century, see Sister Mary Jean Dorcy, OP, *St. Dominic's Family* (Tan Books and Publishers: Rockford, IL and Dominicana Publications: Washington, D.C. 1983). Selected writings of early Dominicans are recorded in Simon Tugwell, OP (ed.), *Early Dominicans* (New York, NY: Paulist Press, 1982).

retire, associate members are beginning to partner with Dominican Sisters to carry on the work and charism of the Order and in some instances, to carry on the administration of the Sisters' institutions.

The story of how some Dominican women ventured out of their cloisters from Europe to become significant leaders, especially in the United States, is a fascinating one. This essay presents a brief history of the life and movement of the pioneers who came to "the new world," whose courageous spirit and exercise of leadership continue to inspire and ground Dominican women leaders today. The essay also showcases the extraordinary work being accomplished by United States Dominican women leaders, most notably throughout the twentieth century and into this twenty-first century, and it considers the present and future challenges now facing Dominican women if the innovative, creative, intellectual, progressive, and practical aspect of the charism is to continue long into the future.

The word 'showcasing' is chosen deliberately, because to date nothing has been written specifically about the Dominica women and their accomplishments in the twentieth and twenty-first centuries. Thus, the struggles and difficulties they faced and the extenuating circumstances and situations they had to cope with remain unknown. Congregational websites and newsletters only highlight their achievements, but the full stories "behind the scenes" wait to be told and recorded.[7] This essay, then, is a starting point that begins the recognition and acknowledgement of Dominican women as leaders in the United States.

From first Cloister to an American Classroom: Dominican Women on the Move, Sailing the Seas (1206-1853)

When Dominic first conceived the idea of the contemplative monastic life for women, it was directly related to the Albigensian heresy which spread quickly and uncontrollably throughout southern France. The leaders of the heretical sect, known as the Cathers or the Albigensians because of the sect's stronghold in Albi, France, taught that there were two gods, one good and one evil, that matter was evil and only the spirit was good, and that the body was the creation of the god of evil. These leaders also denied what Christians considered to be

---

[7] Only in February of 2021 is this lacuna coming to light when the editor of *U.S. Catholic Historian*, Fr. David Endres, noted that 2022 marks the bicentennial of the establishment of Dominican women religious in the United States. To commemorate this landmark, one full issue of the journal in 2022 will feature articles that showcase the history of Dominican women and their contributions.

three foundational doctrines of Christianity: the Trinity, the Incarnation, and the Resurrection. Pope Innocent III wanted to rid France of this heresy, and thus he commissioned Dominic to combat these heretics. In trying to convert the heretics, Dominic used the Albigensians' own methods: powerful preaching and disputation, and simplicity and austerity of lifestyle. He also made himself available to anyone who would seek him out with a sincere heart.

In one instance when Dominic had finished preaching a rousing and inspiring open-air sermon, nine wealthy women who had heard him preach approached him in a church where he was praying. These women were believers in all that they had been taught by the leaders of the Albigensian sect, and as members of the sect, they were considered "perfect" in the eyes of their leaders who had placed them in charge of colleges, other centers of learning, and retreat centers so that they could mold and form others in the Albigensian teachings. The lifestyle of these women was poor, austere, and chaste. Dominic's open-air sermon moved them deeply and tossed all their beliefs into chaos, to the point that they questioned their faith, abandoned their beliefs deemed heretical, and converted to Christianity. Understanding their plight, Dominic knew that he would have to offer them an alternative community and an experience of leadership somewhat similar to what they had known as part of the Albigensian sect. After Dominic unexpectantly received a piece of property, specifically, the deserted church of Notre Dame de Prouille, given to him by the Bishop of Toulouse, Dominic immediately converted it into a monastery, and it became a safe haven for the nine women converts and others who would enter through its doors. On November 22, 1206, these nine women, along with two Catholic penitents from Fanjeau, became the first members of the Dominican Order. Their life was strictly contemplative, but they did engage in teaching and other apostolic work on an occasional basis. A benefactor, Berenger of Narbonne, provided the monies needed to sustain their monastic lifestyle.[8]

Dominican women's monastic contemplative life can also be traced to Italy where Pope Honorius III tasked Dominic with uniting six small communities in Rome that soon became one large reformed community modeled after the Prouille community. Under the direction of Blessed Jordan of Saxony, Dominic's successor and the Order's second Master General, the Friars established monasteries of Dominican women in Spain and Germany. The most notable

---

[8]   Letters written by Dominic and his successors to the Nuns in the monasteries have been compiled in Tugwell (ed.), *Early Dominicans*, 387-431.

of these monasteries is the Convent of the Holy Cross in Regensburg, Bavaria, Germany (which Dominicans historically called "Ratisbon," the French alternative). This monastery, founded in 1233, officially became part of the Dominican Order in 1245. Since that time, the Dominican women residing there experienced several major events: the Lutheran Revolution (1517-1648), the Thirty Years War (1618-1648), and the Napoleonic Wars (1803-1815). This community of strong women, along with their monastery, became a notable example of life lived through adversity and uncertainty, a life continually renewing itself with grace, dignity, courage, and fortitude, and one that has stood the test of time through the centuries. Even when Prince Bishop von Dalburg issued a decree in 1803 that the nuns must teach in the city school or be suppressed, the nuns integrated the active and contemplative lifestyles in a new way. Their present circumstances dictated change, and their courage to embrace something "new" laid a firm foundation for what Dominican women would face in the American Catholic Church in the twentieth and twenty-first centuries. To this day, Holy Cross Convent is the only German convent with a continuous history free from suppression or secularization.

In 1836, with the strong leadership of Mother Benedicta Bauer, the Prioress, the community at Regensburg underwent a successful internal reform. It resulted in the monastery being placed under diocesan jurisdiction of the local bishop. Mother Benedicta also established new foundations at Niederviehbach and Mintraching, Germany. A woman of vision, complemented by daring boldness, she let neither personnel nor financial struggles and hardships deter her from what she set out to do, and she accomplished her work of founding new monasteries with zeal, zest, and vigor. Her vision, however, would not be complete until she established monasteries in the United States. For Mother Benedicta Bauer, the Dominican charism in the form of the contemplative life, was to know no bounds. After establishing the new monasteries, she searched out viable opportunities to send Sisters to "the new world." One opportunity came in 1851 when Sister Benedicta learned through a Benedictine Abbot, Dom Wimmer, of the need in the United States. It involved neglected Catholic children, particularly those of German immigrants. Immediately, Mother Benedicta wrote to the bishop of Regensburg who agreed to grant Mother Benedicta's "dismissorial" of four of their community members. Thus, on July 25, 1853, four courageous Dominican women of Holy Cross Convent left the confines of their monastic cells, embarked on the *Germania*, sailed across the Atlantic, to "the new world," to New York, and reached it on August 28,

1853. On August 2, 1853 the news of their departure appeared in the foreign news column of the *Katholische Zeitung* of New York. An excerpt from the article states:

> A new order has followed the orders of the Bavarian Sisterhoods, who are interesting themselves in the welfare of the poor German Americans. Yesterday four women departed from the Convent of Holy Cross here, for a mission in North America provided with everything which the establishment of such a convent requires, and followed by the heartfelt good wishes of their companions in religion...[9]

Historian Lois Curry, OP, captures the sentiments and spirit of the four Dominican women who had now become German immigrants working among the children of German immigrants:

> The journey of the four took them to the docks on Fulton Street in New York. The awakenings of faith in the hearts of the German immigrants began in confusion and apprehension since they were left stranded, but the journey reached the desired end through their adamant spirit to dare, to dream, to envision, and to plan for a new life in the new world and to help build something that would endure.[10]

The names of these four women who brought the Order to America are: choir nuns Josepha Witzlhofer and Augustine Neuhierl, and lay Sisters, Francesca Retter and Jacobina Riederer. They never looked back; they never returned to their German monastery; and their daring and courageous spirit set the tone and pace for those who would later join them in the Order, charting new destinies and blazing new trails.[11]

Dominican Women Expand the Order and Lead as Lights of the Church, Lights of the World
Growing in number
After the four German Dominican women settled in the United States, those who joined them grew in number, embraced an apostolic spirit firmly rooted in contemplation, and like their ancestors, set out across the country to establish

---

[9] As quoted by Lois Curry, OP, *Women after His Own Heart* (New City Press: Brooklyn, NY 1981), 18-19.

[10] Ibid., 19.

[11] For the full descriptive study on the journey of the Dominican Nuns from Europe to the United States, see ibid., 7-41.

additional motherhouses and congregations. To date, US Dominican women have founded 19 congregations whose members have been engaged in mission and ministry throughout the world.

As the apostolic nature of the Order's charism and mission expanded and developed, so did the Order's contemplative branch. In 1880, four nuns from Oullins in France, a monastery whose origins went back to Prouille, came to Newark, NJ, where they made the first permanent American foundation of cloistered nuns, the Monastery of St. Dominic. By 1889, members of the Newark foundation opened a second monastery in the Bronx, NY. In 1906, they opened another one at Farmington Hills in Michigan. In 1891, a second monastic foundation from Europe took root in New Jersey. Four nuns of the Perpetual Rosary, founded in Belgium, opened a monastery in Union City. By 1910, they had established five more.[12] Today, Dominican women have founded 16 monasteries that continue in the same spirit of the contemplative life as when Dominic founded this branch of the "Family."[13]

Education

Since the time when the four German Dominican women sailed to the United States to help educate the children of German immigrants, Dominican women have been leaders in the field of education especially. Currently throughout the United States, the Dominican Sisters administer 27 high schools founded and

---

[12] These five monasteries were established in Milwaukee, WI in 1897; Catonsville, MD in 1899; Camden, NJ in 1900; Buffalo, NY in 1905; and La Crosse, WI in 1909. The La Crosse monastery moved to Washington, D.C., in 1984 and in 2008 to Linden, VA.

[13] To date, no substantial and comprehensive study exists that describes collectively the life and work of the apostolic Dominican women in the United States. In an essay entitled "Dominicans (O.P.)," Mary Nona McGreal, OP, includes a section that traces the women's foundations, tracks their migration across the United States and highlights the institutions they founded: see Michael Glazier and Thomas J. Shelly (eds.), *The Encyclopedia of American Catholic History* (The Liturgical Press: Collegeville, MN 1997), 440-448. Many of the individual Dominican congregations throughout the United States have the specific histories of their own particular congregations written by their own community historians. See, e.g., http://adriandominicans. org/Our-Story/A-Walk-Through-History, 01 May 2021. Most of the current accomplishments of the present-day Dominican women exists in the oral tradition, specific congregational websites, on the national Dominican Life USA website https://domlife.org/, 01 May 2021 which is described as a "web crossroads for the Order of Preachers," or on websites associated with the organizations to which they have made or are making contributions. The latest published volume on recent accomplishments of the Dominican "family" in general is Margaret M. McGuinness and Jeffrey M. Burns (eds.), *Preaching with Their Lives: Dominicans on Mission in the United States after 1850* (Fordham University Press: New York, NY 2020).

sponsored by 10 different congregations. In these schools, the Sisters have served as presidents and principals while others have served on the schools' faculties. True to the Dominican spirit of subsidiarity and collegiality, the schools, though independent of one another, are joined together in the Dominican Association of Secondary Schools. Dominican women from the different congregations have also founded colleges and universities where many Sisters are presidents, vice-presidents, and board members. Presently, 17 Dominican institutions of higher education exist, and like the Dominican high schools, the colleges and universities participate in the Dominican Colloquium for Higher Education.[14]

Even though many administrators and leaders engaged in education are adept at negotiation, consensus-building, finances, fund-raising, and passing on the Dominican charism, not all have vision. *Vivien Jennings, OP*, of the Dominican Sisters of Caldwell, NJ, however, had vision. At age 35, she was the youngest member ever to be elected prioress of a religious women's congregation. Her election to leadership required special approval from the Vatican since Canon Law sets the minimum age for elected Major Superiors and Prioresses at 40. Approval was granted immediately upon the congregation's petition to Rome. One of the hallmarks of her leadership was to expand her congregation's understanding of and deep commitment to justice. This commitment to justice, complemented by a strong professional commitment to education led Jennings to found Project Link Educational Center in Newark in 1969. This alternative middle and junior high school was for the purpose of helping disenfranchised Black students from Newark, NJ, after the civil unrest of 1967 devastated the city. Jennings believed strongly in civil rights and in education as a way of advancement out of poverty. Together, Jennings and the Dominican Sisters designed a caring, private school environment for children of all religions, as well as a successful educational experience to students in those crucial years of early adolescence. From 1969 to 1998, the Sisters served as administrators and faculty members of the school, providing first rate educational opportunities to high-need Black students, all of whom went on to high school and many on to colleges and universities where they began to achieve their hopes and dreams that led to successful professional careers. The school, now administered by lay leadership and its Board of Trustees, continues to thrive while making a positive contribution to its Black community and in the lives of countless graduates.

---

[14] For a description of this colloquium, its history, its mission statement, and a sample of their programs, see http://www.domlife.org/2010Stories/DominicanColloquium.htm, 01 May 2021.

Serving Catholic institutions and graduate schools of Theology
In addition to founding and working in their own schools, Dominican women also serve as *administrators* and faculty members in other Catholic institutions and graduate schools of Theology. In 2020, *Barbara E. Reid, OP*, a Dominican from Grand Rapids, was named the first woman President of the Catholic Theological Union in Chicago, IL. She is also the first Dominican to hold this position. Formerly, Dr. Reid was the institution's Academic Dean, another first for Dominican women.[15]

Besides being gifted leaders in educational institutions, Dominican women are also renowned theologians and Bible scholars. *Theologians* include Mary Kay Oosdyke, OP, Anne Sullivan, OP, Mary Ann Fatula, OP, Mary Catherine Hilkert, OP, Loretta Devoy, OP, Patricia Benson OP, Kathleen McManus, OP, Sara Fairbanks OP, Kathleen Cannon, OP, Colleen Mary Mallon, OP, and Jamie Phelps, OP. and Maura Campbell, OP.

Maura Campbell, OP was one of the first women in the United States to receive a Ph.D. in Theology from St. Mary's College, Notre Dame, IN. The following accomplishments are a testament to her outstanding leadership. Since 1976 she served as permanent representative at the United Nations for the International Catholic Education Office. She was a member of the United Nations Committee on Aging and Committee on Disarmament and served as delegate to numerous conferences for OIEC (Office International de l'Enseignement Catholique) in Thailand, the Philippines, Egypt, Kenya, Spain, Italy, England, India, Peru, Ecuador, and Belgium. She was on the Executive Board of the United Nations Department of Public Information, the American Academy of History, the Catholic Historical Society, and the Ecumenical/ Interfaith Commission – Pastoral Council (Newark, NJ). A member of the US Women's Leadership Conference, she was the Roman Catholic representative for the World Council of Religion; chairperson of the World Concerns Committee; president of the board of directors of the International Catholic Organization at the United Nations; and president of the United States Dominican Educational Association. Her many awards include: the Ambassador for Peace Award (Women's Federation for Peace), Fidelity to the Mission of the Office International de l'Enseignement Catholique (OIEC) Award, the Soroptimist International Woman of Distinction Award, CIO Award for Service at the

---

[15] For an announcement and description of Reid's historic appointment, see https://www. globalsistersreport.org/news/news/news/ctu-names-first-woman-president-dominican-sr-bar- bara-reid, 01 May 2021.

United Nations, Who's Who of Women in the World and the United States, State of New Jersey Faculty Recognition for Outstanding Achievement in Higher Education, and listed in the Directory of American Scholars of Religion.[16]

Bible scholars include Mary Margaret Pazdan, OP, Barbara Green, OP, Maribeth Howell, OP, Barbara E. Reid, OP, Laurie Brink, OP, and Carol J. Dempsey, OP. Barbara E. Reid, OP initiated the new Wisdom Commentary Series and serves as its General Editor.[17] This international 58 volume series is by Liturgical Press and the first scholarly collaboration that offers detailed feminist interpretations of every biblical book. Barbara is also one of the editors for the New Jerome Biblical Commentary for the Twenty-first Century.

Carol J. Dempsey, OP, Old Testament scholar has published 8 volumes, edited 11 volumes, currently serves on the Wisdom Commentary Editorial Board, and is one of six general editors of *The Paulist Biblical Commentary*.[18] She is also an associate editor of the *Catholic Biblical Quarterly*[19] and *Old Testament Abstracts*.[20] Three scholars have held office in their respective professional societies: Mary Catherine Hilkert, OP, president of the Catholic Theological Society of American (2005-2006);[21] Barbara E. Reid, OP, president of the Catholic Biblical Association of America (2014-2015);[22] Joan A.

---

[16] For a full description of Campbell's accomplishments, see https://obits.nj.com/obituaries/starledger/obituary.aspx?n=maura-campbell&pid=148277492, 01 May 2021.

[17] For a full description of the commentary series, see https://litpress.org/wisdom-commentary-series, 01 May 2021 which also features a video presentation by Reid as General Editor.

[18] See Jose Enrique Aguilar Chiu, Richard J. Clifford, SJ, Carol J. Dempsey, OP, Eileen M. Schuller, OSU, Thomas Stegman, SJ, and Ronald Witherup, PSS (eds.), *The Paulist Biblical Commentary* (Paulist Press: Mahwah, NJ 2018). Among Dempsey's latest works are "The Bible and Justice" and "Isaiah 55-66" to be published in the *New Jerome Biblical Commentary for the Twenty-first Century* (Bloomsbury Press: New York, NY; in press, 2021-2022) and "Catholic Androcentric Bible Translations as Global Missionary Tools?" in: Susanne Scholz (ed.), *The Oxford Handbook of Feminist Approaches to the Hebrew Bible* (Oxford University Press: New York, NY 2020) 37-52. She is currently working on *Isaiah* for the Wisdom Commentary Series and *Beyond Christian Anthropocentrism: What it Means to Be Catholic in the New Diaspora* for the series Dispatches from the New Diaspora, eds. Marc Ellis and Susanne Scholz.

[19] Leslie Hoppe, ed. *The Catholic Biblical Quarterly* (The Catholic Biblical Association of America: Washington, D.C.).

[20] Christopher T. Begg, ed. *Old Testament Abstracts* (The Catholic Biblical Association of America: Washington, D.C.).

[21] See https://ctsa-online.org/resources/CTSA.PDFs/BoardOfDirectors/PastPresidents.pdf, 01 May 2021.

[22] See https://www.catholicbiblical.org/cba-presidents, 01 May 2021.

Leonard, OP and Loretta Devoy, OP, presidents of the College Theology Society (1992 and 2002, respectively); Carol J. Dempsey, OP vice-president of the College Theology Society (2004-2006).[23]

Leadership Conference of Women Religious

Dominican women are not only in the forefront of education but also leaders among all the women's religious congregations represented in the Leadership Conference of Women Religious (LCWR). This conference has about 1,350 members, who represent nearly 80 percent of the approximately 49,000 women religious in the United States. The conference's concerns are broad and deep and include "collaborating in Catholic church and societal efforts to influence systemic change, studying significant trends and issues within the church and society, working with organizations to effect and utilizing its corporate voice in solidarity with people who experience any form of violence or oppression"[24] in the United States and throughout the world. Four Dominicans have served as Presidents of this conference: Nadine Foley, OP, Ph.D., (1988), Donna Markum, OP, Ph.D. (1991), Mary Hughes, OP, Ph.D. (2010), and Elise Garcia, OP who is the current President (2020-2021).[25]

Mary Hughes' tenure as president during the papacy of Benedict XVI involved continued conversations about the LCWR with Vatican representatives who had first initiated the dialogue in 2008. At that time, LCWR leaders were informed that the Vatican's Congregation for the Doctrine of Faith would begin to conduct a doctrinal assessment of the LCWR to evaluate three major areas of concern. The first concern focused on speakers' addresses at the LCWR assemblies that "manifest problematic statements and serious theological even doctrinal errors" and call into question "core Catholic beliefs" that are both "a rejection of faith" and "a serious source of scandal and is incompatible with religious life."[26] The second concern involved policies of dissent on the part of the sisters that do not adhere to Church teaching "regarding the question of women's ordination and of a correct pastoral approach to ministry to homosexual persons."[27] The third concern highlighted the

---

[23] See http://www.collegetheology.org/Past-Presidents, 01 May 2021.

[24] See the LCWR description at lcwr.org, 01 May 2021.

[25] For a list of past presidents, see https://lcwr.org/about/officers, 01 May 2021.

[26] See *Congregation for the Doctrine of the Faith (2012-04-18). "Doctrinal Assessment of the Leadership Conference of Women Religious"*, 01 May 2021 (archived, 01 May 2021 from the original on 02 July 2012).

[27] Ibid.

"prevalence of certain radical feminist themes incompatible with the Catholic faith, including theological interpretations that risk distorting faith in Jesus and his loving Father," along with commentaries that not only "distort the way in which Jesus has structured sacramental life in the Church," but also "undermine the revealed doctrines of the Holy Trinity, the divinity of Christ, and the inspiration of Sacred Scripture."[28] This Vatican doctrinal assessment coincided with the announcement by Cardinal Franc Rode, CM, prefect of the CICLSAL, that the Vatican's Congregation for the Institutes of Consecrated Life and Societies of Apostolic Life (CICLSAL) would conduct an apostolic visitation of US women religious to examine their quality of life, ministries, vocation efforts, and financial status.[29] Many women saw this investigation as an indictment against some of the less traditional communities within the LCWR and a means to obtaining the soundness of doctrine held and taught within religious congregations.[30] Hughes and the leadership team of LCWR traveled to Rome to receive the Vatican's final report. The Vatican's assessment was juridical, condescending, and insulting to both the LCWR as an organization and to the thousands of women religious who are the backbone of Catholic education, health care, and social justice. The leaders of women's religious congregations have since received a more positive response from Pope Francis who addressed the LCWR membership directly and affirmed the sisters' work throughout the decades.[31]

Economic, corporate, and ecological justice
The work of economic and corporate justice continues to be an avenue where Dominican women exercise leadership today in profound ways. For more than 30 years, *Patricia A. Daly, OP*, has worked in corporate responsibility and socially responsible investing.[32] For 24 years, she served as Executive Director of Investor Advocates for Social Justice (1994-2017), an organization founded in 1975 by Catholic congregations involved in the movement to encourage

---

[28] Ibid.
[29] See https://www.nytimes.com/2009/07/02/us/02nuns.html, 01 May 2021.
[30] See https://usatoday30.usatoday.com/news/religion/2009-08-05-catholic-sisters_N.htm, 01 May 2021.
[31] See https://www.ncronline.org/news/vatican/vatican-ends-controversial-three-year-oversight-us-sisters-leaders, 01 May 2021.
[32] See http://www.domlife.org/2010Stories/opcaldwell_pat_daly.htm and https://iasj.org/celebrating-sr-pat-dalys-24-years-leadership-tri-state-coalition/, 01 May 2021.

corporations to leave apartheid South Africa.[33] Today the organization advocates on behalf of investors with faith-based values to promote human rights, climate justice, racial equity, and the common good. Daly represents institutional investors to the national Interfaith Center on Corporate Responsibility,[34] which encompasses 300 Roman Catholic, Protestant, Jewish and Buddhist organizations holding more than $500 billion in investments. She has worked with companies on issues including human rights, labor, ecological concerns, militarism, equality, health, tobacco, debt, international capital flows, and corporate governance. Together with many women's religious congregations as investors, she has confronted and taken on powerful industries such as inclusive of pharmaceutical companies, fossil fuel companies, agriculture commodities, and big banks guilty of serious human rights abuses. Members regularly engage management in a series of strategies: dialogue with corporate executives, shareholder resolutions, proxy voting, investor letters, public policy advocacy, and participation in annual meetings, all in an effort to identify and mitigate social and environmental risks resulting from corporate operations and policies. She persistently convinces many corporate leaders to change their behavior and to create more socially responsible and profitable companies. In 2014, Ceres and Trillium Asset Management awarded Daly the prestigious Joan Bavaria Award, conferred on her by William Clay Ford Jr., Executive Director of Ford Motor Corporation.[35] This award honors unique investor, business, and NGO leaders who are working to transform the capital markets into a system that balances economic prosperity with social and environmental concerns. In 2017, the Interfaith Center on Corporate Responsibility presented Daly with their Legacy Award.[36] Her crowning work, however, occurred in 2020 when Alternative Investment Partners Private Markets (AIP Private Markets), part of Morgan Stanley Investment Management, announced

> it has built upon its $800 million impact investing platform by closing on a fund which will focus on climate solutions. The $110 million fund seeks to address critical climate issues including global warming and pollution, depleting resources and eco diversity. This globally diversified private markets offering was launched

---

[33] See https://iasj.org/history/, 01 May 2021.

[34] See https://www.iccr.org/about-iccr, 01 May 2021.

[35] See https://www.3blmedia.com/News/Sister-Patricia-Daly-Visionary-Leader-Dedicated-Environmental-Justice-Wins-Joan-Bavaria-Award, 01 May 2021.

[36] See https://www.humanthreadcampaign.org/blog/sr-patricia-daly-and-fr-michael-crosby-winners-of-iccrs-2017-legacy-award/, 01 May 2021.

in a first of its kind collaboration with the US congregations of Dominican Sisters to find investment solutions which focus on climate change and aiding marginalized communities that are disproportionately impacted by global warming.[37]

Daly helped create the fund together with 16 congregations of United States Dominican sisters who, in 2018, had begun pooling an initial $46 million taken from their own assets. In collaboration with Morgan Stanley, the initial monies grew to $130 million to debut a "climate solutions fund."[38]

When not in the corporate board rooms, Dominican women work on behalf of justice at the United Nations. *Margaret Mayce*, OP of Amityville, New York, made peace and justice issues the focus of her work since she first joined the Dominicans in 1975. Since 2008, Mayce has served as the representative of the Dominican Leadership Conference, a nongovernmental organization, a position she has held since 2008.[39] At the United Nations, she has been engaged in a wide range of issues, including poverty eradication, climate change, the plight of women and girls worldwide, and financing for sustainable development. Eileen Gannon, OP, was the first United Nations representative for the Dominican Leadership Conference.[40]

Dominican women also work on behalf of *ecological justice*. Their concern for the planet and its sustainability, along with the commitment to educating people on the sacredness of the earth and the benefits of raising food organically and making it available throughout local bioregions, has led many Dominican congregations to establish organic farms throughout the United

---

[37] Lauren Bellmare, "Morgan Stanley Investment Management's AIP Private Markets Team Expands $800 Million Impact Investing Platform with Global Climate Impact Fund," https://www.businesswire.com/news/home/20200504005100/en/Morgan-Stanley-Investment-Management%E2%80%99s-AIP-Private-Markets, 01 May 2021; see also https://www.motherjones.com/environment/2020/07/meet-the-nuns-who-created-their-own-climate-solutions-fund/, 01 May 2021.

[38] See https://www.businesswire.com/news/home/20200504005100/en/Morgan-Stanley-Investment-Management%E2%80%99s-AIP-Private-Markets, 01 May 2021; http://adriandominicans.org/News/us-dominican-sisters-and-morgan-stanley-launch-climate-solutions-funds, 01 May 2021; https://grist.org/justice/meet-the-dominican-nuns-who-created-their-own-climate-solutions-fund/, 01 May 2021 and https://www.motherjones.com/environment/2020/07/meet-the-nuns-who-created-their-own-climate-solutions-fund/, 01 May 2021.

[39] See https://www.sistersofstdominic.org/non-governmental-organization-ngo-representative-at-the-united-nations/; https://www.dominicansisters.com/justice/, 01 May 2021.

[40] See https://dominicanleadershipconference.org/did-you-know-dominicans-have-four-un-offices/, 01 May 2021.

States. The first of these farms, Genesis Farm, located in Blairstown, NJ, and begun by the Dominican Sisters of Caldwell, NJ in 1980, is an international ecological center dedicated to understanding the Universe and Earth as a single, unfolding process. Since 1980, Miriam Therese MacGillis, OP has been the Farm's director. People from all over the world come to study in the many programs offered there. The Farm is also home to the legendary and world-renowned Community Supported Garden.[41] This garden, with more than 300 members, is true to the Community Supported Agriculture (CSA) model and is one of the first of its kind in the United States.

Healthcare, arts, spirituality
Other areas where Dominican women have exercised leadership include healthcare, law, corporate boards, spirituality, and the arts, to name but a few endeavors. Specifically, in the area of healthcare, *Mary Flood, OP, MD* practices medicine at Columbia University Medical Center/New York-Presbyterian Hospital where she is also an associate professor of medicine.[42] Her research focuses on clinical infectious diseases, in particular HIV primary care and infections in immunocompromised patients. Recognized as a "Super Doctor" in the New York Times Magazine and listed as one of New York City's top doctors by New York Magazine, Mary mentored Uchenna Okereke, OP, MD, originally from Nigeria and now a Dominican of Caldwell, NJ, who practices medicine at Conemaugh Memorial Medical Center in Pennsylvania. Uchenna is the youngest Dominican medical doctor, specializing in and researching infectious disease and epidemiology.[43]

Attuned to the "artistic spirit" once alive in such Dominican creative artists as Fra Angelico, Dominican women jointly founded the *Institute for the Arts*[44] that supports the Order's poets, potters, film makers, composers, musicians, photographers, writers, sculptors, painters, and creative designers. Artists such as *Gerardine Mueller, OP, MFA,*[45] design and create stained glass windows for cathedrals, chapels, educational institutions, along with a whole host of other artistic contributions that have graced the world locally and globally.

---

[41] http://csgatgenesisfarm.com/, 01 May 2021.
[42] See https://domlife.org/2015Stories/blauvelt_sister_doctor.html, 01 May 2021.
[43] See https://domlife.org/2020/12/08/dr-uchenna-okereke-fulfills-her-dream/, 01 May 2021.
[44] See https://www.diartsop.org/, 01 May 2021.
[45] For an interview with Gerardine Mueller, OP and a profile of her work, see https://www.caldwell.edu/interview-with-sr-gerardine-mueller-o-p-professor-emerita-caldwell-university-art-department/, 01 May 2021.

At 99 years of age, Mueller is the longest living artist in the Dominican Order to date who remains fully engaged in her work. Poet and literary scholar, *Elizabeth Michael Boyle, OP, Ph.D.*, received the Institute's Fra Angelico Award for her creative literary works. Her first book, *Preaching the Poetry of the Gospels A Lyric Companion to the Lectionary*,[46] received a first place award from the Catholic Press Association. Her second book, *Science as Sacred Metaphor: An Evolving Revelation*,[47] contains reflections on the liturgical seasons through the prism of science and using everything from evolution to string theory as poetic texts. Her third book, *The Bible and Literature*,[48] co-authored with Carol J. Dempsey, OP, is an interdisciplinary work that explores the intersection between biblical stories and international works of literature. She has also published two volumes of poems, *The View from the Ruin*[49] and *Gift Exchange*.[50] Dr. Boyle is a member of the Academy of American Poets.

In sum, women who are members of the Dominican Order of Preachers in the United States are extraordinary gifted and talented leaders whose many contributions have left an indelible mark on the fabric of life and in the lives of countless people. As they leave a gentle footprint on the earth wherever they go, they are conscious of the planet's deep need and yearning for healing, rejuvenation, and restoration. They are also conscious of their aging population, their dwindling numbers, and the increasing rise of the Christian-Catholic right, all of which challenge their mission as Dominicans and the passing on of the charism to future generations.

Leaning into the Future: Dominican Women Restructure, Reunite, and Revision

Gone are the days when the many individual congregations of Dominican women each boasted 600, 700, or even 800 members. Today, the median age for most congregations is approximately between 75-82 years old. Despite the reality of the aging process, the Dominican spirit remains resilient among its members, and for some women even well into their 90s as they continue to

---

[46] Elizabeth Michael Boyle, *Preaching the Poetry of the Gospels A Lyric Companion to the Lectionary* (Liturgical Press: Collegeville 2003).

[47] Elizabeth Michael Boyle, *Science as Sacred Metaphor: An Evolving Revelation* (Liturgical Press: Collegeville 2006).

[48] Elizabeth Michael Boyle and Carol J. Dempsey, *The Bible and Literature* (Orbis Books: Maryknoll, NY 2015).

[49] Elizabeth Michael Boyle, *The View from the Ruin* (North Star Press: Saint Cloud, MN 2011).

[50] Elizabeth Michael Boyle, *Gift Exchange* (Pudding House Publications: Columbus, OH 2010).

live creative and productive lives. The leadership teams, together with their respective congregations, however, face many challenges today, some of which they have already begun addressing.

The following seven challenges are important to consider. First, several small congregations have had to restructure because of dwindling numbers and the unnecessary duplication or resources. Either they merged or became a new entity altogether, allowing for a broader sense of community and shared resources.

Second, congregations have increased and developed their popular and sought-after associate programs. They allow non-vowed members committed to the mission, charism, and vision of the Order to participate in the life of the Dominican community, their institutions, and the mission as a whole.

Third, because of their dwindling numbers, congregations have begun the process of relinquishing control and leadership of the institutions that they own. The institutions, such as schools, hospitals, farms, educational and spiritual centers are now "sponsored" by the congregations, but the women maintain a strong presence through their full participation in the institutions' two-tiered Boards of Trustees. The sisters no longer staff or serve in administrative positions in many of these institutions. They entrusted the institutions to lay leadership, educating all constituents to the four pillars of Dominican life – prayer, study, community and preaching – and simultaneously immersing them into the charism so that the flame remains alive and the torch can be passed from one generation to the next. Some congregations have also completely divested of their institutions. For financial reasons and increased rates of retirement, some hospitals and schools had to be sold; retreat centers closed.

Fourth, the leadership teams, together with OP members, have begun tackling the question of how to support younger members in aging communities. While plans for increased retirements are under way, so are plans for sustaining the Order's younger women members, with an eye to attracting new members. In October 2020, all Dominican women 70 years and younger participated in a three-day zoom conference to discuss the present reality of Dominican life and to plan for its future. Several ideas have emerged: the need for new models of community life; the need for progressive and solid theological education to be incorporated into formation programs for new and newer members, with opportunities for ongoing education and the study of global issues made available for all members. Because Dominican intellectual life is both speculative and practical, study is to lead to personal transformation and a deeper commitment to justice, especially with regard to topics like racism and sexism, two divisive and unjust realities prevalent in today's world.

A fifth challenge that Dominican women face today is the need to create communication structures that allow for United States members to communicate easily with one another and with other Dominican women globally. The members need to develop stronger interpersonal relationships with one another for the sake of a broader, deeper, and more "organic" sense of community that is less institutionally centered. Complementing the need for deeper interpersonal bonds among members, Dominican women need to have a greater awareness of and engagement in each other's work and ministry so that the mission of preaching, with justice as its cornerstone and contemplation as its foundation, can flourish in new creative and collaborative ways.

Sixth, the leadership teams, together with OP members, continue to address the need for vocations. With so many professional avenues now open to women, Dominican women are going to have to re-think and re-claim the most attractive part of their lives and lifestyle other than their success as leaders and their diversified ministries. One possibility is to re-claim the foundational Dominican pillar, namely, contemplation, and understand it and experience it in new ways inclusive of and also beyond the norms of Christianity. Contemplation can be transformative, energizing, and life-giving. It can also lead to insight, vision, a deeper awareness of the oneness of all, and life lived in union with the Divine.

Seventh and finally, as an Order called to be the "Light of the Church," Dominican women are faced with the challenge of revisioning for themselves what it means to be Catholic-catholic within the context of Roman Catholicism. History has borne out that male church leaders continue to challenge, ostracize, erase, and even silence powerful women who lead not only by example but also by active engagement in the critical issues of the day, such as racism, sexism, sexual orientation, reproductive rights of women, classism, sexual violence, militarism, poverty, and other forms of socio-political alienation and marginalization. Dominican women have not escaped the snares of sexism, patriarchy, hierarchy, clericalism, colonization by a male clergy, as well as abuse. Many have internalized these oppressions that have even affected how their life is structured, and today, Dominican women and their congregations continue to work through them together. Women can now officially be lectors. With the stroke of the papal pen, canon law was changed. Dominican women are preachers, and even though they preach in a myriad of ways, they cannot preach "from the pulpit." How long must they wait for the papal pen to make another change to canon law that will allow them to preach homilies during Catholic Masses and other services reserved for priests by virtue of their ordination? Clearly, for Dominican women, church law has become a hindrance to their God-given charism and has kept it from being fully realized in their lives. Just as their ancestors pushed the boundaries to prepare for the Dominican woman of today, so Dominican women have to continue pushing the boundaries for those who will come after them. Pushing the boundaries is the only way forward.

Venturing into the Future: Concluding Comments

Since their arrival into the United States from Germany, Dominican women have made countless contributions to the life of the Church and world in the United States, and many have emerged as recognized leaders. Like most people's and group's histories, the Dominican women's history has been neither easy nor rosy. Like most people in the United States, they have weathered such challenges as the 1918 influenza pandemic, the 1929-1939 Great Depression, and today the Covid 19 pandemic which has taken the lives of some congregations' sisters. Post-Vatican II 1960s into the 1970s offered many challenges as congregations went through a "renewal" process. Not all women could accept the renewal changes; others became frustrated with their congregations not moving through the renewal process quickly enough to support their vision and ministry aspirations. Still others found themselves re-assessing their commitment to the vowed life. These turbulent times of growth, renewal, and reassessment led some women to choose paths other than Dominican life. As Therese Catherine, OP so aptly stated: "To study the history of any community in the throes of reform is to look deeply into the heartbreak of many souls."[51]

The important work being done by so many Dominican women leaders today, however, attests to the reality that the way forward is neither to retreat back to the cloister nor to adapt to the rising conservatism present in both the United States and in the Catholic Church within the United States. Dominican women are called to be pioneers and trailblazers like their ancestors. Their course is to be an unchartered one, and their presence in the world is to be a prophetic one that exposes injustice and unearths what is dead and no longer life-giving for the twenty-first century. As prophetic leaders, Dominican women are called to lead in new ways with a new vision that offers hope to the outcast, the marginalized, the erased one, and the one who does not "fit

---

[51] As quoted in Lois Curry, OP, *Women after His Own Heart* (New City Press: New York, NY 1981), 197.

in." Many Dominican women are already lights of the church and world, but their light has to shine ever more brightly which can happen if they make their work better known to wider audiences than they are currently doing. In a church, world, and Order heavily male dominated and male privileged, the Sisters have been able to maintain a healthy and strong autonomy. They have successfully expanded the Catholic church's understanding of "preaching" to encompass more than the pulpit. Well educated and now experienced beyond the cloister and the monastery, Dominican women take their place beside other women leaders as they speak truth to power and work to blaze new pathways. They need to celebrate their many accomplishments.

The time has come, and perhaps is already quickly passing, for Dominican women to re-think their identity and renew themselves, but this time to renew themselves as feminists, for surely strains of the feminist spirit were alive in women like Catherine of Siena and in the early foundresses of the various United States congregations. Dominican women have a deep and rich legacy from which to draw their strength for a new vision. It is time to tap into that legacy. The church and world are waiting, ever hopeful and ever ready, for them to begin a new chapter in the storied experience of life.

Carol J. Dempsey, OP, Ph.D. is Professor of Theology (Biblical Studies) at the University of Portland, OR. She has authored 8 books, edited 11 books, and is on the editorial boards of the Wisdom Commentary Series, *The Catholic Biblical Quarterly*, *Old Testament Abstracts*, and *The Paulist Biblical Commentary*. Currently she is working on three book manuscripts: *Isaiah* for the feminist Wisdom Commentary Series (Liturgical Press), *Moving Beyond Anthropocentrism: What It Means to Be Catholic in the New Diaspora* (Lexington/Fortress Books), and *Responding to Climate Crisis: Hope at the Margins* (Lexington/Fortress Books), a co-edited volume. Her latest articles include "Catholic Androcentric Bible Translations as Global Missionary Tools?" in *The Oxford Handbook of Feminist Approaches to the Hebrew Bible* (ed. Susanne Scholz, Oxford University Press, 2021), "Metaphor and the Minor Prophets," in *The Oxford Handbook of Minor Prophets* (ed. Julia O'Brien, Oxford University Press, 2021), "The Bible and Justice" and "Isaiah" for *The New Jerome Biblical Commentary for the Twenty-first Century* (Bloomsbury Press, 2022). Carol has delivered more than 70 scholarly papers at national and international professional conferences, and lectures nationally and internationally for various colleges, universities, and other groups. She has been a member of the Order of Preachers (Dominicans) for 46 years.

Journal of the European Society of Women in Theological Research 29 (2021) 85-111.
doi: 10.2143/ESWTR.29.0.3289662

Friederike Eichhorn-Remmel

Taugt Maria zur Revolte?
Feministisch-exegetische Blicke auf medial kommunizierte Marienkonstruktionen

Zusammenfassung

Bei der in der Überschrift gestellten Frage „Taugt Maria zur Revolte?" handelt es sich um die Headline eines Artikels der ‚Zeit'-Beilage ‚Christ und Welt'. Die Beantwortung dieser Frage ist nicht das primäre Ziel der vorliegenden Untersuchung. Vielmehr ist die konkrete mediale Einbettung der Frage selbst an ihren spezifischen Orten Gegenstand der (wiederum) kulturhermeneutischen und exegetischen Beobachtungen eines solchen Phänomens ‚sichtbarer Religion'.

Die darin begegnenden ‚Blicke', die angeregt sind von der aktuellen Debatte um emanzipatorische Frauenbewegungen in der Katholischen Kirche – vor allem ‚Maria 2.0' –, zeigen in ihren jeweiligen Konstruktionen nicht zuletzt einen Konflikt um religiöse Führungspositionen. Denn an die Frage, wer diese ‚Maria' eigentlich ist und damit auch was sie kann und darf, wird nicht selten eine generalisierende Aussage für alle Frauen angeschlossen. Es ist deshalb nicht verwunderlich, dass ausgerechnet anhand der – die literarische ‚Maria' der Bibel rezipierenden – oft stereotypen Darstellung und Deutung dieser ‚Frau' die Frage nach dem religiösen Führungspotenzial von Frauen im Generellen in der Katholischen Kirche diskutiert wird. In hier exemplarisch analysierten, medialen Lesarten wird also nicht nur die dort herangezogene literarische ‚Maria' des Lukas, sondern werden alle Frauen ihres prophetischen und befreienden Potenzials entweder enteignet oder aber *empowered*. Insofern solche Deutungen dem biblischen Befund – auf den sie in ihren (teils vermeintlich) geteilten Annahmen von ‚Maria' verweisen, um in normativer Absicht gegenwärtige (Frauen-)Fragen zu beantworten – zuwiderlaufen, wird der religionswissenschaftliche Blick auf das vorliegende Moment sichtbarer Religion mit der exegetisch-kritischen Sicht auf den zugrundeliegenden Text korreliert. Denn gerade gegenüber den Einsichten feministischer und befreiungstheologischer Auslegung wird darin nicht selten medial polemisiert, obwohl – oder womöglich wohl wissend – hier und gerade heute diese oppositionellen Lesarten (nicht nur) Frauen ermächtigen könnten, binäre Wahrnehmungsschemata zu durchbrechen.

Abstract

The question raised in the title of this text: 'Would Mary be suited for (a) rebellion?'
is originally the headline of an article in the 'Christ und Welt' supplement of the news-
paper 'Die Zeit'. Answering this question is not the primary goal of the present enquiry,
though. For it is the concrete medial embedding of the question itself in its specific
sites which is the subject matter of the cultural-hermeneutical and exegetical observations of this phenomenon of 'visible religion'.

The views and opinions which can be distinguished in the media and which are
inspired by the topical debate around the emancipatory women's movement in the Catholic Church – not in the last instant by 'Maria 2.0' – do show in their current constructions a conflict around religious leadership positions. For sweeping statements about all
women are often added to the questions about who this Mary is exactly, and hence about
what she can do and is allowed to do. Small wonder that precisely on the basis of fre-
quently stereotypical representations and interpretations of this 'woman' – representations
which are often based on receptions of the literary Mary of the Bible – the question is
raised whether women are capable to be religious leaders in general and in the Catholic
Church in particular. In the analysis of these medial readings, which are exemplary for
the debate, it will become clear that the references to this literary Mary of Luke either
expropriate her prophetic power or empower her, as well as all (other) women in the same
gesture. Insofar as such interpretations contradict the biblical findings – to which they
refer in their (partly supposedly) shared suppositions of Mary to answer contemporary
(woman) questions normatively – the religious studies view-point on the moment of visible religion in question will be correlated with the exegetical-critical perspective on the
biblical text. For these medial readings often polemicize precisely against the insights of
feminist and liberation theological interpretation, although – or maybe intentionally –
these oppositional readings might precisely empower (not only) women to break through
these binary perception-schemes here and now.

Resumen

La pregunta planteada en el título de este texto, «¿estaría María hecha para (una)
rebelión?», es el titular original de un artículo del suplemento *Christ und Welt* del
periódico *Die Zeit*. No obstante, responder a esa pregunta no es el objetivo principal
de la presente investigación. Cómo la propia pregunta aparece incrustada en los
medios de comunicación en sus lugares específicos constituye el tema de las observa-
ciones culturales-hermenéuticas y exegéticas de este fenómeno de la "religión visible".
Las visiones y opiniones que pueden distinguirse en los medios de comunicación y que
están inspiradas por el debate acerca del movimiento emancipatorio de las mujeres en
la Iglesia Católica (especialmente María 2.0.) muestran, en sus construcciones actuales,
un conflicto en torno a las posiciones de liderazgo religioso, ya que se añaden afirma-
ciones generalizadas sobre todas las mujeres a las cuestiones de quién es exactamente
esta María y, por ende, lo que puede hacer y está permitido hacer. No es de sorprender

que, precisamente en base a representaciones frecuentemente estereotipadas e interpretaciones de esta «mujer» (las cuales a menudo están basadas en recepciones de la María literaria de la Biblia), la pregunta que se plantea es si las mujeres son capaces de ser líderes religiosas en general y dentro de la Iglesia Católica en particular. En el análisis de estas lecturas de los medios de comunicación, que son paradigmáticas del debate, se hará evidente que las referencias a esta María literaria de Lucas o bien expropian su poder profético o bien la empoderan, así como a todas las (demás) mujeres. En la medida en la que dichas interpretaciones contradicen los descubrimientos bíblicos (a los cuales se refieren en sus compartidas suposiciones de María) para contestar normativamente a la cuestión de la mujer contemporánea, la mirada de los estudios religiosos al movimiento de la religión visible en cuestión se correlacionará con la perspectiva exegética-crítica del texto bíblico. Estas lecturas de los medios de comunicación a menudo polemizan precisamente con las interpretaciones feministas y de la teología de la liberación, aunque (o quizá de forma intencionada) estas lecturas oposicionistas podrían precisamente empoderar, aquí y ahora, a (no solo) las mujeres para romper esos esquemas de percepción binarias.

Keywords: Visuality; circuit of culture; Mary; Luke 1:46-55; gender.

‚Maria' voll im Blick? – Methodische Vorentscheidungen

Wird nach den Bedingungen aktuell diskutierter Mariendeutungen und ihrer medialen Visualisierungen gefragt, so handelt es sich dabei um die Frage nach „Blickkulturen" auf „sichtbare Religion",[1] und hier auf kommunizierte Marien-Konstruktionen. Als ‚sichtbar' werden im Folgenden nicht nur jene Marienbilder bezeichnet, die eine Materialisierung erfahren haben (etwa in Artefakten), sondern auch die ihnen zugrundeliegenden mentalen Bilder der Gottesmutter. Vorausgesetzt wird damit das Konzept einer ‚Visuellen Kultur', die intermedial[2] „eine Vielzahl von sozialen Feldern und Tätigkeiten [...] [umfasst,] alte, neue und neueste Medien ein[schließt], die nicht erst heute keineswegs nur ‚visuell' sind und nur den Augensinn ansprechen, sondern mit Texten, mit Sprache, mit Zu-hören-Gegebenem notwendig verknüpft sind."[3]

---

[1] Natalie Fritz et al., *Sichtbare Religion: Eine Einführung in die Religionswissenschaft* (De Gruyter: Berlin und Boston 2018), De Gruyter Studium, 215.

[2] Eine Analyse der Hierarchien und Wechselwirkungen zwischen den verschiedenen Kommunikationsformen wie auch unterschiedlichen Medien kann und soll an dieser Stelle nicht geleistet werden, wenngleich aufgrund der exegetischen Herkunft der Forscherinnenperspektive ein Fokus auf dem biblischen Text eingeräumt werden muss.

[3] Sigrid Schade und Silke Wenk, *Studien zur visuellen Kultur: Einführung in ein transdisziplinäres Forschungsfeld* (Transcript: Bielefeld 2011), 9.

Das angestrebte ‚Sehen' dieses „materiellen und immateriellen Fundus, der mit den Erwartungen, Repräsentationen, Vorstellungen, Geschichten, Ideen und Praktiken einer Gruppe oder einer Gemeinschaft"[4] verbunden ist, bezieht sich nicht nur auf ein einzelnes Objekt, sondern ein Gesamtgeschehen – einen ständigen „kommunikativen Prozess".[5]

Dass es sich dabei keineswegs um eine diffuse und systemisch nicht zu fassende Analyse solcher Dynamiken handelt, gewährleistet Stuart Halls Modell des *circuit of culture*:[6] Hinwege zum Verstehen der in Bildern kommunizierten Be-Deutung(en) sind dort – wie hier – jene Verweise, die in den interagierenden Kategorien Repräsentation, Produktion, Rezeption, Identität und Regulierung „hergestellt und transformiert"[7] werden. Mit diesem methodischen Vorgehen wird aber keineswegs ein „Anspruch auf Vollständigkeit hinsichtlich der besprochenen Medien, Materialien und ihrer kulturellen Kontexte" beansprucht, sondern nur „Momente eines Kommunikationsprozesses"[8] hervorgehoben.

Sind also exemplarische Blickkulturen auf ‚Maria' Gegenstand der Untersuchung, so „lassen sich *emische* Blicke von involvierten Akteuren und Akteurinnen, *medial-öffentliche* Blicke auf religiöse Gemeinschaften, Traditionen und Motive sowie *wissenschaftliche* Blicke […] unterscheiden."[9] Keineswegs sind diese drei heuristischen Zugänge klar getrennt, sondern vielmehr „interagieren [sie] ständig miteinander"[10]. Dennoch wird sich – auch in Hinblick auf ‚Maria' – aufzeigen lassen, dass „[w]ährend emische Perspektiven

---

4 Fritz, *Religion*, 219.

5 Fritz, *Religion*, 104; dort weiter (103-104): „Aussagen werden mittels Zeichen kodiert, per Medien übermittelt und vom Empfänger wiederum dekodiert. Dieses stetige Kodieren-Dekodieren wird von Stuart Hall als kommunikativer Prozess umschrieben. Medien konstruieren demzufolge Wirklichkeit, indem sie Bedeutungen, Werte und Inhalte repräsentieren, die von gesellschaftlicher Gültigkeit sind und dazu beitragen die Realität zu ordnen und zu verstehen."

6 Vgl. Stuart Hall, „Introduction," in: Ders., Jessica Evans und Sean Nixon (ed.), *Representation* (Sage: London [2]2013), xvii-xxvi.

7 Fritz, *Religion*, 39.

8 Fritz, *Religion*, 214. Weil Bilder vielfältig sind und Kommunikation komplex ist, ermöglicht es gerade das exemplarische Vorgehen, „dieser Vielfalt Raum zu lassen und der Komplexität zu begegnen, ohne sie in vorgefertigte Schemata zu zwängen" (ebd., 214). Wenn hier also bestimmte Bildaspekte ausgewählt oder hervorgehoben werden, so liegt das am Gemenge emischer, medialer und wissenschaftlicher Blicke der Autorin: „Würde eine sichtbare Religion, die in einem anderen akademischen Kontext entsteht und mit Bildern aus anderen Kulturen arbeitet, anders sein? Ganz bestimmt" (ebd., 215).

9 Fritz, *Religion*, 10 (Hervorhebung im Original).

10 Fritz, *Religion*, 16.

durch eine große Variabilität und Vielfalt charakterisiert sind, [...] sich mediale Diskurse zu Religion durch eine Tendenz zur Generalisierung aus[zeichnen]."[11]

Das müssen sie auch, denn sie funktionieren (nur) aufgrund des genannten „geteilten Fundus an mentalen und materiellen Bildern".[12] Dies gilt insbesondere für das Bild ‚Maria', welches solch ein Beispiel eines durch Zeit und Raum wandernden Nomaden[13] ist, mit dem stets Traditions- und Innovationsprozesse[14] einhergehen. Solche Dynamiken können Gemeinschaften herausfordern, denn insofern diese „auf ‚geteilten Bildern' beruhen, sind die jeweiligen Bedeutungszuschreibungen abhängig von der Kommunikation, die vor dem Bild entsteht, und dem gesellschaftlichen Kontext, der sie prägt."[15] Gemeinschafts- und identitätsstiftende Bilder – wie das von ‚Maria'[16] – gehen von daher immer auch – insofern es um Bedeutungsgenerierung geht – mit „machtpolitischen Überlegungen"[17] einher und evozieren Regulierung.

Verhandlungen und Neuzuweisungen werden dort sichtbar, wo sich Bedeutungszuweisungen wandeln,[18] wo neue Lesarten alte ablösen und dies – in dieser Binnenperspektive zurecht – als „Destabilisierung der Gemeinschaft"[19] wahrgenommen wird. Marker für solches Verstehen sind oft Grenzziehungen zwischen ‚uns' und den ‚anderen', die im Konflikt um Deutungshoheit arrangiert werden als ‚wahr' beziehungsweise ‚falsch'. Das hat Konsequenzen für die Darstellung der Bilder:

> [D]iejenigen, die innerhalb einer Gesellschaft die Machtposition besetzen, [geben] nicht nur die Lesart [vor], sondern auch Darstellungskonventionen bezüglich gemeinschaftsstiftender und Macht legitmierender [sic] Bildmotive [...]. Dadurch

---

[11] Fritz, *Religion*, 13.
[12] Fritz, *Religion*, 231.
[13] Vgl. Fritz, *Religion*, 198.
[14] Fritz, *Religion*, 198-199: „Tradierung [ist] ein Prozess [...], der nicht auf die bloße Wiederholung von Motiven reduziert werden darf, sondern stets mit einer Weiterentwicklung und Aktualisierung einhergeht" und zwar „auf der Ebene der Produktion", „der Regulation" und „der Rezeption".
[15] Fritz, *Religion*, 199.
[16] Vgl. Fritz, *Religion*, 203: „Die Mutter Jesu fungiert in der christlichen Überlieferung als eine Projektionsfläche, auf die je nach Kontext divergierende Eigenschaften übertragen worden sind."
[17] Fritz, *Religion*, 200.
[18] Vgl. Fritz, *Religion*, 194.
[19] Fritz, *Religion*, 155.

unterdrücken sie zumindest zeitweilig oppositionelle und subversive Interpretationen oder Repräsentationsformen.[20]

Begründet wird diese (ästhetische) Konventionalisierung religiöser Bilder nicht allein mit den „Autoritätsansprüche[n] einer dominierenden Sicht", sondern – bei Einhaltung der mit diesen Bildern eingeforderten Handlungsanweisungen – auch mit dem (Heils-)Versprechen „gesellschaftliche Konstanz sowie Kohäsion"[21] zu garantieren. Diese medial vermittelte Normativität wird den Gruppenmitgliedern auch durch Vorbilder wie ‚Maria' kommuniziert. Insbesondere die in diesem Frauen-Bild konstruierten Erwartungen entsprechen dabei „einem etablierten, kulturell spezifischen Konventionskanon bezüglich der Darstellung von Geschlecht".[22]

Die dargestellten Aspekte sichtbarer Religion werden im Folgenden zusammengeführt. Alle hierzu verwendeten Bilder ‚Marias' verbindet die durch ‚Maria 2.0' (neu) angestoßene Auseinandersetzung um Lesarten und die daraus je abgeleiteten unterschiedlichen Antworten auf die erweiterte Frage: Taugt das Bild von Maria zur Revolte?

Marienvergiftung – Sehgewohnheiten und ihre Brechungen

Die katholische Initiative ‚Maria 2.0' hat sich den Namen eines Updates gegeben und setzt mit dieser Metapher einer aktualisierten Version von ‚Maria' voraus, dass bei der konventionalisierten Sicht auf ‚Maria' ein zu behebender Interpretationsfehler vorliegt: „Frauenlob wird gerne von Kirchenmännern gesungen, die aber allein bestimmen, wo Frauen ihre Talente in der Kirche einbringen dürfen. In ihrer Mitte dulden sie nur eine Frau: Maria. Auf ihrem Sockel. Da steht sie. Und darf nur schweigen."[23] Das Bild der entmündigten[24] Gottesmutter wird gekoppelt an dasjenige der überhöhten ‚Maria'. Hier treffen sich nicht nur emische, sondern auch wissenschaftliche Blicke, denn die

---

[20] Fritz, *Religion*, 204.

[21] Fritz, *Religion*, 204.

[22] Fritz, *Religion*, 104.

[23] Petition ‚An: Papst Franziskus und die Synode der Bischöfe. Offener Brief aus Anlass des Sondergipfels zum Thema der sexualisierten Gewalt in der Kirche', (https://weact.campact.de/petitions/offener-brief-an-papst-franziskus-aus-anlass-des-sondergipfels-uber-missbrauch-in-der-kirche, 10 August 2020).

[24] Vgl. Lisa Kötters Bild der Maria mit zugeklebtem Mund, (http://www.mariazweipunktnull.de/wp-content/uploads/2019/03/Maria20Ikone.jpg, 11 Februar 2021).

Ablehnung der skizzierten ‚Maria' hat in der feministischen Theologie eine lange Tradition:[25]

> Maria – das erste Bild, das ich vor mir sehe, ist das Gipswesen aus der Grotte von Lourdes, niedergeschlagene Augen, den Körper bis zur Unkenntlichkeit verhüllt: Entsexualisierung plus Demut, das weibliche Ideal. Ein Symbol, geschaffen, den Unterdrückten die Selbstunterdrückung beizubringen, den Verunsicherten die Selbstzensur, den doppelt Ausgebeuteten die Selbstausbeutung.[26]

Selbstzensur – in der Theologie also die bewusste Nichtbeschäftigung mit ‚Maria'[27] – lag „bis vor kurzer Zeit" darin begründet, dass „die Darstellung der Maria im NT frauenabwertende Interpretationen zu unterstützen"[28] schien. Das Bild, mehr noch die darin wahrgenommene normative Botschaft eines „Prototyp[s] aller Frauen", der „die ‚Berufung' der Frau vorrangig in Mutterschaft und Jungfräulichkeit"[29] erkennt, wurde und wird hier abgelehnt. Diese Nichtrezeption gründet aber nicht nur in den mit der ‚Gips-Madonna' konfligierenden Weltansichten und Werten, die sich der Demokratisierung und Emanzipierung verpflichtet wissen, sondern ebenso in den errungenen Erkenntnissen „feministische[r] Theologie bzw. Exegese, [die] auch und gerade im Blick auf Maria, zu ganz anderen Ergebnissen"[30] kommt.

---

[25] Vgl. Regina Radlbeck-Ossmann, „Maria in der Feministischen Theologie," in: Wolfgang Beinert und Heinrich Petri (ed.), *Handbuch der Marienkunde* (Pustet: Regensburg [2]1996), 1: Theologische Grundlegung: Geistliches Leben, 435-465.

[26] Dorothee Sölle, „Maria ist eine Sympathisantin," in: Karl-Josef Kuschel (ed.), *Und Maria trat aus ihren Bildern: Literarische Texte* (Herder: Freiburg 1990), 185-190, hier 185.

[27] Vgl. Renate Wind, „Madonna, Muttergöttin, Menschenfrau? Zur Geschichte der Maria aus Nazareth," in: Dies., *Maria aus Nazareth aus Betanien aus Magdala: Drei Frauengeschichten* (Kaiser: Gütersloh 1996), 9-41; Rosemary Radford Ruether, *Maria: Kirche in weiblicher Gestalt* (Kaiser: München 1980), 8-15; Elisabeth Schüssler Fiorenza, „Maria und die Frauenbefreiungsbewegung: Eine kritisch-feministische Sichtung," in: Josef Pfammatter und Eduard Christen (ed.), *Was willst du von mir, Frau? Maria in heutiger Sicht* (Paulusverlag: Freiburg 1995), 91-119.

[28] Heike Bee-Schroedter, „Lesarten der Bibel aus feministischer Perspektive: Wie nehmen Exegetinnen beispielsweise Maria aus Nazareth wahr?," in: Hubert Frankemölle (ed.), *Lebendige Welt Jesu und des Neuen Testaments* (Herder: Freiburg 2000), 167-171, hier 169-170.

[29] Bernhard Heininger, „Geschlechterdifferenz im Neuen Testament: Eine methodische und inhaltliche Skizze," in: Ders. (ed.), *Geschlechterdifferenz in religiösen Symbolsystemen* (Lit: Münster 2003), Geschlecht – Symbol – Religion 1, 26-49, hier 26.

[30] Heininger, „Geschlechterdifferenz," 26.

Statt einer „Marienvergiftung"[31] durch Nichtrezeption zu entgehen, voll-
zieht also die Theologie den emanzipatorischen Akt einer transformierten
Blickkultur, indem sie ‚eigene' Marienbilder kommuniziert. Bevor im Detail
– exemplarisch anhand der ‚Maria' des Magnifikat – auf diese wissenschaftlichen Lesarten und ihre (Nicht-)Rezeption geschaut werden soll, gilt das über-
geordnete Interesse zuerst wieder ‚Maria 2.0' und den von ihr evozierten Blicken. Denn im Gegensatz zur hoch spezifizierten und deshalb nur begrenzt
wirksamen Theologie, gelingt der Initiative, trotz ähnlichem Marienbild, eine
hohe mediale Aufmerksamkeit. Das liegt nicht zuletzt auch in ihrer Ausma-
lung eines identitäts- und gemeinschaftsstiftenden (Vor-)Bildes begründet:
„Holen wir sie vom Sockel! In unsere Mitte. Als Schwester, die in die gleiche
Richtung schaut, wie wir".[32]

„Alle Ladies in Gottes Gemeinden: Es ist Zeit, unsre Stimmen zu verei-nen"[33] – wie Bilder Identität und Gemeinschaft stiften

Diese Lesart von ‚Maria' greift auch Carolin Kebekus (eben nicht nur) satirisch in ihrer Comedyshow auf. In ihrem Redebeitrag, der dezidiert an ‚Maria
2.0' anschließt, teilt sie nicht nur den Wertekanon[34] der Initiative, sondern
zugleich das identitäts- und gemeinschaftsstiftende Moment:

> Warum […] treten diese Frauen nicht einfach aus […]? […] [E]igentlich wollen
> die bleiben, weil diese Frauen in ihren Gemeinden verwurzelt sind, weil die ihren
> Glauben leben und dieser Teil ihrer Identität ist […]: Wie kann ich heute als
> moderne, unabhängige Frau gleichzeitig Mitglied der katholischen Kirche sein?
> […] Ich bin aus der Kirche ausgetreten, weil ich das vor mir selber irgendwann
> nicht mehr rechtfertigen konnte. Aber ich bin katholisch getauft und fühle mich

---

[31] Sabine Demel, „Jungfrau und Mutter: Maria und ihre Auswirkungen auf das Frauenbild (in)
der katholischen Kirche," in: Inge Kroppenberg und Martin Löhnig (ed.), *Fragmentierte Fami-*
lien: Brechungen einer sozialen Form in der Moderne (transcript: Bielefeld 2010), 15: *Lite-*
ralität und Liminalität, 39-69, hier 60.

[32] Maria 2.0, Offener Brief.

[33] Carolin Kebekus, „Im Namen der Mutter," 00:00-00:26, (https://www.youtube.com/
watch?v=wXV7oiM566I, 28 Juli 2020).

[34] Carolin Kebekus, „Die Carolin Kebekus Show," 09 Juli 2020, 20:16-20:22: „Gleichberech-
tigung ist nämlich kein momentaner Trend, den die Kirche einfach aussitzen kann", (https://
www.ardmediathek.de/ard/video/die-carolin-kebekus-show/die-carolin-kebekus-show-vom-
9-juli-2020/das-erste/Y3JpZDovL2Rhc2Vyc3RlLmRlL2RpZS1jYXJvbGluLWtlYmVrd-
XMtc2hvdy9mOWJmNFiNy05YzFlLTQ0OGMtODUzOC11YTljYz5YTdkMDA/, 12 Februar 2021).

natürlich immer noch als Christin [...], ich kann diese Verbundenheit mit der Gemeinde und den Glauben der Frauen von Maria 2.0 absolut nachvollziehen. Für mich ist es einfach nur ein riesiges Rätsel, warum man nicht das Engagement dieser Frauen nutzt. Euer Laden geht den Bach runter und da stehen schlaue, hochintelligente, studierte Frauen, voller Liebe für ihre Kirche und wollen helfen. [...] Ich hoffe auf Veränderung und ich hoffe, dass jetzt alle Frauen die Kirchen stürmen und sie zu neuem Leben erwecken.[35]

Im Anschluss daran präsentiert Kebekus in einem Videoclip ihre Sicht weniger auf ‚Maria‘, als vielmehr auf die mit diesem Bild einhergehende Kritik an geschlechtsgebundenen Rollenzuschreibungen.[36] Sie arrangiert diesen Blick professionell im Format populärer Musik[37] unter dem Titel ‚Im Namen der Mutter‘. Diese Inszenierung von Religion lässt sich auf vier Ebenen analysieren:

Auf Produktionsebene handelt es sich bei dem Videoclip erstens um das Ergebnis kollektiver Herstellungs- und Vermarktungsprozesse,[38] an denen eine große Anzahl an Personen beteiligt ist.[39] Zur Produktion herangezogen wurde offensichtlich auch eine feministisch-theologische Beratung. Denn die konkrete Darstellung sucht textlich wie visuell nicht nur den Schulterschluss mit namhaften Theologinnen feministischer Forschung,[40] sondern spielt auf verschiedene in diesem Feld geführte Debatten an, die ein bestimmtes, nämlich theologisch bewandertes Publikum voraussetzen: Wenn der CIC etwa im Papierkorb landet (Kebekus, „Mutter," 3:02-3:03), dann geht es um die kirchenrechtlichen Begründungen zum Ausschluss von Frauen vom

---

[35] Kebekus, „Show," 20:41-21:02; 21:48-22:32; 23:00-23:07.

[36] Tätigkeiten, die Priestern in ihrem Amt (zumeist) vorbehalten sind, werden analogisiert mit (meist) von Frauen vollzogenen Berufen der Care-Arbeit (vgl. Kebekus, „Mutter," 0:36-0:38; 0:41-0:48; 0:51-0:53; 1:06-1:10).

[37] Vgl. zur Korrelation von Religion und Popkultur: Andreas Kubik, „Das Interesse der christlichen Theologie an einer Hermeneutik der populären Kultur," in: Frank Thomas Brinkmann (ed.), *Pop goes my heart: Religions- und popkulturelle Gespräche im 21. Jahrhundert* (Springer: Wiesbaden 2016), pop.religion: lebensstil – kultur – theologie, 99-122.

[38] Vgl. Fritz, *Religion*, 159.

[39] Hinter dem Musikvideo steht die Produktionsfirma ‚bildundtonfabrik‘ (btf GmbH; vgl. https://btf.de/, 12 Februar 2021), sowie die Musikproduktionsfirma Score Squad (http://www.scoresquad.com/, 14 Februar 2021).

[40] Vgl. die Bildergalerie mit Uta Ranke-Heinemann oder Mary Daly, die textlich unterlegt wird mit: „Gott schuf am achten Tag den Feminismus: Wir sind die Sisters von Jesus Christus" (vgl. Kebekus, „Mutter," 1:51-1:55).

Priesteramt.[41] Rappt Kebekus: „Wegen Schwesta Eva müsst ihr uns dissen? Adam hat doch auch in den scheiss Apfel gebissen" (Kebekus, „Mutter," 0:56-1:01), dann steht im Hintergrund die exegetische Beschäftigung mit der Auslegungs- und Wirkungsgeschichte von Gen 1-3.[42] Ähnliches gilt für die Stigmatisierung von (biblischen) Frauen zu Huren im Laufe der christlichen Auslegungs- und Wirkungsgeschichte.[43] Wird das Fresko von Urschalling verwendet (Kebekus, „Show," 14:08-14:15),[44] dann liegt dem die theologische Diskussion um ‚weibliche' Aspekte der dritten trinitarischen Person, sowie grundsätzlich die (Nicht-)Darstellbarkeit des trinitarischen Gottes zugrunde.

All diese im Videoclip adaptierten, dort aber keinesfalls ausdiskutierten, theologischen Narrative setzen also, zweitens, bestimmte Sehgewohnheiten voraus, ohne die sie nicht funktionieren würden. Über den schon aufgezeigten (begrenzten theologischen) Kreis hinaus ist das Musikvideo vor allem deshalb wirkungsvoll,[45] weil mit der Inszenierung im Format eines auf YouTube geteilten Clips die Filterblase des (deutschen) Katholizismus weit überschritten und ein Publikum adressiert wird, „das bestimmten Werten wie […] Demokratisierung verpflichtet ist."[46] Von diesem intendierten Adressat*innenkreis wird erwartet, dass er kollektive Erfahrungen „hinsichtlich Religion und ihrer Repräsentation"[47] teilt, sodass diese adaptiert werden können. Im Musikvideo werden solche vorausgesetzten und gemeinschaftlichen Einsichten – hier der Ausschluss von Frauen von geweihten Ämtern – mittels liturgischer Kleidung eingeholt. Gekoppelt werden diese mit der kollektiven Erwartung einer in der

---

[41] Vgl. Sabine Demel, *Frauen und kirchliches Amt: Vom Ende eines Tabus in der katholischen Kirche* (Herder: Freiburg im Breisgau, Basel und Wien 2004).

[42] Vgl. Helen Schüngel-Straumann, „,Von einer Frau nahm die Sünde ihren Anfang, ihretwegen müssen wir alle sterben' (Sir 25,24): Zur Wirkungs- und Rezeptionsgeschichte der ersten drei Kapitel der Genesis in biblischer Zeit," in: *Bibel und Kirche* 53 (1/1998), 11-20.

[43] Vgl. exemplarisch Sabine Bieberstein, „Maria Magdalena: Jüngerin und Apostelin oder Sünderin und Hure?: Bilder einer neutestamentlichen Frauenfigur im Wandel," in: Marion Bayerl, Verena Gutsche und Bea Klüsener (ed.): *Gender – Recht – Gerechtigkeit* (Winter: Heidelberg 2012), 5: Regensburger Beiträge zur Gender-Forschung, 125-152.

[44] Vgl. Verena Wodtke-Werner, „Heiliger Geist oder Heilige Geistin im Trinitätsfresko von Urschalling?," in: Elisabeth Moltmann-Wendel (ed.), *Die Weiblichkeit des Heiligen Geistes* (Kaiser: Gütersloh 1995), 77-114.

[45] Vgl. die hohe Zahl an Likes (28.739), Dislikes (1334), Views (729.987) und Kommentaren (2.655), zu Kebekus, „Mutter," Stand: 14 Februar 2021, 19:21 Uhr.

[46] Fritz, *Religion*, 158.

[47] Fritz, *Religion*, 158.

Kirche demütigen und auf das Dienen reduzierten Frau, welche allerdings im Laufe der Inszenierung durch die sich selbst ermächtigenden Frauen konterkariert werden: Statt sich wie bei einer Priesterweihe passiv einkleiden zu lassen, ziehen sich die zuvor auf feste Rollen verwiesenen Frauen die liturgischen Gewänder selber an (Kebekus, „Mutter," 2:13-2:19). Aber nicht nur in der Vergangenheit etablierte Erwartungen werden hier vorausgesetzt, sondern diese werden zudem „gemäß dem Zeitgeschmack, also zeitlich gebundener kollektiver Moden"[48] neu verwendet, wenn zum Beispiel die junge und ‚Schwarze' Schauspielerin Adrielle Isabelle in weißer Soutane, Zingulum, Mozetta und Pileolus im Hip Hop Urban Style performt.

Drittens ist im Videoclip ein Bezug zu religiösen Gemeinschaften mittels Inszenierung eines Kollektivs erkennbar. Als identitätsstiftendes Merkmal dient hier, neben der vorausgesetzten Zugehörigkeit zur Katholischen Kirche, einerseits *gender* und andererseits *race*, die je von Einzelcharakteren repräsentiert und mit denen zugleich die als ‚real' gesetzten Begebenheiten „visuell hinterfragt werden":[49] Neben dem schon genannten Beispiel von Adrielle Isabelle kann noch auf Thelma Buabeng verwiesen werden, die im Video als ‚Schwarze' Göttin rappt (Kebekus, „Mutter," 2:33-2:34). Eine solche Darstellung[50] Gottes ist nicht erst die Erfindung von Kebekus,[51] dennoch erscheint sie als so sehr den ikonographischen Erwartungen an Gott als einem ‚Weißen' alten Mann zuwiderlaufend, dass sie im ‚besten' Fall erklärt,[52] im schlechtesten Falle als ‚blasphemisch'[53] gebrandmarkt wird.

Insofern der Rückgriff auf bestimmte Sehgewohnheiten eines Bildes der Wiedererkennung und damit der vereinfachten Rezeption dient, ist mit dem

---

[48] Fritz, *Religion*, 158.

[49] Fritz, *Religion*, 158.

[50] Auch in dieser Inszenierung Gottes als ‚Schwarzer' Frau kann – in Ergänzung zur ersten Produktionsebene – theologisch die Debatte um die Nicht-Abbildbarkeit Gottes bei dennoch bleibend menschlich-defizitärem Versuch, das Unsichtbare sichtbar zu machen, aufscheinen.

[51] Vgl. die Neuinterpretation der ‚Erschaffung Adams' durch Harmonia Rosales, die alle ‚Weißen' Männer – so auch Gott – durch *Women of Color* ersetzt (https://www.bento.de/art/erschaffung-adams-warum-diese-frau-gott-als-schwarze-frau-darstellt-a-00000000-0003-0001-0000-000001374150, 10 August 2020).

[52] Vgl. https://www.katholisch.de/artikel/26132-kabarettistin-kebekus-nimmt-erneut-katholische-kirche-aufs-korn, 17 Februar 2021: „Eine schwarze ‚Göttin' tritt auf und betont unter anderem: ‚Was Vatikan, das kann Mutti schon lange'."

[53] Vgl. etwa zum Werk von Rosales: https://katholisches.info/2020/07/14/revolution-durch-die-hintertuer/, 10 August 2020). Eine solche Bewertung ist nicht nur sexistisch, sondern auch rassistisch.

Videoclip ‚Im Namen der Mutter‘ auch die Irritation dieser Erwartungen ein-kalkuliert und zwar in dezidierter Form der Empörung.[54] Als vierte Ebene kollektiver Prozesse sichtbarer Religion können von daher „gruppendynami-sche Prozesse […], beispielsweise innerhalb von Fangruppen oder konträr dazu in kritischen Kreisen"[55] sichtbar gemacht werden: Während ‚Maria 2.0‘, die ‚Katholische Frauengemeinschaft Deutschlands‘ und der ‚Katholische Deutsche Frauenbund‘ sich Kebekus gegenüber wertschätzend positionieren,[56] zeigen Johanna Stöhr für ‚Maria 1.0‘[57] und Julia Rosner für die Social Media-Redaktion der Deutschen Bischofskonferenz[58] in ihren „Reaktionen […], dass [sie] sich aus ihrer Sicht [– nämlich als katholische Frauen –] medial nicht korrekt wiedergegeben"[59] fühlen: Die beiden zuletzt Genannten verstehen den Videoclip, bzw. „die [dortige] Verwendung und Wahrnehmung religiöser Symbole und Narrative"[60] als Gotteslästerung, nämlich als Beleidigung des „katholische[n] Glaube[ns] und übelste Hetze gegen die Kirche",[61] bzw. als „Äußerungen, die blasphemische Elemente enthalten, […] [und] auch verlet-zend sein"[62] können.

Diese Aufteilung der Bewertungen verwendeter Motive und ihrer Umset-zung „im Clip [–] entweder positiv als Ergänzung der bestehenden Bedeutung

---

[54] Vgl. Fritz, *Religion*, 204.
[55] Fritz, *Religion*, 158.
[56] Vgl. https://www.katholisch.de/artikel/26301-kfd-lobt-erneut-kirchenkritisches-video-von-kabarettistin-kebekus, 17 Februar 2021.
[57] Vgl. ihr Facebook-Eintrag am 10 Juli 2020 um 12:51 Uhr: „Dieses Video von Frau Carolin Kebekus offenbart genau, wo das katholische Grundproblem in Deutschland ist. Denn wie kann man für Frauen ein heiliges Amt einfordern wollen, während man gleichzeitig zeigt, dass einem nichts heilig ist." (https://www.facebook.com/MariaEinsPunktNull/, 15 Februar 2021)
[58] Vgl. Julia Rosners – zumindest anfänglich satirisch wirken wollender – Post auf Facebook am 10 Juli 2020 um 03:40 Uhr: „Liebe Frau Carolin Kebekus, Grüße vom ‚ältesten Männerverein der Welt‘. Vielen Dank für diese Zusammenfassung unserer Geschichte und Wertvorstellun-gen. Ja, zweifellos arbeiten wir noch immer hart daran, unsere Verfehlungen der vergangenen Jahre und Jahrzehnte aufzuarbeiten. […] Vielleicht noch eine kleine Bitte: bei aller Liebe zur Satire – Äußerungen, die blasphemische Elemente enthalten, können auch verletzend sein. Vielleicht sollten Sie hier auch die Katholiken und Katholikinnen im Blick behalten, die mit ihrem Herzen in der Kirche sind und zu dem stehen, woran sie glauben." (https://www.face-book.com/dbk.de, 15 Februar 2021)
[59] Fritz, *Religion*, 158.
[60] Fritz, *Religion*, 159.
[61] Stöhr, „Maria 1.0".
[62] Rosner, DBK.

[...] oder negativ als blasphemisch[e]"[63] Verwerfung – spiegelt sich neben den genannten Gruppierungen auch in den individuellen Kommentaren zu den herangezogenen Posts wider und ist ein Indikator dafür, dass die Inszenierung des Clips, die auf „Orientierung und Bedeutungsproduktion"[64] zielt, sowohl in die eine wie die andere Richtung und zudem individuell wie kollektiv funktioniert. Zugleich verweist die Bewertung von ‚Maria 2.0' und den in diesem Kontext erzeugten Bedeutungen als ‚blasphemisch' auf den Aspekt der Regulierung und damit der Machtausübung[65] im *circuit of culture* hin. Denn wird den Aktualisierungen religiöser Traditionen durch ‚Maria 2.0' unterstellt, sie berge die „Gefahr, den ‚wahren', also über Epochen tradierten Glauben, zu verfälschen, was zu Konflikten zwischen Individuen oder Gruppen und zu Abspaltungen führen könnte",[66] so wird in diesem Vorwurf weniger – bzw. überhaupt nicht – Maria selbst, als vielmehr eine als verbindlich vorgegebene Bild-Tradierung diskutiert: Wie ‚Maria' auszusehen hat,

> weiß ‚man' aufgrund einer spezifischen regulierten Bildtradition, die sich über Jahrhunderte und via unterschiedlichster Medien ausgebildet hat, und nicht aufgrund der archäologischen und anthropologischen Rekonstruktionen des Durchschnittsmenschen im 1. Jahrhundert in Palästina. Diese Bildtradition ist so ausgeprägt, dass eine durchschnittliche Europäerin (die nicht zwingend ein aktives Mitglied einer christlichen Gemeinschaft sein muss) eine [...] [Marienfigur] auf Anhieb erkennt, auch wenn sie außerhalb des biblischen Kontexts vorkommt.[67]

Wird nach der Regulierung Bedeutung generierender Mariendarstellungen gefragt, so kommt insbesondere der Theologischen Wissenschaft als einer hier fachlich prädestinierten Disziplin die Rolle der Kontrolleurin zu. Wie stark sich mediale Darstellung mittels Selbstinszenierung von Wissenschaftlichkeit einer Bilder konventionalisierenden Repräsentationsmacht bedient, dabei aber keineswegs auf wissenschaftlich-theologische – hier konkret exegetische –

---

[63] Fritz, *Religion*, 159.

[64] Fritz, *Religion*, 158f.

[65] Vgl. Herman L. Beck, „Gotteslästerung, religionsgeschichtlich," in: *Religion in Geschichte und Gegenwart* (Mohr Siebeck: Tübingen ⁴2000), 3, 1226-1227, 1227: „Die Gesch[ichte] des Christentums lehrt, daß jede Form weitergehender Kritik oder auch nur Kommentierung von Glaubensauffassungen und Lehrsätzen jenes Teils der Christenheit, zu dem die herrschende Elite gehörte [...] als G[otteslästerung] aufgefaßt werden konnte und entsprechend bestraft [...] [und] in einem engen Zusammenhang mit Häresie gesehen" wurde, bzw. noch immer wird.

[66] Fritz, *Religion*, 162.

[67] Fritz, *Religion*, 163; dort aber in Bezug auf Jesus.

Erkenntnisse rekurriert, zeigt das folgende Beispiel von Blickkulturen auf die ‚Maria' des Magnifikat.

Taugt das Bild von Maria zur Revolte? – wie Macht inszeniert und Bilder reguliert werden

Ebenfalls angestoßen von ‚Maria 2.0' wurde in der ‚Zeit'-Beilage ‚Christ und Welt', danach gefragt, ob ‚Maria zur Revolte' tauge.[68] Zwei Antworten – die einer Frau und eines Mannes – werden den Lesenden als (vermeintlich) konträre Reaktionen aus dem fachspezifischen Journalismus präsentiert:

Christina Rietz, Redakteurin bei ‚Christ & Welt' beantwortet die Frage, die in der Unterüberschrift dezidiert in die Thematik ‚Symbolik in der Kirche' eingeordnet wird, mit einem klaren „Nein".[69] Denn ‚Maria' sei das Gegenteil einer emanzipierten Frau, weil sie ihr Schicksal nicht in die eigene Hand nehme, sondern in die Hand Gottes lege. Sie begründet ihre Antwort mit einer Deutung des Magnifikat:

> Maria […] taugt nicht zur Galionsfigur einer Emanzipationsbewegung im 21. Jahrhundert. Emanzipation kommt vom lateinischen Ausdruck *ex manu capere*, was so viel bedeutet wie ‚aus der Hand entlassen'. Maria begibt sich doch im Gegenteil ganz in die Hand Gottes. Nirgends wird das deutlicher als in der berühmten, aber auch fast einzigen größeren Bibelstelle, die ganz der Madonna gehört: ‚Und Maria sprach: Meine Seele erhebt den Herrn, und mein Geist freuet sich Gottes, meines Heilandes; denn er hat die Niedrigkeit seiner Magd angesehen. Siehe, von nun an werden mich seligpreisen alle Kindeskinder. Denn er hat große Dinge an mir getan, der da mächtig ist und dessen Name heilig ist.' Sie ist alles durch ihn, aber nichts durch sich. Zwar [strahlt] das sogenannte Magnificat […] als vermeintliche Erhöhung Mariens durch die Jahrhunderte. Aber die Eigenschaft der Gottesmutter, die durch das Magnificat doch am prominentesten ausgestellt wird, das ist die Demut, die Einsicht in die Nichtswürdigkeit ihrer selbst, bevor Gott der Herr sie angesehen.[70]

Rietz unterscheidet nicht zwischen dem lukanischen Text und seiner Wirkungsgeschichte und folgert deshalb, dass ‚Maria' dort nur vermeintlich erhöht, tatsächlich aber erniedrigt würde, weil ihre ‚Nichtswürdigkeit' hervorgehoben werde. Diese problematische Gleichsetzung von ‚Demut' mit

---

[68] Vgl. Christina Rietz und Andreas Öhler, „Taugt Maria zur Revolte? Symbolik in der Kirche," in: *Christ & Welt* (Beilage zur *Zeit* 29/2019).

[69] Rietz; Öhler, „Revolte".

[70] Rietz; Öhler, „Revolte".

‚Nichtswürdigkeit' versperrt aber den Blick auf das im Magnifikat Erzählte: Lukas betont eben nicht Marias ‚Nichtswürdigkeit', sondern Gottes Aufhebung und Neuzuweisung überkommener „Statuszuweisungen".[71]

Als Gegenpart beantwortet Andreas Öhler – dortiger Redakteur und Kulturkorrespondent der Katholischen Nachrichten-Agentur – die Frage der symbolischen Tauglichkeit von ‚Maria' für eine Revolte ebenfalls unter Einholung des Magnifikat vorgeblich mit „Ja"[72] – unterschwellig[73] aber mit „Nein":

> Seit Urzeiten wird das Weiche dem Weiblichen zugeordnet. Das ist bei Maria nicht anders. Sie hat nur wenige Auftritte in der Bibel, aber einer hat es in sich. Da wird sie laut, da klingt sie politisch. Im Magnificat nach Lukas heißt es: ‚Gott stößt die Gewaltigen vom Thron und erhebt die Niedrigen. Die Hungrigen füllt er mit Gütern und lässt die Reichen leer ausgehen.' Feministische Theologinnen machten aus ihr eine sozialkritische Prophetin. Dabei gehört sie nicht zu alttestamentlichen Propheten wie etwa Jesaia, der seine Sozialkritik in die Wüste schrie. Maria kämpft als Mutter.[74]

Öhler diffamiert die feministische Auslegung des Textes als eine eisegetische Konstruktion. Er entkoppelt damit die lukanisch erzählte ‚Maria' aus ihrem ersttestamentlichen Verstehenshintergrund, ohne welchen eine Annäherung an diese Mariendarstellung nicht möglich ist und reproduziert damit ein Rollenbild ‚Marias', das nicht mehr dem lukanischen Textbestand entspricht.

Zugleich suggeriert er mit der Unterstellung, erst feministische Theologinnen hätten aus ‚Maria' eine sozialkritische Prophetin – hier läge ja das Potenzial für eine Tauglichkeit zur symbolischen ‚Revolte'[75] – gemacht, dass die

---

[71] Vgl. Michael Wolter, *Das Lukasevangelium* (Mohr Siebeck: Tübingen 2008), Handbuch zum Neuen Testament 5, 100.

[72] Rietz; Öhler, „Revolte".

[73] In metakommunikativer Perspektive wirkt rhetorisch perfide, dass ausgerechnet der für ‚Marias' Führerschaft durch sein ‚Ja' Partei ergreifende Mann mit seiner Auslegung und der damit einhergehenden Frauenkonzeption eine Mariengestalt konstruiert, die sich tatsächlich keine Emanzipationsbewegung als Gallionsfigur auswählen würde. Das vorausgegangene ‚Nein' seiner Kollegin Rietz wirkt unter Einbezug der Perspektive Öhlers dann geradezu bestätigend: Diese ‚Maria' taugt nicht als ‚Galionsfigur einer Emanzipationsbewegung im 21. Jahrhundert'. Während die normativen Aussagen Öhlers so „camoufliert" werden und ihn „vor Kritik hinsichtlich [...] Frauenfeindlichkeit" (Fritz, *Religion*, 118) schützen, wirkt das Anliegen von ‚Maria 2.0' – unausgesprochen – absurd.

[74] Rietz; Öhler, „Revolte".

[75] Bereits der im Titel gewählte Begriff der ‚Revolte' als eines „Aufruhr[s] oder meist von einer kleinen Gruppe getragener Aufstand" (Manfred G. Schmidt, „Revolte," in: *Wörterbuch zur*

dieser ‚Umdeutung' vorausgegangene Lesart ‚Marias' die ursprünglichere sei.
Darauf deutet auch seine essentialistische, nur vermeintlich zeit- und kultur-
transzendierende („seit Urzeiten … [; d]as ist bei Maria nicht anders") Rollen-
zuweisung von Frauen zu Müttern („weich, weiblich, mütterlich") hin, die er
exklusivistisch auf die literarische Figur der ‚Maria' überträgt. Diese Regulie-
rungsversuche Öhlers zeigen deutliche Parallelen zu jenen Gruppierungen, die
ebenfalls mittels (wissenschaftlichem) Anspruch auf Deutungshoheit kontrol-
lieren wollen, „was gezeigt werden kann und was nicht" und im extremsten
Fall solche „Bilder [von Maria], die einem [– nämlich dem eigenen –] Werte-
system widersprechen, zerstör[en]":[76]

Der Luganer Dogmatik-Professor Manfred Hauke etwa stellt in der ‚Tagespost' zu den „Irrungen" des Synodalen Weges folgende dualistische Differen-
zierung in authentische und nicht-authentische Marien- und – für ihn damit
einhergehend – Frauendeutungen auf: „Unter dem Stichwort ‚Maria 2.0' haben
sich feministische Aktivitäten versammelt, denen es um das Weihepriestertum
der Frau geht, während gläubige katholische Frauen, die Maria in der Originalfassung annehmen, dagegen die Initiative ‚Maria 1.0' gesetzt haben".[77] Er
fordert: „Die Kirche braucht die Originalfassung von Maria".[78] Einzige
‚originale' Deutung ist in Haukes Perspektive die Hervorhebung von „Jungfräulichkeit und […] Mutterschaft als zwei zentrale[n] Dimensionen für die

---

Politik [Kröner: Stuttgart ³2010], 695) wird dem von ‚Maria 2.0' erhobenen Anliegen, gleich-
würdige und -rechtliche Partizipation für Frauen als der Hälfte aller Christ*innen einzufordern,
nicht gerecht, sondern suggeriert, etwa im Gegensatz zur ‚Revolution' als einer „tief greifenden
Umgestaltung der [als ungerecht empfundenen] politischen, gesellschaftlichen oder wirtschaft-
lichen Verhältnisse in einem Gemeinwesen" (vgl. Manfred G. Schmidt, „Revolution," in:
Wörterbuch zur Politik [Kröner: Stuttgart ³2010], 265), das Scheitern einer nur kleinen Opposition. Insofern ‚Revolten' ‚Revolutionen' allerdings meist vorausgehen, entscheidet erst die
nachträgliche Einordnung des Geschehens, um was es sich je gehandelt hat. In dieser Perspektive erscheint die Frage nach der Tauglichkeit des Symbols ‚Maria' nicht nur als unlogisch,
sondern zugleich als manipulativ, beansprucht sie doch die Antwort schon liefern zu können.
[76] Fritz, *Religion*, 121.
[77] Manfred Hauke, „Die Kirche braucht die Originalfassung von Maria," in: *Die Tagespost*, 16
Juli 2020, vgl. https://www.die-tagespost.de/gesellschaft/feuilleton/die-kirche-braucht-die-ori-
ginalfassung-von-maria;art310,210231, 19 August 2020; vgl. ‚Maria 1.0 schreibt an Maria
2.0': „Maria ist die Gleiche, gestern und heute und morgen. Sie braucht kein Update und ihr
Name darf auch nicht instrumentalisiert werden." (https://www.domradio.de/themen/
glaube/2019-09-17/eure-forderungen-sind-nicht-gut-maria-10-schreibt-maria-20, 17 August
2020)
[78] Hauke, „Originalfassung".

Berufung der Frau [...], die in Maria ihr Vorbild findet."[79] Alterierende Deutungen können in dieser Perspektive nur falsch sein: Die „Inkubationszeit des Synodalen Weges" sei, so Hauke, „im Grund nichts anderes als bischöflich geförderter Vulgärmarxismus."[80] Denn „der ideologische Gegner der biblischen Sicht ist vor allem der Marxismus", der in „bestimmte[n] Kreise[n] des Synodalen Weges" wirke, die darauf zielten „die Familie ab[zu]schaffen wegen der besonderen Leitungsverantwortung des Mannes."[81] Mit diesen Äußerungen verortet Hauke sich nicht nur im Sprachjargon „nach Art des amerikanischen Antifeminismus und des katholischen Fundamentalismus".[82] Er pflegt darüber hinaus mit seiner ‚Originalfassung von Maria' einen „fundamentalistischen Umgang mit der Heiligen Schrift", denn „diese [Ideologie] verlangt ein totales Einverständnis mit starren doktrinären Haltungen und fordert als einzige Quelle der Lehre im Hinblick auf das christliche Leben und Heil eine Lektüre der Bibel, die jegliches kritisches Fragen und Forschen ablehnt".[83] Dass „[f]eministische Aktivitäten"[84] kirchlich gewollt „feministische Exegese"[85] sein könnten, die dazu gefordert ist, „geläufige Interpretationen [aufzudecken], die tendenziös waren und darauf hinausliefen, die Herrschaft des Mannes über die Frau zu rechtfertigen",[86] wird von Hauke schlicht ignoriert.

Das Postulat eines ‚originalen' Bildes von ‚Maria', an dem sich Rechtgläubigkeit von Blasphemie scheidet, wird auch von Stefano M. Manelli in der von Hauke herausgegebenen ‚Biblischen[n] Mariologie' vertreten, mit dem Anspruch „‚religiöses Kapital' in Form von explizitem religiösen Wissen [...] [und] theologischer Reflexion [...]"[87] zu repräsentieren. Wie Öhler und Hauke greift auch Manelli – mit dem Ziel der Regulierung von Blickkulturen – auf das lukanische Marienbild des Magnifikat zurück, um zu behaupten ‚Maria' im Original darstellen zu können: Die historisch-kritische „Hypothese", dass

---

[79] Hauke, „Originalfassung".

[80] Hauke, „Originalfassung".

[81] Hauke, „Originalfassung".

[82] Rebeka Jadranka Anić, „Gender, Politik und die katholische Kirche: Ein Beitrag zum Abbau der alten Geschlechterstereotypen," in: *Concilium* 48 (2012), 373-382, hier 380.

[83] Päpstliche Bibelkommission, „Die Interpretation der Bibel in der Kirche," in: Sekretariat der Deutschen Bischofskonferenz (ed.), *Verlautbarungen des Apostolischen Stuhls 115* (Bonn ⁴2004), 61.

[84] Hauke, „Originalfassung".

[85] Bibelkommission, „Interpretation," 59.

[86] Bibelkommission, „Interpretation," 60.

[87] Fritz, *Religion*, 127.

dieses Lied „eine Konstruktion des Evangelisten" sei, ist für Manelli „selbst-
verständlich unannehmbar".[88] Denn Maria habe als „Tochter des semitischen
Volkes [...] die Fähigkeit zu improvisieren und besonders viel im Gedächtnis
behalten zu können, gleichsam im Blut"[89] gelegen. Zu vergessen sei auch
nicht, „dass Maria, [...] seit dem Ereignis der Verkündigung mehrere Tage
Zeit hatte, in ihrem Herzen den Gesang des Magnifikat zu überlegen und zu
erdichten".[90] Zwar habe Lukas bei der Übersetzung aus dem Semitischen ins
Griechische auch ein wenig „vermittelt",[91] ohne dabei aber am Inhalt etwas
zu ändern.[92] Im Gegensatz zu Manellis Auffassung kann aber keinesfalls resü-
miert werden, dass „[d]ie Mehrheit der Exegeten [...] [mit der These der
wörtlichen Authentizität des Magnifikat] einverstanden ist".[93] Denn es herrscht
zwar „Konsens" darüber, „[d]ass das Magnifikat insgesamt oder zum größten
Teil vorlukanischer Herkunft ist und ursprünglich als selbstständiger Hymnus
existierte".[94] Das entbindet aber keinesfalls von der Tatsache, dass „[a]lle[...]
Aussagen über eine wie auch immer geartete Vorgeschichte des Magnifikat
[...] hochspekulativ sind und die jeweiligen Entscheidungen sich durchweg
außerhalb eines objektivierbaren methodischen Plausibilitätssystems bewe-
gen".[95] Deshalb gilt für jede „Interpretation [...] von einer möglichen Vorgeschichte abzusehen [...] [und] das Magnifikat [...] ausschließlich als lk
Komposition"[96] zu kommentieren.

Gegen verkürzende Bewertungen historisch-kritischer Auslegung wendet
sich das folgende Kapitel, als eine Form des „Querlesen[s] von Botschaften [,
die es] erlaubt [...] umgedeutete Codes wieder in den Prozess von Produktion
und Rezeption zu reintegrieren, Bedeutungen zu verschieben und die Regulie-
rungsansprüche der Produktion zu unterwandern."[97] Denn die soeben aufgezeigten Bedeutungsproduktionen verfehlen – mit ihren Versuchen feministische Auslegungen durch (nur beanspruchte) Wissenschaftlichkeit als

---

[88] Stefano Maria Manelli, *Biblische Mariologie* (Pustet: Regensburg 2018), Mariologische Studien 27, 185.
[89] Manelli, *Mariologie*, 185.
[90] Manelli, *Mariologie*, 186.
[91] Manelli, *Mariologie*, 188.
[92] Vgl. Manelli, *Mariologie*, 187-188.
[93] Manelli, *Mariologie*, 189.
[94] Wolter, *Lukasevangelium*, 99.
[95] Wolter, *Lukasevangelium*, 99.
[96] Wolter, *Lukasevangelium*, 99.
[97] Fritz, *Religion*, 122.

Machtdemonstration zu regulieren – sowohl das Thema (nämlich Kontinuität der göttlichen Heilsinitiative an Israel) als auch das Objekt (nämlich Gott) des Magnifikat.[98]

Blicke, die ‚Maria' in der Auslegung des Magnifikat zum Verhängnis wurden und werden

Maria oder ‚Maria'?
Biblische Texte sind niedergeschriebene Erfahrungen des göttlichen Offenbarungsgeschehens. Diese Zeugnisse konkreter Menschen sind nicht misszuverstehen als histori(sti)sche oder biologi(sti)sche Berichte. So erhebt auch das Magnifikat keinesfalls den Anspruch, einen Zugang zu der ‚Originalfassung von Maria' ermöglichen zu wollen. Denn „[ü]ber Maria als historische Gestalt wissen wir wenig".[99] Das hier analysierte Gotteslied ist – wie jeder andere biblische Text – eine theologische Aussage über das auf Heil hin orientierte Handeln Gottes am und für den Menschen. Damit ist es aber immer schon menschliche Deutung dieses Geschehens, also Konstruktion. Das mindert in keinem Fall seinen Aussagewert, sondern das Bewusstsein um dieses Konstitutivum ermöglicht vielmehr eine Entgrenzung der darin enthaltenen Frohbotschaft: „Die Frage, die wir an die Evangelientexte richten sollten, lautet nicht: Ist das wirklich so passiert? sondern: Was hat dieser Text zu bedeuten?"[100] Histori(sti)sche Ableitungen aus diesem poetischen Text zu ziehen, verbietet sich nicht nur aus den eben genannten theologischen, sondern auch aus logischen Gründen: Wer davon ausgeht, dass das Magnifikat Rückschlüsse auf ein realhistorisches Geschehen liefert, der muss so (theologisch unnötige) Fragen beantworten, wie nach den historischen Bedingungen der Inhalte dieser „extravagante[n] Erzählung".[101]

‚Maria' oder Israel?
Christina Rietz begeht nicht den soeben aufgezeigten Fehler eines wörtlichen Verständnisses, also einer fundamentalistischen Lesart. Ihre Deutung der nicht

---

[98] Wolter, *Lukasevangelium*, 100.

[99] Silke Petersen, „Maria aus Nazareth: Eine Geschichte der Verwandlung," in: Irmtraud Fischer und Andrea Taschl-Erber (ed.), *Evangelien: Erzählungen und Geschichte* (Kohlhammer: Stuttgart 2011), Die Bibel und die Frauen: Eine exegetisch-kulturgeschichtliche Enzyklopädie 2.1, 320-339, hier 320.

[100] Wind, „Madonna," 28-29.

[101] Wolter, *Lukasevangelium*, 97. So wäre etwa zu klären, wie der Evangelist zu seinem intimen Wissen über den rein gynozentrischen Dialog zwischen Maria und Elisabeth kommt oder woher er das Wissen über die inneren Beweggründe seiner Protagonist*innen hatte.

emanzipierten ‚Maria', die sich in die ‚Hand Gottes' begibt und ihr Schicksal nicht in die ‚eigene Hand' nimmt, ist unter dem Aspekt von ‚Selbstständigkeit' oder ‚Selbstbefreiung' zuerst einmal nachvollziehbar. Diese oberflächliche Perspektive ändert sich aber, wenn die ersttestamentlichen Kon-Texte des lukanischen Loblieds der ‚Maria', also die heilsgeschichtlichen Befreiungstaten JHWHs, miteinbezogen werden. Denn ersttestamentlich[102] wie im Magnifikat ist das, was Maria nicht nur rückblickend dankend, sondern auch gegenwärtig und zukünftig in vollkommener Gewissheit antizipierend besingt,[103] emanzipatorisches Handeln im besten Format, nämlich die schon geschehene und gegenwärtig wie in Zukunft weiterhin geschehende Befreiung der (ökonomisch) Ausgebeuteten (V. 51.53) und (hegemonial) Unterdrückten (V. 52).[104]

Nun könnte eingewendet werden, dass es sich bei der Lukaserzählung um eine „vollständig gynozentrisch[e]"[105] Situation handelt, die ausschließlich im „innerhäusliche[n, also] nicht öffentliche[n]"[106] Raum stattfindet. Dennoch kann von einer ‚privaten Geschichte' keinesfalls die Rede sein. Denn die beiden Jüdinnen Maria und Elisabeth repräsentieren ihr Volk Israel, sodass ihr Ergehen eng „mit dem Geschick des Volkes verwoben"[107] ist. Wenn also Gott

---

[102] Ex 15,1-18.19-21; Dtn 32,1-43; Ri 5,1-31; 1 Sam 2,1-10; 2 Sam 22,2-51; 1 Chr 16,8-36; Jon 2,3-10; Jdt 16,1-17.

[103] Vgl. das Futur: μακαριοῦσίν με in V. 48 und die Aoriste: ἐπέβλεψεν, V. 48; ἐποίησέν, V. 49.51; διεσκόρπισεν, V. 51; καθεῖλεν, ὕψωσεν, V. 51; ἐνέπλησεν, ἐξαπέστειλεν, V. 53; ἀντελάβετο, μνησθῆναι, V. 54; ἐλάλησεν, V. 55. Insbesondere die Aoriste können auf mehr hinweisen, als nur eine „normale Feststellung [...] vergangenen Geschehens": vgl. François Bovon, *Das Evangelium nach Lukas (Lk 1,1-9,50)* (Benzinger und Neukirchner: Zürich 1989), Evangelisch-Katholischer Kommentar zum Neuen Testament [EKK] III/1, 83. Die lukanische „Maria *hat* die Aufmerksamkeit Gottes schon erlebt" (ebd., 92, Hervorhebung durch Eichhorn-Remmel), zugleich aber weiß Lukas „mehr [...] als Maria", weil er „*nach* der Mission Jesu, *nach* Kreuz und Auferstehung lebt" (ebd., Hervorhebung im Original). In lukanischer, wie unserer Zeit bleibt „die Spannung: Die Reichen und die Herrscher haben heutzutage weniger denn je ihre Machtstellung verloren. [...] So könnte Lukas die Aoriste auch inchoativ verstanden haben" (ebd., Hervorhebung im Original); vgl. Kerstin Schiffner, *Lukas liest Exodus: Eine Untersuchung zur Aufnahme ersttestamentlicher Befreiungsgeschichte im lukanischen Werk als Schrift-Lektüre* (Kohlhammer: Stuttgart 2008), Beiträge zur Wissenschaft vom Alten und Neuen Testament [BWANT] 172, 234.

[104] Vgl. Schiffner, *Exodus*, 287-290; vgl. Bovon, *Lukas*, 87-92; Wolter, *Lukasevangelium*, 100.

[105] Luise Schottroff, *Lydias ungeduldige Schwestern: Feministische Sozialgeschichte des frühen Christentums*, (Kaiser: Gütersloh ³2013), 280.

[106] Schottroff, *Sozialgeschichte*, 281.

[107] Schottroff, *Sozialgeschichte*, 281, dort weiter: „Im Magnifikat der Maria wird ihre Erniedrigung nicht erläutert, aber als Bestandteil der Erniedrigung des Volkes gesehen."

auf Maria schaut (V. 48), so gilt diese Hinwendung nicht nur ihr und ihrer individuellen ταπείνωσις, sondern immer auch dem von ihr repräsentierten Volk Israel und seiner ‚Erniedrigung'. Rettet Gott Maria, so rettet er/sie damit (wieder bzw. weiterhin) sein/ihr ganzes Volk: „Die *Erniedrigung der Frauen* [Maria und Elisabeth] gehört […] mit der *Erniedrigung des Volkes* zusammen."[108] Eine „in der westlichen Kultur eingeübte Sichtweise der Demut vor Gott und der Intimität und Privatheit der Begegnung zwischen Elisabeth und Maria [steht] im Widerspruch zur beschriebenen Situation".[109]

Aktiv oder passiv?

Diese Gewissheit in Gottes Befreiungshandeln ist auch Anstoß für die aktive Handlung ‚Marias', „auf die Pauke der Weltrevolution Gottes zu hauen".[110] Denn sie hätte, wie die (typisch für Lukas) erzählte männliche Entsprechung zur weiblichen Erzählfigur – Zacharias – auch ablehnend auf Gabriels Botschaft reagieren können. Aber: Die lukanische ‚Maria' „ist stark, wo Zacharias schwach war (Lk 1,20)."[111] Im Gegensatz zu seiner verspäteten Einsicht (Lk 1,59-65) ist das berüchtigte ‚fiat' (Lk 1,38, eigentlich: γένοιτο) der erzählten ‚Maria' aber nicht, wie Rietz es liest, ‚Einsicht in die Nichtswürdigkeit ihrer selbst, bevor Gott der Herr sie angesehen', sondern aktive Zustimmung und Beteiligung.[112]

Aber nicht nur das ‚Ja' der lukanischen Erzählfigur ist hier hervorzuheben, sondern auch die lukanische Inszenierung dieser ‚marianischen' Antwort: Lukas lässt seine Leser*innen wissen, dass Maria ohne Mann schwanger wird und zwar gegen die auch schon in der Antike durchaus verbreitete Auffassung,

---

[108] Schottroff, *Sozialgeschichte*, 281 (Hervorhebung im Original).

[109] Schottroff, *Sozialgeschichte*, 282; vgl. Leonardo Boff: *Das mütterliche Antlitz Gottes: Ein interdisziplinärer Versuch über das Weibliche und seine religiöse Bedeutung* (Patmos: Düsseldorf 1985), 204.

[110] Schottroff, Sozialgeschichte, 282.

[111] Schottroff, *Sozialgeschichte*, 282.

[112] Catharina J. M. Halkes, „Maria – inspirierendes oder abschreckendes Vorbild für Frauen?," in: Elisabeth Moltmann-Wendel, Hans Küng und Jürgen Moltmann (ed.), *Was geht uns Maria an?* (Gütersloher Verlagshaus: Gütersloh ²1991), 113-130, hier 123: „[I]hr ‚Fiat' [wurde] durch eine Männerkirche als jene furchtsame und passive Reaktion auf ein überwältigendes Wort Gottes ausgelegt […] Das sagt aber schon alles über die Interpreten. Maria gibt doch frei und aktiv ihr Jawort als eine autonome Person, die in gläubiger Empfänglichkeit offen ist für Heil von Gott her und die darauf antwortet. Wenn man hier überhaupt von Abhängigkeit sprechen will, dann machte Gott sich abhängig von den Menschen, und der Mensch war empfänglich für Gott."

dass zu einer Zeugung sowohl Mann als auch Frau notwendig sind: „Der Text setzt diese gängige Meinung ja voraus. Maria setzt sich kühn über diese – ihr selbst vorher auch selbstverständliche Meinung – hinweg (Lk 1,34)."[113] Wenn ‚Maria' einer Schwangerschaft zustimmt, die nicht Menschen-, aber auch nicht „Gotteszeugung"[114] ist, dann ist wieder nach dem Sinn einer solchen Darstellung zu fragen: Die lukanische Erzählung ist „keine historische Erklärung oder gar Schilderung des biologischen Vorgangs der Jungfrauengeburt. Denn nicht Biologie, auch nicht Historiografie, sondern Theologie, also die Rede von Gott und über den Glauben an ihn, ist das Thema hier wie in der gesamten Bibel":[115] ‚Maria' garantiert die menschliche Herkunft ihres Sohnes, des erwarteten Messias „aus der Sippe Davids".[116]

‚Unterdrückung' oder ‚Demut'?

Lk 1,38 ist aber auch deshalb für die Auslegung des Magnifikat von – für Frauen verhängnisvoller – Bedeutung, weil das hier ‚Maria' in den Mund gelegte Stichwort der ‚Magd des Herrn' (ἡ δούλη κυρίου), das in Vers 48 (‚seine Magd') wieder aufgegriffen wird und zwar in Bezug auf deren ‚Niedrigkeit' (τὴν ταπείνωσιν τῆς δούλης αὐτοῦ), oft als Diskreditierung gedeutet wurde: ‚Maria' als ‚Magd' (wörtlicher: ‚Sklavin') hat ergebungsvoll und sich selbst verleugnend zu dienen. Dabei ist die ‚Magd' – und ihr maskulines Pendant, der ‚Knecht'[117] (V. 54: Ἰσραὴλ παιδὸς αὐτοῦ) – nicht als herabwürdigende Prädikation, sondern vielmehr als Ehrentitel, der die heilsgeschichtliche Kontinuität anzeigt, zu verstehen, zum Beispiel für Mose oder Josua.[118]

In diesem Sinne weist auch Luise Schottroff zu Recht daraufhin, dass „kein christliches Ohr ‚Demut'" hört, „[w]enn Paulus sich Gottes Sklaven (meist

---

[113] Schottroff, *Sozialgeschichte*, 283, und zwar gegen die verbreitetere Tradition, dass „allein der Vater der Hervorbringer des Kindes ist".

[114] Schottroff, *Sozialgeschichte*, 284; vgl. Gerhard Ludwig Müller, *Katholische Dogmatik: Für Studium und Praxis der Theologie* (Herder: Freiburg [10]2016), 490.

[115] Demel, „Jungfrau und Mutter," 41.

[116] Otto Knoch, „Maria in der Heiligen Schrift," in: Wolfgang Beinert und Heinrich Petri (ed.), *Handbuch der Marienkunde* (Pustet: Regensburg [2]1996), 1: Theologische Grundlegung: Geistliches Leben, 15-98, hier 89.

[117] Das griechische παῖς kann auch mit ‚Kind' wiedergegeben werden. In beiden Begriffen (‚Kind' und ‚Knecht') zeichnet sich ihre je rechtliche Stellung in der patriarchalen Gesellschaft der Antike ab, zu der aber auch die Pflichten des Herrn bzw. Vaters, hier also Gottes gehören.

[118] Vgl. Schiffner, *Exodus*, 234.

‚Diener' übersetzt) nennt (z.B. Röm 1,1)", sondern „vielmehr wird dort ‚Amtsträger' gehört."[119] Anders bei der Frau:

> Wenn Maria sich Sklavin nennt, hören die christlich geprägten Ohren ‚Magd' im Sinne von ‚Demut'. Die[se] [...] Übersetzung von Lk 1,48 birgt eine offensichtlich tiefsitzende christliche Ideologie: ‚die Niedrigkeit seiner Magd': demütige Frauen, die Demut des Frommen vor Gott usw.[120]

Die abwertende Konnotation von ‚Niedrigkeit' (V. 48) lässt (erst) die moderne Leserschaft eine gänzlich unemanzipierte ‚Maria' annehmen, auch weil ‚Niedrigkeit', also ‚ταπείνωσις', (fälschlicherweise) mit ‚Nichtswürdigkeit' (vgl. Rietz) gleichgesetzt wird: Die lukanische ‚Maria' lobt aber keineswegs ihre ‚Demut [als] Einsicht in ihre Nichtswürdigkeit'.[121] Genau umgekehrt ist ihr Danklied zu verstehen, nämlich als Lob der durch Gott erkämpften Aufhebung von Unterdrückung und Diskriminierung. Nicht Gott erniedrigt Maria, sondern er/sie befreit diese aus irdischer Erniedrigung. Das antwortende Lob auf die Rettungserfahrung geschieht also keineswegs zurückhaltend oder in der Einsicht der eigenen Nichtswürdigkeit. Die ‚Maria' des Magnifikat ist sich ihrer Sache stattdessen – ihrer Ermächtigung, ihrer Emanzipation, ihrer Befreiung aus „Unbedeutendheit, Machtlosigkeit, Ohnmacht, Schwäche, [...] [niedrigem] Stand, Ärmlichkeit" oder auch „Erniedrigung [...] [und] Demütigung"[122] – so sicher, dass sie diese/n mit ihrem/ seinem machtvollen Arm die Feinde zerschlagenden[123] Gott (V. 51) ganz für sich – also Israel – in Anspruch nimmt.

Für eine solche repräsentative Interpretation von ταπείνωσις spricht auch, dass eine individuelle Erniedrigung ‚Marias' im Text nicht erläutert wird, wohl aber des Volkes Israel: Dieses – und damit auch ‚Maria' – leidet unter Fremdherrschaft,

---

[119] Schottroff, *Sozialgeschichte*, 292.

[120] Schottroff, *Sozialgeschichte*, 292.

[121] So suggerieren es aber folgende Übersetzungen: Hoffnung für alle, Neue Genfer Übersetzung, Gute Nachricht Bibel, Neues Leben. Die Bibel, Neue evangelistische Übersetzung; vgl. Wilfried Eckey, *Das Lukasevangelium: Unter Berücksichtigung seiner Parallelen 1: 1,1-10,42* (Neukirchener: Neukirchen-Vluyn [2]2006), 107.

[122] „ταπεινότης," in: Menge-Güthling: *Griechisch-deutsches und deutsch-griechisches Hand- und Schulwörterbuch* (Langenscheidtsche Verlagsbuchhandlung: Berlin [9]1913), 1: Griechisch-deutsch, 674.

[123] Zum anthropomorphen und -pragmatischen Bild des Kriegergottes vgl. Andreas Wagner, „Arm (AT)," in: Das Wissenschaftliche Bibellexikon im Internet (https://www.bibelwissenschaft.de/stichwort/41407/, 27 August 2020).

Hunger, Armut und Unterdrückung.[124] Wird „der Text des Magnifikat [...] ent-
politisiert",[125] indem er „einer privatisierenden und verinnerlichten Spiritualität
unterzogen"[126] wird, so kann „die Erniedrigung der Maria nicht als reale Erfahrung von Unterdrückung verstanden"[127] werden: „ταπείνωσις darf also in 48b
auf keinen Fall mit ‚Demut' wiedergegeben werden".[128]

V. 48 hat aber noch eine weitere frauenunterdrückende Lesart nach sich gezo-
gen: Es macht einen großen Unterschied, ob Gott *auf* die Unterdrückung der
‚Maria' ‚schaut' oder aber ‚genau hinsieht'. Eine räumliche, hierarchische Kon-
stellationen abbildende Aussage wird mit ἐπισκέπτομαι hier nicht getätigt: Der
erhöhte Gott schaut nicht herab auf die niedrigere Magd, die sich demütig unter-
wirft. Vielmehr bedeutet „[d]as ‚Schauen' Gottes [...] im Alten Testament, daß
Gott ‚Mitleid' hat angesichts der Bedrängnis, in der die Menschen als einzelne
(Ps 13,4; 25,16; 69,17-18; 119,132) oder als Volk (Ex 14,24; Ri 6,14; Lev 26,9;
1 Kön 9,16) leben."[129] Eine solche Auslegung wird auch durch den „weiteren
Verlauf des lukanischen Doppelwerks [ersichtlich, in dem] immer wieder Gottes
besondere Aufmerksamkeit für sein Volk zum Ausdruck"[130] gebracht wird.

Prophetische Konstruktion ‚Marias' durch Feministinnen oder Lukas?
Die Behauptung Öhlers, erst feministische Theologinnen hätten aus ‚Maria'
eine sozialkritische Prophetin gemacht, übersieht die theologische Leistung
des Lukas als Komponenten dieses Hymnus. Nicht erst die (auch nicht nur
feministischen) Ausleger*innen von Lk 1,46-55 haben ‚Maria' diese sozial-
kritischen und in der prophetischen[131] Tradition verorteten Worte in den Mund
gelegt, sondern schon der Evangelist hat das Ineinander der individuellen
Heilsgeschichte ‚Marias' mit der des Volkes Israel – im besten Sinne des
Wortes – konstruiert.[132]

---

[124] Boff, *Antlitz*, 204, Anm. 7.
[125] Schottroff, *Sozialgeschichte*, 291.
[126] Boff, *Antlitz*, 208.
[127] Schottroff, *Sozialgeschichte*, 291.
[128] Wolter, *Lukasevangelium*, 102.
[129] Boff, *Antlitz*, 204, Anm. 7.
[130] Schiffner, *Exodus*, 253; mit Verweis auf Lk 1,25.78; 7,16.
[131] Vgl. Irmtraud Fischer, *Gotteskünderinnen: Zu einer geschlechterfairen Deutung des Phäno-*
mens der Prophetie und der Prophetinnen in der Hebräischen Bibel (Kohlhammer: Stuttgart
2002), 124-126.
[132] Vgl. Schiffner, *Exodus*, 219-220, die betont, dass sich Mariae „Prophetinsein [...] schon in der
Namengebung abzeichnet: Sie trägt den Namen Mirjam, den Namen der ersten namentlich

Der lukanischen ‚Maria‘ das Prophetische abzusprechen, ist theologisch unsinnig. Noch unsinniger aber ist es, stattdessen aus dem Magnifikat ein essentialistisches Lob des ‚seit Urzeiten[133] Weiche[n,] [...] Weiblichen‘ ‚Marias‘ zu machen, das ihren ‚Kampf als Mutter‘ auszeichne. Nirgends wird im Magnifikat oder seinem textlichen Umfeld irgendeine Aussage über die Weiblichkeit, Weichheit oder Mütterlichkeit ‚Marias‘ gemacht. Warum auch? Wie unnötig erscheint die Frage nach (vermeintlich) weiblichen oder mütterlichen Charakteristika, wenn doch gerade das Heilshandeln Gottes am Menschen, sein/ihr Vollzug von Gerechtigkeit und das schon angebrochene Gottesreich thematisiert wird?

Die ‚Maria‘ des Magnifikat ‚klingt‘ auch nicht nur politisch, wie etwa Öhler suggerieren möchte, sondern ist es. Denn sie ist es, die als Repräsentantin ihres Volkes Israel und als Frau, die Erfahrung und Gewissheit verbalisiert, dass Gott vorherrschende, also konkrete ungerechte Herrschaftsstrukturen nicht nur aufhebt, sondern umkehrt (V. 51-53). Sie bezieht also, wie schon die Prophet*innen des Ersten Testaments, öffentlich Stellung zu gesellschaftlichen Fragen ihrer Zeit: „Die Unterdrückung des jüdischen Volkes unter römischer Herrschaft ist die Situation der Rede Marias – eine Lektüre, die individuelle Demut und Mutterglück ins Zentrum stellt, verkürzt die politische Dimension dieses Textes.“[134]

‚Maria‘ mit Trillerpfeife und Megaphon – (k)ein Fazit

Die Frage nach der Tauglichkeit von ‚Maria‘ als Galionsfigur einer Emanzipationsbewegung im 21. Jahrhundert kann je nach Blickkultur unterschiedlich ausfallen. Aus exegetischer Perspektive aber sollte sie mit einem eindeutigen ‚Ja‘ beantwortet werden, ohne dabei essentialistische Rollenzuschreibungen bedienen zu müssen. Denn versteht man Gott als Gerechtigkeit Verwirklichende/n und die biblische Heilszusage als zeittranszendierend und damit auch als

---

genannten Prophetin des Ersten Testaments [.] (...) So wie Mirjam singt auch Maria [...] ein Lied, ein Loblied der Befreiung“.

[133] Keinesfalls exklusiv lässt sich ‚[s]eit Urzeiten [...] das Weiche dem Weiblichen‘ zuordnen, wie Öhler meint. Ein Blick in die heute noch greifbaren Belege aus diesen ‚Urzeiten‘ zeigt vielmehr das nicht zu differenzierende Ineinander von ‚männlichen‘ und ‚weiblichen‘, von ‚weichen‘ und ‚harten‘, von ‚väterlichen‘ und ‚mütterlichen‘ Eigenschaften. Vgl. Friederike Eichhorn-Remmel, „‚Schützen‘ (עיר) oder ‚in Bewegung bringen‘ (עור)? – Ein neues Missverständnis: Theriomorphe und -pragmatische Darstellungen elterlichen Handelns JHWHs in Deuteronomium 32,11 in de-konstruktiver Perspektive,“ in: *lectio difficilior* (2/2019).

[134] Petersen, „Nazareth,“ 337; vgl. Schottroff, *Sozialgeschichte*, 281.

gegenwärtig und zukünftig bedeutsam, so muss Geschlechtergerechtigkeit aus guten (biblischen) Gründen als ein Handlungsfeld göttlichen Heilshandelns verstanden werden.

Nach den referierten Blicken auf medial kommunizierte Marienbilder, möchte ich mit einer weiteren Inszenierung enden: Dem hier analysierten Doppel-Artikel in ‚Christ & Welt' war eine Mariendarstellung der Illustratorin Christine Rösch beigegeben, die sich wesentlich von der zu Beginn skizzierten ‚Gipsmadonna' unterscheidet. ‚Maria' hat ein ärgerliches Gesicht und einen zum Protest geöffneten Mund. Vor ihrem Bauch trägt sie in einer praktischen Bauchtrage – natürlich verziert mit Buttons des um eine geballte Faust ergänzten Gendersymbols für Weiblichkeit – das ebenfalls protestierende Jesuskind. Ihre Hände hat sie also frei, um die Linke als geballte Faust in die Luft zu strecken und in der Rechten eine Trillerpfeife zu halten. Neben ihren Füßen steht ein Megaphon. Von ‚Maria' als solch einer als „Sympathisantin"[135] ging aber nicht nur die feministische Theologin Sölle, sondern auch schon Papst Paul VI. aus, wenn er der

heutige[n] Frau, die danach strebt, mit Entscheidungsvollmacht an den zu treffenden Wahlen der Gemeinschaft teilzunehmen, [attestiert] mit inniger Freude Maria [zu] betrachten, die, da sie in den Dialog mit Gott aufgenommen wird, ihre aktive und verantwortungsbewußte Zustimmung gibt [...]; [und] [...] mit freudiger Überraschung feststellen [werde], daß Maria von Nazaret, obwohl sie sich vollkommen dem Willen des Herrn überließ, alles andere war als eine passiv unterwürfige oder von einer befremdenden Religiösität geprägte Frau, sondern eine Frau, die nicht zögerte zu verkünden, daß Gott der Rächer der Niedrigen und Bedrückten ist und die Mächtigen dieser Welt von ihren Thronen stürzt (vgl. *Lk* 1, 51 – 58); sie wird an Maria, die ‚*unter den Demütigen und Armen des Herrn hervorragte*', eine starke Frau erkennen, die Armut und Leid, Flucht und Exil kannte (vgl. *Mt* 2, 13 – 23); Situationen, die der Aufmerksamkeit dessen nicht entgehen können, der die befreienden Kräfte des Menschen und der Gesellschaft im Geist des Evangeliums unterstützen möchte.[136]

Friederike Eichhorn-Remmel, Fulda (Deutschland), geb. 1986, ist Wissenschaftliche Mitarbeiterin am Institut für Katholische Theologie der Universität Koblenz-Landau, Standort Koblenz, am Arbeitsbereich Praktische Theologie bei Frau

---

[135] Sölle, „Sympathisantin," 189.

[136] Paul VI.: Apostolisches Schreiben *Marialis cultus*, 37, (Hervorhebung im Original) (http://www.vatican.va/content/paul-vi/de/apost_exhortations/documents/hf_p-vi_exh_19740202_marialis-cultus.html, 8 September 2020, 10 September 2020).

Prof.[in] Angela Kaupp. Sie studierte Katholische Theologie mit dem Abschluss des Diploms an der Philipps-Universität Marburg, an der Theologischen Fakultät Fulda, im 35. Theologischen Studienjahr Jerusalem, an den päpstlichen Universitäten San Anselmo, Gregoriana und Augustinianum in Rom und an der Philosophisch-Theologischen Hochschule Sankt Georgen in Frankfurt. Sie war Kollegiatin am interuniversitären, -religiösen und -disziplinären Graduiertenkolleg ‚Theologie als Wissenschaft‘ an der Goethe-Universität in Frankfurt und promoviert im Bereich des Neuen Testaments an der Theologischen Fakultät Fulda bei Herrn Prof. Christoph Gregor Müller zur Polemik des Paulus im 2. Korintherbrief und der daraus resultierenden (De-)Konstruktion von Gegner*innen. An der Universität Koblenz ist sie in der Lehre für die Veranstaltungen der Bibeldidaktik zuständig. Sie ist verheiratet und hat drei Kinder.

Journal of the European Society of Women in Theological Research 29 (2021) 113-134.
doi: 10.2143/ESWTR.29.0.3289663

Elizabet Gurdus

Ritual Impurity and Invisibility of Women in the Russian Orthodox Church

Abstract
In spite of the fact that today women are involved in the life of Church more than men, they do not have same opportunities due to their menstruation, which is seen as impure. This ritual impurity is one of the biggest reasons for the invisibility of women in the Orthodox tradition. In this article, I will explain reasons of restrictions based on the idea of ritual impurity in the Russian Orthodox Church and propose solutions which could help to overcome the invisibility of women and make them feel visible, worthy and proud to be women in the Church.

Keywords: Ritualism, ritual impurity, Christianity, Russian Orthodox Church

Resumen
Actualmente las mujeres parecen ser invisibles en la Iglesia Ortodoxa Rusa debido a su impureza ritual. A pesar de que las mujeres de hoy en día están involucradas en la vida de la Iglesia en mayor medida que los hombres, no gozan de las mismas oportunidades. Una de las principales razones de la invisibilidad de las mujeres en la tradición ortodoxa se debe a la impureza ritual. En este artículo, explicaremos las razones de las restricciones basadas en la idea de la impureza ritual en la Iglesia Ortodoxa Rusa y propondremos soluciones que podrían ayudar a superar dicha invisibilidad y hacer que las mujeres se sientan visibles, valiosas y orgullosas de ser mujeres en la Iglesia.

Zusammenfassung
Heute scheinen Frauen in der russisch-orthodoxen Kirchen aufgrund ihrer rituellen Unreinheit unsichtbar zu sein. Trotz der Tatsache, dass Frauen heute in das Leben der Kirche viel mehr als Männer involviert sind, haben sie nicht dieselben Möglichkeiten. Einer der Hauptgründe für die Unsichtbarkeit von Frauen in der orthodoxen Tradition ist rituelle Unreinheit. In diesem Artikel erkläre ich die Gründe für die Einschränkungen, die auf der Vorstellung ritueller Unreinheit basieren, in der russisch-orthodoxen Kirche und schlage Lösungen vor, die dazu beitragen könnten, die Unsichtbarkeit von Frauen in der russisch-orthodoxen Kirche zu überwinden, sodass Frauen sich sichtbar und wertvoll fühlen und stolz sind, eine Frau in dieser Kirche zu sein.

Introduction: Tradition justifies invisibility of women in the Russian Orthodox Church

The mystery of menstruation with bleedings which do not kill has always been perceived as a problem and labelled as impurity. Hinduism, Buddhism, Islam, Judaism and Christianity still have restrictions for women because of menstruation. The sacred Mount Ōmine in Japan, the Golden Rock in Burma and the Athos Mountain in Greece are the best-known religious places in the world forbidden for women because of their impurity caused by their biology.

It may seem strange to talk about invisible women in Christianity, for a lot of women are fervent Christians in contrast to men.[1] They devote their lives to pastoral missions, singing in choirs and assisting at masses.[2] The Russian Orthodox Church accepts their services, but it does not mean that women are accepted as women with their biology. Some positions are still strictly destined for men, for example, the priesthood or the diaconate. The Church justifies these restrictions only on the basis of existing tradition.[3] From childhood onwards, women do not occupy the same liturgical place as men. Orthodox women cannot receive communion in the altar zone while men can without restrictions. Only women after 40 years, or girls, or extraordinarily pious women may be accepted in that zone as exceptions[4], for normally only priests can enter the altar zone. These restrictions are based on the rules issued by the different councils: canon 69 from the Sixth ecumenical Quinisext Council in Trullo[5] and rule 19 and 45 from the Council of Laodicea[6]. The majority of priests cannot explain why these

---

[1] In 2016, there were 3% more fervent Christian Women than Men in the ROC. 53% of women and 47% of men identified themselves as Christians. Travis Mitchell, "Religion is equally or more important to women than men in most countries," in: *Pew Research Center: Religion & Public Life* (https://www.pewforum.org/2016/03/22/religion-is-equally-or-more-important-to-women-than-men-in-most-countries/, 25 April 2021).

[2] Nadezhda Kizenko, "Feminized Patriarchy? Orthodoxy and Gender in Post-Soviet Russia," in: *Signs* 38,3 (2013), 595-621.

[3] Andreï Kuraev, *Церковь в мире людей* [Church in the World of People] (Сретенский ставропигиальный мужской монастырь: Москва 2009).

[4] Resolution of the united presence of the patriarch, synod and the All-Union Central Council of June 20, 1919, in Evgeniya Beliakova, Nadezhda Beliakova and Elena Yemchenko (eds.), *Женщина в православии: Церковное право и российская практика* [Woman in the Orthodoxy: Canon Law and Russian practice] (Кучково поле: Москва 2011), 559-561.

[5] Rule 69 from the Quinisext Council, in: *azbyka* (https://azbyka.ru/otechnik/Nikodim_Milash/pravila-svjatyh-apostolov-i-vselenskih-soborov-s-tolkovanijami/220, 25 April 2021).

[6] Canons of the Russian Orthodox Church (https://ktds.org.ua/-/media/files/1/4/1450022520-kanoni-pravoslavnoi-cerkvy.pdf, 25 April 2021).

limitations still exist. On the Russian internet, we can find many forums with questions from women about ritual impurity. They ask if they can receive the sacrament of the Eucharist. The majority of priests forbid communion because of the biblical interdiction that is figured in Lev 15:18-24.[7]

In this paper I shall discuss the problem of the ritual impurity of women in the Russian Orthodox Church and propose some solutions which, I think, could help to overcome the problem of the 'invisibility' of women. I decided to use the term 'invisibility' because nowadays it is commonly used in discussions about the role and position of women in society, in social sciences, in different areas like politics, demographic and arts.[8] I choose this term to attract attention to the necessity of the full-fledged recognition of women as members of the Church, which is especially important for the Russian Orthodox Church. I will discuss why ritual impurity of women can be perceived as a problem and reinforces women's invisibility in the Russian Orthodox Church nowadays. I will outline how Jesus recognizes a bleeding woman (Mark 5:25-34) and helps her to find her confidence and dignity.[9]

Finally, I will offer some personal reflexions on the way which according to me can help women to take up much more visible position in the Russian Orthodox Church, for instance through specific women's liturgies which propose to highlight women's biology. The aim of this article is to show that a woman can find her place in the Church with recognition of her body. The Church is invited to follow Jesus' example which makes a woman visible and distinguished.

Holy Scriptures as a basis of women's impurity restrictions in the Russian Orthodox Church

Restrictions based on women's ritual impurity came from the rules described in the scriptures of Leviticus and Mark (Lev 15:19-24, Mark 5:25-34). The

---

[7] Forum of the Church of Saint Nicola in Magadan (http://mag-nikolas.cerkov.ru/voprosy-svy-ashhenniku/, 29 January 2021); forum *pravmir* (https://forum.pravmir.ru/showthread.php?t=11988, 29 January 2021); The article about the visiting of church, "О посещении храма" (about visiting the temple), in: *Pravoslavnoe obrazobvaniye* (https://pravobraz.ru/1-o-poseshhenii-xrama/, 25 April 2021).

[8] Caroline Creado Perez, *Invisible Women: Exposing Data Bias in a World Designed for Men* (Abrams Press: New York 2019).

[9] Camille Focant, "Opérer une brèche dans les règles de pureté en vue d'être sauvée: Le cas de la femme qui souffrait d'hémorragie (Mc 5,24-34)," in: Barbara Baert and Niels Schalley (eds.), *The Woman with the Blood Flow (Mark 5:24-34)*, 35-51.

Russian Orthodox Church perceives menstruation as ritual impurity on the basis of the second rule of Dionysius of Alexandria[10] and the seventh rule of Timothy of Alexandria[11] which approve those restrictions, making exceptions only for extreme situations (sickness, danger of death).

Dionysius of Alexandria was a patriarch of Alexandria (3rd century). He specified some points of the Christian Doctrine in his work "Rules". In the Second Rule, he explained why menstruating women could not receive the Eucharist and enter churches. He based this interdiction on the Old Testament tradition and on the example of the bleeding woman who did not touch Jesus's body but only his clothes because of her impurity (Mark 5:25-34). On the basis of this example and the restrictions in the Leviticus 15, Christian women should not receive communion and visit the Church during their menstruation. However, Dionysius encouraged women to pray in their homes during those days.

Timothy of Alexandria was a patriarch in Alexandria (4th century), too, and had a large spiritual authority. He responded to questions of Christians about restrictions concerning communion. His response 7 was about the restriction for menstrual women. He explained that women could not receive communion because of their impurity which could not guarantee the efficacy of the Eucharist. Both bishops concluded that women suffering from gynaecological problems (bleedings) could receive the Eucharist without any restrictions.

On the second and third of February, 2015, the Bishop's Meeting of the Russian Orthodox Church in Moscow approved the restriction of the Eucharist for women during the days of their impurity: "The canons prohibit communion in a state of female impurity (2nd rule of St. Dionysius of Alexandria, 7th rule Timothy of Alexandria). An exception is possible in case of mortal danger and if bleeding lasts for a long time due to a chronic or acute disease".[12] Thus the Orthodox church explains its restrictions by referring to women's biology. But in the online Orthodox Journal "Foma", the Russian Orthodox priest Andreï Ephanov connected this interdiction with the idea of the unacceptability

---

[10] The Second Rule of Dionysius of Alexandria, in: *azbyka* (https://azbyka.ru/otechnik/Nikodim_Milash/pravila-svjatyh-ottsov-pravoslavnoj-tserkvi-s-tolkovanijami/97, 25 April 2021).

[11] The rule of Timothy of Alexandria about the ritual impurity, response 7, in: *azbyka* (https://azbyka.ru/otechnik/pravila/pravila-i-sobory-pravoslavnoj-cerkvi-kanonicheskie-otvety-timofeja-aleksandrijskogo/, 25 April 2021).

[12] The document about the participation of the Christians in the Eucharist, in: *patriarchia* (http://www.patriarchia.ru/db/text/3981166.html, 25 April 2021).

of blood in the church, because the only acceptable sacrifice in the Church were the body and the blood of God through the Eucharist.[13]

It is difficult to change the Orthodox Church tradition, because the interpretation of the biblical menstrual laws is not clear in the writings of the Christian sages. Some of them support the communion rules for menstruating women of Dionysius of Alexandria[14] and Timothy of Alexandria.[15] Others oppose that position and consider communion possible for a menstruating woman. Gregory the Great said that women can have communion any time with no interdictions. In his letter to Augustin of Canterbury, who asked him about the status of menstruating women in the Church, he explained that biological impurity ought to have been distinguished from spiritual and ontological impurity. On the basis of the example of the bleeding woman (Mark 5:24-35), he showed that the woman was cured via physical contact with Jesus. According to him, women can always enter the church with no restrictions and may have communion. At the same time, he honored women who deprived themselves from the Eucharist by religious piety.[16] Athanasius of Alexandria authorized women to enter the church and participate in the liturgy without communion. He explained that menstruating did not make women ritually impure.[17] Pope Clement I encouraged women to enter the church any time, because the bleeding woman touched Jesus while being ritually impure.[18]

The Holy Scriptures are the main basis of the restrictions based on ritual impurity in the Russian Orthodox Church. The origins of the ritual impurity problem can be found in the above-mentioned Leviticus 15. For better

---

[13] Andreï Ephanov, "Можно ли причащаться и ходить в храм во время месячных?" [Is it possible to receive communion and go to the church during menstruation?], in: *Foma* (https://foma.ru/mozhno-li-prichashhatsya-hodit-v-hram-vo-vremya-mesyachnyih.html, 25 April 2021).

[14] The Second Rule of Dionysius of Alexandria, in *azbyka* (https://azbyka.ru/otechnik/Nikodim_Milash/pravila-svjatyh-ottsov-pravoslavnoj-tserkvi-s-tolkovanijami/97, 25 April 2021).

[15] The rule of Timothy of Alexandria about the ritual impurity, response 7, in *azbyka* (https://azbyka.ru/otechnik/pravila/pravila-i-sobory-pravoslavnoj-cerkvi-kanonicheskie-otvety-timofeja-aleksandrijskogo/, 25 April 2021).

[16] Margaret Deanesley, "The capitular text of the Responsiones of Pope Gregory I to St. Augustin," in: *Journal of Ecclesiastical History* 12 (1961), 231-234.

[17] The message of Saint Athanasius of Alexandria to the monk Amun from Bishop Nicodemus, 354, in: *azbyka* (https://azbyka.ru/otechnik/Afanasij_Velikij/poslanie-k-ammunu-monakhu/?=нечистота, 25 April 2021).

[18] The message of Pope Clement I to the Corinthians (http://khazarzar.skeptik.net/books/clem_rom/clem_r_1.htm, 25 April 2021).

understanding of this restriction, it is important to go back to the Bible and understand what the woman's ritual impurity means in the Book.

Leviticus 15

In her famous book "Purity and Danger: An Analysis of the Concepts of Pollution and Taboo"[19], Mary Douglas shows how important it was to respect the purity laws in the Jewish society. The social order could only be guaranteed by separation of the pure and the impure. Impurity was considered dangerous because it could lead to disorder.[20]

Leviticus 15 is focused on the ritual impurity of men and women.[21] The chapter starts with prescriptions about men's ejaculation process (Lev 15:1-18) and then moves on to women's bleedings (Lev 15:19-30).[22] Leviticus 15:19-24 deals with the rules for women during their menstruation and Leviticus 15:25-30 is focused on women with gynaecological problems. A period of impurity due to menstruation is fixed for seven days, a regular period of menstruation. If the period of menstruation continues, the period of impurity is extended until the bleeding stops. This is the case of women with irregular periods (Lev 15:25-30).[23] The Bible does not say whether women should purify themselves. The prescription of purification in a ritual bath or *miqveh* can be found in Tannaitic literature. In that body of literature, it is said that a woman should immerse her whole body in a *miqveh* on the seventh day after cessation of menstrual flow.[24] Jewish Orthodox women accomplish this ritual still today. It presupposes that a woman washes her body thoroughly.[25]

At the beginning of Leviticus 15:19-24 different types of women's secretions are described and the duration of the impurity which can be passed to another is defined: this person becomes impure until sunset (Lev 15:19). In

---

[19] Mary Douglas, *Purity and Danger: An Analysis of Concepts of Pollution and Taboo* (Routledge: London 1980).

[20] Tracy Maria Lemos, "Where There Is Dirt, Is There System? Revisiting Biblical Purity Constructions," in: *Journal for the Study of the Old* Testament 37,3 (2013), 265-294, here 265-267.

[21] Jacob Milgrom, *Leviticus 1-16: A New Translation with Introduction and Commentary.* (Yale University Press: Yale 1998), The Anchor Yale Bible Commentaries 3, 902-1009.

[22] Charlotte Fonrobert, *Menstrual Purity: Rabbinic and Christian Reconstructions of Biblical Gender* (Stanford University Press: Stanford 2000), 43-45.

[23] Milgrom, *Leviticus 1-16*, 942-944.

[24] Tirzah Meacham, "Female Purity (Niddah)," in: *Jewish Women's Archive* (https://jwa.org/encyclopedia/article/female-purity-niddah, 25 April 2021).

[25] Fonrobert, *Menstrual Purity*, 85.

Leviticus 15:20, it is enumerated what kind of objects will be contaminated by an impure woman if she has a contact with them: "any bedding" and "any furniture". If anyone touches a woman's furniture or bed during her menstruation, this person and his/her clothes become impure. A person is obliged to wash and clean his/her clothes (Lev 15:21-22). Objects which are on a woman's bed are automatically impure (Lev 15:23). Leviticus 15:24 deals with the impurity of sexual intercourse with a woman during her menstruation. If a man has intercourse with his wife during this period, he becomes impure for seven days and transmits his impurity to "whatever bed he sleeps on". [26] An impure woman is called *niddah* in the Bible. This word can be understood in two ways as "a woman during her period" or as "a person excluded or deported".[27]

The state of impurity of a woman with bleeding problems is called *zabah* and is described in Leviticus 15:25-30.[28] All secretions, which could be considered to be deviating from the normal menstrual cycle, were considered unhealthy and dangerous. Those women were to adopt the same rules as for the period of normal menstruation. In contrast to a regular menstruation, such a woman was in a much more ambiguous situation because of her irregular bleedings which did not stop. She could not know when she would be able to become pure and reintegrate into normal social life. She was therefore impure for an undetermined period of time. When the *zabah* woman had no more secretions, she could reintegrate religious life after seven "white" days and a purification ritual.[29]

Leviticus 15 explains the crucial role of ritual purity in religious Jewish life and reflects realities of ancient Judea. The problem of Leviticus 15 is its misogynistic interpretation by rabbi's from the Middle Ages and by the apocryphal pseudo-Talmud "Baraïta Niddah". In this book, menstruation is seen as a really dangerous period in which contacts with women and contacts of women with others should be limited as much as possible. For example, during this period a woman should not sit with members of her family at the table, fill a glass of wine if others intend to drink from it, or touch common dishes.[30]

---

[26] Milgrom, *Leviticus 1-16*, 934-941.

[27] Fonrobert, *Menstrual Purity*, 16-19.

[28] Milgrom, *Leviticus 1-16*, 942-948.

[29] Philip S. Tarja, *Menstruation and Childbirth in the Bible: Fertility and Impurity* (Peter Lang: Bern 2006), 55-57.

[30] Baraïta-de-Niddah II:5, in Evyatar Marienberg, *Le Baraïta de-Niddah: Un texte juif pseudo-talmudique sur les lois religieuses relatives à la menstruation*, 107-109.

A bleeding woman story (Mark 5:25-34) and its interpretations
Mark's story helps us to understand Jesus' message concerning ritual impurity. This story about a bleeding woman (Mark 5:25-34) had a real influence on woman's status in Christianity. The exegetes underline the physical and moral sufferings of the bleeding woman. She felt excluded from her community because of her *zabah* impurity.[31] So she suffered not only because of her physical sickness but also because of the psychological and social rejection by society. In Mark 5, the woman looked for Jesus as her last hope for recovery. She touched only Jesus' clothes. Jesus, however, knew that someone had touched him (Mark 5:30), because he felt that his power left him, and asks 'who has touched me?'. Because Jesus asked: "Who touched me?" (Mark 5:30b-31) and not "Who touched my clothes?", Barbara Baert suggests that in ancient culture, clothes were an integral part of the person and that Jesus' followers made no difference between Jesus' clothes and Jesus' body.[32] After her recovery (Mark 5:33), the woman revealed her identity. She did not need to hide herself anymore. It was not only her body which had finally recovered, but her social status was also restored. Jesus recognized the woman as an integral person (5:34). Finally, she was no longer invisible for society, she became a visible person who could participate in the active religious life of her society and community. Jesus gave her a new identity, a new birth. He recognized the faith and trust of this woman, which she presented by seeking her recovery in Jesus.[33]

The story of the bleeding woman has different interpretations. On the one hand, a feminist scholar like Marla Selvidge wrote that the gospel according to Mark drew the reader's attention to the status of women who were socially rejected due to their *zabah* status (Lev 15:25-30).[34] Selvidge is convinced that the story of the bleeding woman was written in order to liberate impure women in Christian communities from following Jewish religious prescriptions concerning women's impurity. For her Jesus should be perceived as an "advocate for equality" who wanted to overcome the oppression of women and establish social

---

[31] Fonrobert, *Menstrual Purity*, 192-195.
[32] Barbara Baert, "General Introduction Touching the Hem," in: Barbara Baert and Niels Schalley (eds.), *The Woman with the Blood Flow (Mark 5:24-34): Narrative, Iconic, and Anthropological Spaces* (Peeters: Leuven 2014), 1-35, here 3-6.
[33] Focant, "Opérer une brèche," 38-40; Susan Haber, *"They Shall Purify Themselves": Essays on Purity in Early Judaism* (Society of Biblical Literature: Atlanta 2008), 134-135.
[34] Baert, *General Introduction Touching the Hem*, 3.

justice.[35] Shaye Cohen, moreover, believes that the goal of the story of the bleeding woman was to show the first Christians that they could never be excluded from the Church because of their physiological diseases.[36] It is important to specify that many early Christians followed Jewish ritual prescriptions according to Torah and that during the first centuries many important discussions took place about whether Torah prescriptions should be kept or not (Acts 11:1-3).

On the other hand, there are exegetes who do not perceive Jesus as the first to have been an advocate for women. Mary Rose D'Angelo looked at the story of the bleeding woman in connection with Mark's Christology, questions of faith, healing and miracles. According to D'Angelo, Mark wanted to show the seriousness of the bleeding woman's illness and her miraculous recovery thanks to her faith in Jesus. The exegete also thinks that Mark wanted to show the contrast between the words of Jesus who advocated faith, and Judaism, the religion of the law.[37]

The story of the bleeding woman was thus understood in two ways and influenced western and eastern traditions differently.

1. The first Christian interpretation (especially in the West with Gregory the Great) explained that this story was an example that showed that we need to cancel the laws of purity. He distinguished biological purity from ontological purity which marked a woman after the first sin.[38] The reflections of Gregory the Great concerning purity have influenced the Catholic tradition. Today there are no longer any restrictions concerning communion of menstruating women in the Catholic Church. Pope John Paul II emphasized that notions of purity and impurity must be perceived morally. The Pope rejected any idea of ritual impurity presented in the Book of Leviticus. He took the Sermon on the Mount (Mt 5-7) as example. According to John Paul II, Jesus spoke about the purity of heart which was realized in a life "according to the Spirit".[39]

---

[35] Marla Selvidge, "Mark 5:25-34 and Leviticus: A Reaction to Restrictive Purity Regulations," in: *Journal of Biblical Literature* 104,4 (1984), 619-623.

[36] Shaye Cohen, "Menstruants and the sacred," in: Sarah B. Pomeroy (ed.), *Women's History and Ancient History* (The University of North Carolina Press: Chapel Hill 1991), 273-299.

[37] Mary Rose D'Angelo, "Power, Knowledge and the Bodies of Women in Mark 5:21-43," in: Barbara Baert and Niels Schalley (eds.), *The Woman with the Blood Flow (Mark 5:24-34): Narrative, Iconic, and Anthropological Spaces* (Peeters: Leuven 2014), 81-109.

[38] Deanesley, "The capitular text of the Responsiones of Pope Gregory I to St. Augustin," 231-234.

[39] John Paul II, *Hommes et femmes il les créa: Une spiritualité du corps*, (Cerf: Paris 2005), 273-278.

2. The second interpretation (especially in tradition of the Eastern Church) associated this story with the idea of women's exclusion from the Church during menstruation period. Tradition has always been important in the Orthodox Church. As I described in the above, discourses of Dionysius of Alexandria and Timothy of Alexandria are part of Canons of the Russians Orthodox Church which forbid menstruating women receiving the Eucharist, because of their impurity. Dionysius explained that the bleeding woman never touched Jesus' body because of her impurity but only his clothes.[40] On the basis of the interpretation of those sages of Leviticus 15:19-30, the Russian Orthodox Church forbids the Eucharist to menstruating women in its official document about the Eucharist.[41] These regulations impact women's status in the Church. Women cannot always receive the Eucharist as men do because of their biology, although for Jesus, the reason of her recovery was the real faith of the woman.

Jesus and impurity

According to Paula Fredriksen, it is not easy to determine from the Gospels if Jesus followed or ignored the laws of purification.[42] This means that he either followed the rules of purity or he did not follow Jewish prescriptions. An argument 'pro' his observance of the laws is the fact that he came to Jerusalem with his disciples five days before Passover with other pilgrims from Galilee (John 12:12-19). Frederiksen concludes that they came earlier to perform the prescribed purification rites.[43]

Others say that Jesus' position on purity and impurity can be perceived as defiance of the social order. In Mark 7:14-23, Jesus speaks about the crucial importance of moral purity. It is interesting to mention the following. The main emphasis throughout Mark 7 is criticism of the dietary laws of Leviticus 11. In Mark 7:19, Jesus speaks about the stomach (κοιλία). Κοιλία means "body cavity," which includes stomach, intestine and uterus. In Jewish anthropology, there is a notion *qerev/beten* (interior/uterus). It is completely legitimate to

---

[40] The Second Rule of Dionysius of Alexandria, in *azbyka* (https://azbyka.ru/otechnik/Nikodim_Milash/pravila-svjatyh-ottsov-pravoslavnoj-tserkvi-s-tolkovanijami/97, 25 April 2021).

[41] About the participation in the Eucharist, in: *azbyka* (https://azbyka.ru/otechnik/dokumenty/ob-uchastii-vernyh-v-evharistii/#0_7, 25 April 2021).

[42] Paula Fredriksen, *Jesus of Nazareth, King of Jews: A Jewish Life and the Emergence of Christianity* (Macmillan: London 2000), 200-206.

[43] Eyal Regev, "Moral Impurity and the Temple in Early Christianity in Light of Ancient Greek Practice and Qumranic Ideology," in: *The Harvard Theological Review* 97,4 (2004), 383-411.

translate κοιλία not as "belly" but as "uterus". If you accept this translation, the meaning of Jesus' sentence changes completely. Michelle Fletcher thinks that from that point of view Mark 7:18-19 refers to the passage of semen through the body after intercourse, childbirth and menstruation.[44] Marcus Borg in turn showed that Jesus created a paradigm of morality and compassion which defined a person's piety better than traditional observance of the ritual law.[45]

For Thomas Kazen, the distinction between the inner/outer impurity in Mark 7 refers to the perception of the order of purity/impurity in 1st century Palestine. According to him, Jewish tradition differed not in ritual and moral purity, but in interior and exterior purity. For Kazen, Jesus then granted interior spiritual purification that was deserved in accordance with justice and compassion.[46]

An additional, but important problem concerning the question of Jesus' observance of the laws of purity is the issue to what type of Judaism he belonged. The Second Temple period is known for its impressive number of different Jewish sects.[47] From that point of view, it is very important that Jesus did not affirm directly that purity/impurity conceptions were not important, but that he drew attention to moral purity first of all. Jesus' attitude towards impurity can be explained in different ways:

1) If he was a Baptist adept, it explains the opposition of the interiority and exteriority. First Christians looked at the difference between the impurity in the interiority and in the exteriority. It means that a person should be pure first in his soul, consciousness, mind and then in his body.
2) Jesus came from a small town of Nazareth where people could have different explanations of purity laws which could be dissimilar from those of people in the city of Jerusalem.
3) Jesus had the eschatological power that could destroy the impurity. It means that impurity could not affect him. On the basis of the Gospels reading, I consider this version to be the closest to reality.[48] Jesus was ready to oppose

---

[44] Michelle Fletcher, "What comes into a Woman and What comes out of Woman: Feminist Textual Intervention and Mark 7:14–23," in: *Journal of Feminist Studies in Religion* 30,1 (2014), 25-41.

[45] Marcus J. Borg, *Conflict, Holiness and Politics in the Teaching of Jesus* (Continuum: London 1998), 136-147.

[46] Thomas Kazen, *Jesus and Purity Halakhah: Was Jesus Indifferent to Impurity?* (Almqvist & Wiksell International: Stockholm 2002), 3-7.

[47] Kazen, *Jesus and Purity Halakhah*, 248-250.

[48] Thomas Kazen, *Scripture, Interpretation or Authority? Motives and arguments in Jesus' Halakic Conflicts* (Mohr Siebeck: Tübingen 2013), 119-122.

impurity and contact with the impure (Mark 1:23-28; 1:40-45; 5:25-34; 5:1-13). He showed that purity is more powerful than impurity. Impurity could not contaminate purity anymore, but purity could overcome impurity. Purification can be possible because of the real faith of people who had the courage to come out of the shadow and oppose and resist impurity. Jesus evaluated the moral status of the person, the purity of his/her heart.[49]

The Russian Orthodox Church's position regarding ritual impurity problem
The Russian Orthodox Church[50] establishes many restrictions for women because of their sexuality. Russian Orthodox women can feel invisible in a church during liturgy. All limitations are explained by the Church's tradition. The Russian Orthodox mentality is like the Russian proverb: "It is better to leave everything as it is than to change something and make it even worse". Even if tradition is wrong, it is better to preserve it. Fear that something can become worse is very strong in the orthodox perception. It is not only canons and scriptures which formulate restrictions, though. It is the collective perception which strives to prove loyal to God through ritualism and not through sincere faith. Contemporary society knows that menstruation is a natural biological process, it is therefore not logical to continue keeping women invisible because of ritual impurity, thus following the ritual laws of the Jewish religious tradition on this point. For that reason, women are not allowed to enter the sacred altar zone, because of their impurity. Canons forbid menstruating Orthodox women to get the Eucharist because of their impurity. You can see this official prohibition of the partaking of the Eucharist in the official document approved at the Bishop's Meeting of the Russian Orthodox Church, in February 2015. In part 4 of the document, you can find the interdiction of the Eucharist for women within their menstruation period based on the Second rule of Dionysius of Alexandria and the Seventh rule of Timothy of Alexandria, although an exception for menstruating women can be made if it is an extreme situation – death or serious sickness problems that provoke endless menstruation.[51]

It is important to understand why women are excluded from the Church because of their impurity. Russian Orthodox tradition has a specific (probably

---

[49] Focant, "Opérer une brèche," 42-44.
[50] In general, the Orthodox Churches have the same regulations concerning women's participation.
[51] The document about the participation of the Christians in the Eucharist, in: *patriarchia* (http://www.patriarchia.ru/db/text/3981166.html, 25 April 2021).

less symbolic) perception of the Eucharist.[52] Only the blood of the Savior in the Eucharistic celebration is admitted. Other types of blood defile the altar zone because they are reminders of pagan sacrifices which are unacceptable in the holy church,[53] and the validity of the sacrament cannot be guaranteed in case of mixture of these elements. Therefore, women cannot get communion during their period, because the sacred blood of the Savior must not come into contact with their impure blood. Exclusion from the altar zone and from communion during the menstruation period creates bad feelings of exclusion from a communal life of the church, as becomes clear from the many questions in the Internet from practicing women who cannot understand the reasons for the interdiction of the communion.[54]

But women are also angry, because the interdiction of the communion for menstruating women can be found in the same chapter of the document about the Eucharist as the interdiction of the communion for people with sins.[55]

In practice, a lot of things depends on the priest and the community. In some churches, there are additional restrictions for women, like the prohibition to kiss the icons, take holy water, or get blessings from the priest and participate in the Sacraments of the Church. They are perceived as sinners because of their gender. Those interdictions do not have any legal authority (as the Holy Fathers or the Scriptures), although conservative members of the Russian Orthodox Church want to justify and confirm them officially. The priest and the dean of the Christian Psychology University Andrey Lorgus, for instance, underlines the idea of God's choice of men over women to serve him.[56]

---

[52] Andreï Ephanov, "Можно ли причащаться и ходить в храм во время месячных?" [Is it possible to receive communion and go to the church during menstruation?], (https://foma.ru/mozhno-li-prichashhatsya-hodit-v-hram-vo-vremya-mesyachnyih.html).

[53] Andreï Kuraev, "Женские вопросы к Церкви" [Women questions to the Church], (Проспект: Москва 2017).

[54] http://mag-nikolas.cerkov.ru/voprosy-svyashhenniku/, https://yandex.ru/q/question/pochemu_zhenshchinam_v_period_nelzia_v_f84a679c/, https://spzh.news/ru/vopros-svyashhenniku/55304-mozhno-li-zhenshhinam-prichashhatysya-i-khodity-v-cerkovy-vo-vremya-mesyachnyh, https://vk.com/topic-7602563_32756356, 25 April 2020.

[55] The document about the participation of the Christians in the Eucharist, in: *patriarchia* (http://www.patriarchia.ru/db/text/3981166.html, 25 April 2021).

[56] Andrey Lorgus, "Брак: призвание или альтернатива?" [Marriage: vocation or alternative?], in: *Neskuchniy Sad* (http://www.nsad.ru/articles/brak-prizvanie-ili-alternativa, 25 April 2021).

Finally, everything depends on the decision of the local priest who takes the decision on the basis of his own understanding and interpretation of the Scriptures and of the Canons.

1. The main observed problem is the freedom of priests in the Russian Orthodox Church. They are free to offer many different interpretations of the same canon. They have real spiritual power of persuasion. The majority of believers do not verify their interpretations. A part of the priests do not understand ritual purity restrictions, but they continue to extend them in their communities. There are priests who forbid women to enter the church and approach the sacred objects during their menstruation, like priest Igor Silchenckov, who even forbids menstruating women to kiss icons in their homes, because the home represents the small Church. He authorized some women who could not wait till the end of their menstruation to go to church, to enter the hall of the church and stay near the front doors without crossing the boundaries of sacred space.[57]

2. The second problem is the lack of will to change in the Orthodox Church. Many priests and followers believe that the age-old tradition is the only one and the best way. All changes are negative because they destroy the tradition. This is an official position of the Russian Orthodox Church which accentuates the importance of tradition and stability in the Church. Stability can be guaranteed by keeping traditions.[58]

3. The third problem is ritualism. This ritualism occupies a very important place in the tradition of the Russian Orthodox Church.[59] The archpriest of the church of Saint Alexiy in Moscow said during my interview with him:

---

[57] Igor Silchenkov, "Можно ли женщине в дни очищения прикладываться дома к иконам" [Is it possible for a woman to kiss icons at home on the days of purification?], (https://www.youtube.com/watch?v=nKgVcctymI4, 25 April 2021). Another conservative priest is Vladimir Golovin, "Как вести себя в храме в дни женской нечистоты?" [How to behave in the church during the days of female impurity?] (https://www.youtube.com/watch?v=fX2VUIqnsgQ&t=1s, 25 April 2021), Vladimir Golovin, "Почему женщинам в дни очищений нельзя участвовать в церковных Таинствах?" [Why should women not participate in Church Sacraments on the days of impurity?], (https://www.youtube.com/watch?v=bnOfZZ9-pgk, 25 April 2021).

[58] N. N. Tkach, "Православная традиция в формировании российской идентичности," [Orthodox Tradition in the formation of Russian] in: *Философия. Социология. Право*, 44, 2 (2019), 351-356.

[59] Yuriy Pidoprigor, Elena Pidoprigor, "Ритуал и Православие" [Ritualism and Orthodoxy], in: *pravmir* (https://www.pravmir.ru/ritual-i-pravoslavie/, 25 April 2021).

"The ordinary Christians prefer to live on the basis of the law, the ritual, and the custom. It is much easier than to learn the real spiritual connection with God."

4. One more problem is the fear of evolution. Many women are afraid of changes which could finally lead to the end of Christian tradition. Elena Fetisova, an Orthodox theologian and the wife of a priest, wrote in an article 'Eucharist and the woman's question' a response to the "liberals" of the Church, saying that all discussions about the problem of non-access of women to the Eucharist had no sense. She explained that women could always come to the church to pray. There was no interdiction in that sense. She opposed re-examination of the ecclesiastic tradition. According to her words, the end of tradition would mean the end of the Christian faith.[60]

Positive changes in the perception of women's ritual impurity in the Russian Orthodox Church
However, there are priests and theologians in the Russian Orthodox Church who oppose outdated and perverted ideas. Here I will present several examples of opinions of priests and theologians who strive for changes. The metropolitan of the Russian Orthodox Church Abroad, Anastasiy Gribanovskiy, authorized in 1963-1964 little girls (before puberty) to help him in altar zone.[61] This was very innovative even for today's context because normally even baby girls cannot enter the altar zone because of their future ritual impurity. During baptism baby girls do not cross the sacred area contrary to baby boys with whom priests enter altar.

Vassa Larin is a theologian and an Orthodox nun. In 2008 she published an article 'What is ritual impurity and Why' in *St. Vladimir's Theological Quarterly*. At that time, she was in a convent in France. As a nun, she faced many restrictions in her community during menstruation. In her article, she described that during periods of menstruation she could not have the communion but not only that. She also could not kiss icons, touch the antidoron, prepare and hold prosphora, clean the church, set fire to lampadas and candles even in her bedroom. When she asked the others, why there were so many restrictions, nobody

---

[60] Elena Fetisova, "Евхаристия и женский вопрос" [Eucharist and the woman's question], in: *pravmir* (http://www.pravmir.ru/evharistiya-i-zhenskiy-vopros1/, 25 April 2021).

[61] From the recollections of Ludmila Assur, one of the girl acolytes under Metropolitan Anastasy, in: *pravmir* (https://www.pravmir.ru/ritualnaya-nechistota-narodnoe-blagochestie-ili-pravilo-ugodnoe-bogu/, 25 April 2021).

could answer her. She decided to search for responses by herself. She found out that ritual impurity could be justified only by the Old Testament, but that those old prescriptions were interpreted in a spiritual way in the New Testament. She explained the annulation of the ritual impurity restrictions on the basis of the episode of the meeting of Jesus and the bleeding woman (Matt 9:20-22). And she outlined that baptism, which gave new life, removed the laws concerning impurity. She concluded that those people who continued to follow purity rites did not have enough faith in God.[62]

Fedor Ludogovskiy, ex-archpriest and professor of ecclesiastic Slavic language till 2019, published an article in 2011 'The pedagogy of no love or once again about ritual 'impurity'.'[63] He analyzed ritual impurity and its justification. Restrictions for non-communion of women could be justified by one of three types of sins: moral, disciplinary, and technical. Moral prohibitions were linked to moral sins which prevented a Christian to be in harmony with himself. Disciplinary prohibitions were linked to sins connected with lack of discipline. Technical prohibitions could be explained by a physical impossibility of a person to have communion. He concluded that ritual impurity was not a matter of any of those categories, although some theologians tried to explain menstruation as a consequence of the original sin and others spoke about the non-fertility of women as a sin. Ludogovskiy criticized those interpretations. He took up the argumentation of the Serbian patriarch Pavel (1990-2009) who showed that women during their menstruation could not be perceived as ritually impure because you could only speak about impurity of soul and heart (1 Pet 3:4) according to the Christian tradition.[64] Ludogovskiy concluded that ritual impurity could be explained by the hatred of women, by which they were reminded of their sinful biology. He argued that in the history of the Old Testament physiological and moral purity were mixed, whereas Jesus only looked at the heart of a person and not to his or her physiological purity.[65]

---

[62] Vassa Larin, "What is ritual impurity and Why?," in: *St. Vladimir's Theological Quarterly* 52,3-4 (2008), 275-292.

[63] Fedor Ludogovskiy, "Педагогика нелюбви" [Pedagogy of objection], (http://www.pravmir.ru/pedagogika-nelyubvi-ili-snova-o-ritualnoj-nechistote-v-xristianstve/, 25 April 2021).

[64] Patriarch Pavel, "Патриарх Сербский Павел о женской "нечистоте" [Patriarch of Serbia about woman's impurity], in: *Palomnik* (http://sampalomnik.ru/soveti/poleznaya-informaciya/soveti/qq.html, 25 April 2021).

[65] Ludogovskiy, "Педагогика нелюбви" [Pedagogy of objection], (http://www.pravmir.ru/pedagogika-nelyubvi-ili-snova-o-ritualnoj-nechistote-v-xristianstve/, 25 April 2021).

Konstantin Parkhomenko, the archpriest of the Cathedral of Trinity in Saint-Petersburg, is a radical opponent of the restrictions for the communion for menstruating women. According to him, Jesus Christ cancelled the question about purity and impurity. He analyzed three causes of interdiction of the Eucharistic explained by Nicodemus the Hagiorite (18th century)[66] and rewritten in modern Canons. Nicodemus explained that a woman was considered impure during menstrual periods due to three factors. The first one was based on the popular perception that all sorts of secretions from a human body were considered impure. The second one was based on a divine perception that the impurity of a body (involuntary sin) caused moral impurity (voluntary sin). The third one was a divine will which wanted to see a woman as impure to avoid sexual intercourse between a man and a woman. It is important to note that Nicodemus' interpretation of God's will has no (scriptural) evidence.[67] The first factor was perceived as an aesthetic aspect. Parkhomenko explained that with the development of the hygiene, a menstruating woman became invisible for the eyes of others and cannot disturb the sacred place. Dealing with the second cause, Parkhomenko declares that there is no connexion between the sin and the natural biology of a body. Concerning the guarantee to avoid sexual relations between a husband and a wife during that period (the third cause), that seems ridiculous and obsolete to him. Parkhomenko gave his blessing to all believers from his community who were called to be always in connection with God because all that God created was pure without any restrictions.[68]

The above-mentioned examples – opinions of personalities who belong to the Russian Orthodox Church and occupy positions of responsibility – show that positive changes in the perception of ritual impurity are possible in the conservative position of the Russian Orthodox Church. The Ecumenical Patriarch of Constantinople, Bartholomew the 1st also regards women favourably.

---

[66] Rule 28, Bishop Nicodemus, in: *pravmir* (https://lib.pravmir.ru/library/readbook/438, 25 April 2021).

[67] Pavel Stoichevich, "Может ли женщина всегда посещать храм?" [Can woman always visit church?], in: *Русская Народная линия* (http://ruskline.ru/opp/2017/iyul/31/mozhet_li_zhenwina_vsegda_posewat_hram/, 25 April 2021).

[68] Konstantin Parkhomenko, "О женской «нечистоте»: Мнение священника" [About female "impurity": The priest's opinion], (https://www.youtube.com/watch?v=Fs-dNg_MlYs, 25 April 2021).

Solutions for visibility of women with their bodies in the Russian Orthodox Church

The first way to eliminate ritual impurity is exegesis. The tradition of the Fathers is important, but the Russian Orthodox Church should not forget God's will and understand the real message of Jesus Christ who came into the world in order to renew the union between God and people. Jesus Christ definitely highlights moral purity and minimizes ritual impurity. Another way to change the perception of women in the Russian Orthodox Church can be found in some religious women's movements, for example in Germany. It proposes to change the paradigm of ritual impurity and not to blame but to venerate woman's body. It is a really interesting approach, because ritualism is a very important part of the Russian Orthodox Church. Change of perception can help women to find real recognition and increase their self-esteem with the help of rewarding rituals. The liturgical women's movement proposes ritualization of important periods of women's life which means recognition of their experiences. The idea is to support a woman after her first menstruation, during her pregnancy, delivery and menopause.[69] An expert in gender studies theology, Grietje Dresen, underlines that rituals connected with a woman's body should be organized by women and be a part of women's liturgy. It should be the initiative of women for women.[70] This approach does not deny female sexuality but perceives it positively through the rites of recognition.

Since the 1990s Orthodox women began raising their voices asking for change, 50 Orthodox feminists came out against the churching of women during the international conference "The women in the life of the Church" (10-17 May 1997). They explained their indignation at the exclusion of women from the church for 40 days after childbirth. They considered the ritual to be oppressive and discrediting for women. Patriarch Bartholomew I of Constantinople responded that he would think about that critique.[71]

---

[69] Brigitte Enzner-Probst, "Waiting for Delivery: Counselling Pregnant Women as an Issue for the Church," in: *International Journal of Practical Theology* 8 (2004), 185-201.

[70] Grietje Dresen, "The Better Blood: On sacrifice and the Churching of New Mothers in the Roman Catholic Tradition," in Judith A. Herbert et al. (eds.), *Wholly Woman, Holy Blood: A Feminist Critique of Purity and Impurity* (Trinity Press International: Harrisburg 2003), 143-164.

[71] Denis Guillaume, "Les débuts de la vie. Pureté rituelle et purification spirituelle," in : *Orthodox Church of Estonia* (http://www.orthodoxa.org/FR/orthodoxie/catechese/adulte/debutsvie.htm, 25 April 2021).

During that Conference, he also admitted the possibility of restoration of the order of deaconesses.[72] From 2006 till today, the American metropolitans propose to patriarch Bartholomew I to establish the ministry of ordained deaconess in the Orthodox Church.[73] And in 2008, a discussion about the restoration of female's diaconate took place during inter-orthodox consultation in Greece.[74] Even if Patriarch Bartholomew I does not take a decision, the question about the female diaconate is more and more discussed in a positive way.

There are many women today who speak loudly about women's position in the Orthodox Church. You can see theologians and philosophers like Élisabeth Behr-Sigel[75], Svetlana Tolstova[76], Vassa Larin[77], Nadezhda Beliakova[78], Elena Chernyak[79], Teva Regule[80], Nadezhda Orlova[81], Eleni Kasselouri-Hateivassiladi[82], Elena Volkova and Irina Karazuba[83] and others who

---

[72] Address of His All-Holiness Ecumenical Patriarch Bartholomew to the Inter-Orthodox Conference for Women (Phanar, Istanbul: 12 May 1997).

[73] Proposal for Introductory Parameters for the Ministry of Ordained Deaconesses in the Orthodox Church, in: *Saint Catherine's Vision* (http://saintcatherinesvision.org/collaborative-work/ rejuvenation-of-deaconesses, 25 April 2021).

[74] Report of the Inter-Orthodox Consultation in Volos, Greece, 8-12 June 2008, in: *World Council of Churches* (https://www.oikoumene.org/resources/documents/participation-of-orthodox-women-in-the-ecumenical-movement, 25 April 2021).

[75] Élisabeth Behr-Sigel, Kallistos Ware, *The Ordination of Women in the Orthodox Church* (WCC Publications: Geneva 2000).

[76] Svetlana Tolstova, *Женщина и церковь: Постановка проблемы* [Woman and Church: Formulation of the problem] (РнД: Профпресс: Ростов-на-Дону 2014).

[77] Larin, "What is ritual impurity and Why?," 275-292.

[78] Evgeniya Beliakova, Nadezhda Beliakova and Elena Yemchenko (eds.), *Женщина в православии: Церковное право и российская практика* [Woman in the Orthodoxy: Canon Law and Russian practice].

[79] Chernyak, "What Is a Woman Created for? The Image of Women in Russia through the Lens of the Russian Orthodox Church," 299-313.

[80] Teva Regule, "Women and the Canons of the Church: A Difficult Relationship," in *The St. Nina Quarterly* (2014), 1-11.

[81] Nadezhda X. Orlova, *О чем молчал Адам: Гендерное измерение христианской антропологии* [What Adam was Silent About: The Gender Dimension of Christian Anthropology] (Дмитрий Буланин: Санкт-Петербург 2012).

[82] Eleni Kasselouri-Hateivassiladi, Petros Vassiliadis and Niki Papageorgiou (eds.), *Deaconesses, the Ordination of Women and Orthodox Theology* (Cambridge Scholars Publishing: Cambridge 2017).

[83] Irina Karazuba and Elena Volkova in the interview with the orthodox priest Yakov Krotov about the place of women in the Russian Orthodox Church, in: *Radio Svoboda* (https://www.svoboda.org/a/27605174.html, 25 April 2021).

offer a revision of certain traditions and controversial Orthodox rites concerning women. Since the publication in 2010 of the article of Vassa Larin in Russian in the Online Journal "Pravmir"[84], you can find many articles about the problem of "ritual impurity" and the interdiction of communion for menstruating women.[85] I notice a positive evolution of the dialogue between priests and orthodox women. Many orthodox women study this question by themselves and claim the Eucharist because they are morally pure.[86] A new generation of young priests study this question in a thorough way and suggest women to make their own choice in this sensitive question.[87] Even if it is just a dialogue, it is a good start directed at overcoming the stagnation of the Orthodox tradition. The question remains, though, how long do women have to wait for their official recognition with their biology in the Church and in society? Official canon law still forbids the Eucharist to menstruating women.

[84] Vassa Larin, "Можно ли с месячными ходить в церковь? Ответ инокини Вассы" [Can I go to the church during menstruation period? The answer of Sister Vassa], in: *pravmir* (https://www.pravmir.ru/o-ritualnoj-nechistote-chto-eto-i-zachem/, 25 April 2021).

[85] Ephanov, "Можно ли причащаться и ходить в храм во время месячных?" [Is it possible to receive communion and go to the church during menstruation?], (https://pravlife.org/ru/content/mozhno-li-prichashchatsya-i-hodit-v-hram-vo-vremya-mesyachnyh, 25 April 2021). Ludogovskiy, "Педагогика нелюбви" [Pedagogy of objection], (http://www.pravmir.ru/pedagogika-nelyubvi-ili-snova-o-ritualnoj-nechistote-v-xristianstve/, 25 April 2021). Sveshnikov, "К вопросу о «ритуальной нечистоте»: ответ сестре Вассе (Лариной)" [About the Question of "Ritual Impurity": An Answer to Sister Vassa (Larin)], in: *pravmir* (https://www.pravmir.ru/k-voprosu-o-ritualnoj-nechistote-otvet-sestre-vasse-larinoj/, 25 April 2021), Sveshnikov, "О так называемой женской нечистоте" [About the female impurity], in: *azbyka* (https://azbyka.ru/parkhomenko/o-tak-nazyvaemoj-zhenskoj-nechistote.html, 25 April 2021).

[86] Alexander Bozhenov, "Можно ли женщинам во время месячных ходить в храм и причащаться?" [Can women go to church and receive communion during menstruation?], in: *Кудымарская епархия* (http://www.komiprav.ru/proekty/kazhdomu-nuzhno-znat/mozhno-li-zhenschinam-vo-vremja, 25 April 2021). In this article, we find questions and contestations of some Russian orthodox women about communion during their menstruation from Russian orthodox forums: "dobroeslovo" and "pravmir".

[87] Andreï Zaytzev, "Как священники узнают о критических днях?" [How do priests know about menstruation days?], in: *predaniye* (https://blog.predanie.ru/article/kak-svyashhenniki-uznayut-o-kriticheskih-dnyah/, 25 April 2021); Igor Ryabko, "Можно ли женщинам причащаться и ходить в церковь во время месячных?" [Is it possible for women to receive communion and go to church during menstruation ?], in: *Союз православных журналистов* (https://spzh.news/ru/vopros-svyashhenniku/55304-mozhno-li-zhenshhinam-prichashhatysya-i-khodity-v-cerkovy-vo-vremya-mesyachnyh, 25 April 2021).

Élisabeth Behr-Sigel explains in her book all the reasons for the ordination of women.[88] After her death, the Orthodox tradition does not have many well-known feminist authors who are standing for a much stronger recognition of women in the Church through ordination. However, you can find feminist orthodox authors in the Russian Orthodox Church in America who support the idea of a stronger recognition of women without their ordination. One of them is Debora Belonick who republished her book about the relationship between feminist and orthodox identity in 2012. The author wants to show that it is possible to be a feminist and a Christian woman without contradictions. [89]

Conclusion: Visibility for women in the Russian Orthodox Church. Feminist perspective

In my opinion, women remain invisible in the Russian Orthodox Church because of three important reasons.

1. *Women's perception of their bodies is the first and the most important factor.* Women do not accept their bodies and sexuality as God's gift. Unconsciously, the majority of women, till today, associate their biological processes and exclusion from the Church with the original sin. So, it is important to show women that their biology is God's creation, and they should love their bodies. Rituals venerating woman's body can help to overcome this wrong perception.
2. *Tradition based on the laws of the Old Testament is the second factor.* It is important to prove that the Gospel message of Jesus Christ underlines that moral purity and faith were of the greatest importance.
3. Opinions of traditionalists who want to preserve tradition at all costs form the third factor. Their interpretation must be questioned by other theologians.

There are many supporters of the visibility of women. The most important thing is that Jesus stands for women's visibility.

Elizabet Gurdus is a PhD student in the Université Catholique de Louvain. The subject of her doctoral research is "Vers un nouveau paradigme de la représentation féminine dans l'anthropologie chrétienne. Analyses du catholicisme et de l'orthodoxie russe dans une perspective d'études de genre" (Towards a New Paradigm of Female

---

[88] Behr-Sigel, Ware, *The Ordination of Women in the Orthodox Church.*
[89] Deborah Belonick, *Feminism in Christianity: An Orthodox Christian Response* (St Vladimir's Seminary Press: New York, 2012).

Representation in Christian Anthropology. Analysis of Catholicism and Russian Orthodoxy from a Gender Studies Perspective). She got her Master degree in religious studies in the UCLouvain in 2018. The subject of her thesis was "La pureté rituelle de la femme dans le christianisme et l'influence de la tradition juive" (The ritual purity of a Woman in Christianity and the influence of the Jewish tradition).

Journal of the European Society of Women in Theological Research 29 (2021) 135-150.
doi: 10.2143/ESWTR.29.0.3289664

Larissza Hrotkó

Dvoyra Fogel: Zwischen zwei Weltkriegen im Kampf um die Identität

Zusammenfassung
Der Artikel handelt von der jüdischen Dichterin und Schriftstellerin Dvoyra Fogel (Debora Vogel) (1900-1942), die die jiddische Sprache zum Symbol ihrer künstlerischen Unabhängigkeit und Identität machte. In der politisch und wirtschaftlich kritischen Zeit zwischen den beiden Weltkriegen widmete Fogel ihr Talent und ihre umfangreichen Kenntnisse der Literatur, bildenden Kunst, Philosophie und Psychologie der Selbstbehauptung jüdischer Kunst und jiddischer Literatur. Als Frau fühlte sie sich auf dem künstlerischen Fachgebiet benachteiligt. Trotzdem gab Dvoyra Fogel ihren individuellen Kampf um Anerkennung jiddischer Lyrik nie auf. Im 21. Jahrhundert wurde Dvoyra Fogel selbst zu einem Symbol des Kampfes um die Anerkennung der Frauen-Identität in der Literatur und Kunst.
Alle Bereiche und Besonderheiten von Fogels künstlerischer Tätigkeit könnten in einem Artikel nicht ausführlich besprochen werden. Deshalb beschränkt sich dieser auf die Schilderung eines besonderen Charakterzuges der Lyrik von Fogel, und zwar den Gebrauch der Wiederholungen im dichterischen Text.

Abstract
The article is about Dvoyra Fogel (1900-1942), a Jewish poet and writer who made the Yiddish language a symbol of her artistic independence and identity. In the politically and economically critical period between the two world wars, Fogel devoted her talent and comprehensive literary, fine artistic, philosophical as well as psychological knowledge to the autonomous endeavours of Jewish art and Yiddish literature. She felt that as a woman she was in a disadvantageous situation in the field of arts. Despite this, she never gave up her individual fight for the acknowledgement of Yiddish poetry. In the 21st century, Fogel herself became the symbol of the battle fought for the appreciation of women's artistic identity. It is impossible to talk about all the fields and features of Fogel's artistic activity in detail; therefore, the article is limited to a single special characteristic of Fogel's poetry, namely, to the use of repetitions in poetic texts.

Resumen

Este artículo versa sobre Dvoyra Fogel (1900-1942), una poetisa judía y escritora que hizo de la lengua yiddish un símbolo de su independencia artística e identidad. En el período crítico comprendido entre las dos guerras mundiales, tanto política como económicamente, Fogel consagró su talento y conocimiento literario, artístico, filosófico y psicológico a los esfuerzos de emancipación de la literatura en yiddish. Sentía que, como mujer, se hallaba en una situación de desventaja en el mundo de las artes. A pesar de ello, nunca se dio por vencida en su lucha por el reconocimiento de la poesía en yiddish. En el siglo XXI, la propia Fogel se convirtió en un símbolo de la batalla por la apreciación de la identidad artística de las mujeres. Es imposible hablar de todos los campos y características de la actividad artística de Fogel en detalle. Por ello, este artículo se circumscribe a un rasgo especial de la poesía de Fogel, a saber, el uso de repeticiones en textos poéticos.

Keywords: Yiddish language, world war, autonomous endeavours, identity, repetition, literature.

Sprache und nationale Identität

Nachdem Galizien 1914 von den russischen Truppen besetzt worden war, flohen tausende Jüdinnen und Juden nach Mähren, Ungarn und Österreich. 50.000 bis 60.000 galizische Flüchtlinge – unter ihnen auch die Familie Fogel – kamen in Wien an. Viele verloren ihr gesamtes Hab und Gut und mussten unter katastrophalen Verhältnissen in Flüchtlingslagern und Massenquartieren leben. Statt der ersehnten Freiheit und Stabilität stießen die „Galizierinnen" in Wien auf Abneigung und waren zahlreichen Diskriminierungen ausgesetzt.[1]

Auch die integrierten Wiener Juden betrachteten die Ostjuden als Fremde, die sich von ihnen sowohl in der Kleidung als auch in der Sprache stark unterschieden. Für einige der galizischen Dichterinnen und Schriftstellerinnen, auch für Dvoyra Fogel, war die jiddische Sprache beim Ankommen in Wien jedoch noch fremd. Anfangs publizierten sie auf Polnisch oder Deutsch, aber in Wien beziehungsweise nach der Rückkehr in ihre Heimat begannen sie auf Jiddisch zu schreiben.[2] Sie wählten Jiddisch, um sich als Jüdinnen zu identifizieren und ihre Individualität als Künstlerinnen zu behaupten.

---

[1] Stimmungsberichte aus der Kriegszeit, Band 1914-1917
  (www.digital.wienbibliothek.at/wbrobv/periodical/titleinfo/607252, 15 November 2020).
[2] Gabriele Kohlbauer-Fritz (ed.), אין א שטאָדט וואָס שטאַרבט
  In a Schtodt woss starbt. Jiddische Lyrik aus Wien (Picus Verlag: Wien 1995), 9-23.

„Sprache und menschliche Identität sind offenbar miteinander verknüpft."[3] Im Judentum ist das jedoch nicht eindeutig, denn es gibt mehrere jüdische Nationalsprachen, die Jüdinnen und Juden – außer der Sprache des Landes, wo sie leben – als eigene akzeptieren. Als jüdische Sprachen gelten Hebräisch, Ladino und Jiddisch in Europa.

Jiddisch war besonders bei den *Aschkenasim*[4] Osteuropas, vor allem in Ost-Galizien die jüdische Hauptsprache, welche die meisten Ostjüdinnen unter sich mündlich oder auch schriftlich benutzten. Die Anhänger der jüdischen Aufklärung, die *Maskilim*, wollten die „Sprache der Sklaverei" – so nannten sie Jiddisch – dem europäisch gebildeten jüdischen Volk abgewöhnen. Im Verlauf des 19. Jahrhunderts ist das Westjiddische mit dem Ende der Ghettos so gut wie verschwunden. Die Ideen der *Haskala* (der jüdischen Aufklärung) verbreiteten sich weiter und erreichten auch das Ostjudentum.[5] Die *Maskilim* bezogen sich bei ihrer Ablehnung der jiddischen Sprache auf die Unvollkommenheit des Jiddischen und versuchten die Sprache zu diskreditieren:

> Hingegen sei das Vokabular [zu] arm, um den Gefühlen der Zärtlichkeit und der Liebe Ausdruck zu verleihen, so als sei das Liebesleben der Juden und besonders das der jüdischen Frauen durch die das Leben regelnden Normen und deren Hüter, die egozentrischen und introvertierten Gelehrten, zu puritanischer Sittsamkeit verdammt und somit völlig ausgelöscht.[6]

Doch konnten die *Maskilim* ihre Ideen dem jüdischen Volk nicht wirklich erklären, weil die meisten Jüdinnen und Juden nur Jiddisch beherrschten.[7] Deshalb bedienten sich die *Maskilim* des Jiddischen, um sich beim Volk verständlich zu machen. Das literarische Beispiel dafür lieferte Itzchok Lejb Perez (1852-1915), der schon 1888 sein Poem gegen Aberglauben in Jiddisch veröffentlichte, um mehr Leser zu gewinnen.[8] 1908 sagte Perez sogar bei der Czernowitzer Sprachkonferenz: „Ein Volk – Juden; eine Sprache – Jiddisch.

[3] Konrad Schröder, „Zur Problematik von Sprache und Identität in Westeuropa: Eine Analyse aus sprachenpolitischer Perspektive" in: *Sociolinguistica: Internationales Jahrbuch für europäische Soziolinguistik* (De Gruyter: Berlin 1995), 9, 56-66, hier 56.

[4] So bezeichnen sich mittel-, nord- und osteuropäische Jüdinnen und Juden.

[5] Vgl. Armin Eidherr, „Das Jiddische als Kultursprache der Askenasim: Außen-und Innenperspektiven" in: *Chilufim: Zeitschrift für jüdische Kulturgeschichte* 1 (Januar/2006), 32-58, hier: 36-37.

[6] Eidherr, „Das Jiddische als Kultursprache," 42.

[7] Eidherr, „Das Jiddische als Kultursprache," 34-35.

[8] Eidherr, „Das Jiddische als Kultursprache," 38.

In dieser Sprache wollen wir unsere Kultur schaffen, und wir wollen darüber hinaus unseren Geist mit ihr stärken."[9] Schließlich wurde Perez zu einer „Galionsfigur" der jiddischen Kulturbewegung, denn er zeigte, wie „die Spannung zwischen der jüdischen Tradition und dem Anspruch, das jüdische Proletariat zu einer universalistisch-humanistischen Kultur zu erziehen, gelöst werden kann."[10]

Die Czernowitzer Sprachkonferenz von 1908 war für die Positionierung des Jiddischen als Kultursprache von entscheidender Bedeutung. Im Hintergrund der Konferenz stand der „Kampf um das nationale Dasein."[11] Nach den Vorstellungen der Jiddischisten sollte Jiddisch „zum Zentrum jiddischer Kulturautonomie gemacht werden".[12] Die Jiddischisten wurden vor allem von den Aktivisten des Jüdischen Arbeiter-Bundes vertreten. Auf der anderen Seite des Sprach- und Identitätskampfes standen die Zionisten,[13] die das Hebräische zur Nationalsprache machen wollten. Durchgesetzt haben sich die „Gemäßigten" und das Jiddische bekam die gleichen Rechte wie das Hebräische. Die jiddische Sprache wurde zwar nicht für die alleinige, jedoch eine jüdische Nationalsprache erklärt.[14]

Aufschwung jiddischer Kultur in Wien

[…] Und Jiddisch nimmt einen Aufschwung. Die erniedrigte Sprache, an der man sich festhält wie an einem leuchtenden Stern, wird tatsächlich ein leuchtender Stern. In der Sowjetunion ist sie eine der Staatssprachen. Und im jungen Polen kämpft man für denselben Status, ja, und man werde für die Sache bis zum Ende kämpfen. Inzwischen ist auch die Ansiedlung Wien nicht mehr zu ignorieren. Wien ist die Brücke zwischen Ost und West, zwischen Amerika und Russland-Polen.[15]

So begeistert schrieb Melech Ravich (Zekharye-Khone Bergner) in seinem *Geschichtenbuch meines Lebens*. Jiddisch wurde in Wien zum Mittel im

---

[9] Eidherr, „Das Jiddische als Kultursprache," 40.
[10] Thomas Soxberger, *Literatur und Politik: Moderne jiddische Literatur und „Jiddischismus"* *in Wien (1904 bis 1938)* (Diss., Wien 2010), unveröffentlichtes Manuskript, 43 (https://core. ac.uk/download/pdf/11594617.pdf, 11 November 2020).
[11] Eidherr, „Das Jiddische als Kultursprache," 46.
[12] Eidherr, „Das Jiddische als Kultursprache," 46.
[13] Die Poale-Zion-Bewegung jedoch schloss die jiddische Publizistik nicht aus. Soxberger, *Literatur und Politik*, 36.
[14] Eidherr, „Das Jiddische als Kultursprache," 46.
[15] Eidherr, „Das Jiddische als Kultursprache," 42.

Kampf um die jüdischen Nationalitätenrechte im Parlament.[16] Die jüdisch-nationalen Gefühle und die religiöse Zion-Bindung sowie eine Art Protest gegen die herrschende obere Schicht der Gesellschaft inspirierten galizische Schriftstellerinnen und Künstlerinnen zum aktiven Gebrauch des Jiddischen in ihrer künstlerischen Tätigkeit.

Die Aufbruchsstimmung jiddischer Kultur bewog Schmuel Jakob Imber und seine Freunde, ein Zentrum der „jungjiddischen" Literatur in Wien zu eröffnen. Das Zentrum funktionierte in den letzten Kriegsjahren und in der schweren Zeit wirtschaftlicher und gesellschaftlicher Krise der Nachkriegszeit bis 1921. Die Veröffentlichung neuer Literatur auf Jiddisch war dem Verlag von Max Hickl zu verdanken, der seinen Sitz 1915 von Brünn (Brno) nach Wien verlegt hatte.[17]

Über Wien und seine jüdische Bevölkerung wurden schon viele Arbeiten geschrieben. Leider trifft man dabei auf nur wenige Frauennamen, obwohl die Jüdinnen sowohl unter den Politikerinnen als auch in den Reihen der Wiener Künstlerinnen zu finden waren. Die Journalistin Anitta Müller-Cohen, zum Beispiel, „eroberte" damals den „bisher nur von Männern dominierten Bereich der Politik" für die Frauen und „propagierte ein neues Frauenbild."[18] Gisela Werbezirk (ursprünglich: Werbesek; geboren in Bratislava/Preßburg/Pozsony) begeisterte das Publikum in Theater, Film und Kabarett. Hilde Spiel debütierte 1928 mit 17 Jahren als jiddische Schriftstellerin in der Wiener Kaffeehaus-Szene. Unter den damaligen Malerinnen sind Tina Blau, Malerin des Wiener Jugendstils, und Broncia Koller-Pinell (Bronislawa Pineles) aus Galizien unbedingt zu erwähnen. Nicht zu vergessen ist die jiddische Dichterin Rokhl Korn aus Sucha Gora in Galizien, die in Wien zuerst ihre Studien absolvierte. Rokhl Korn gehörte später zum literarischen Kreis der Lemberger Zeitschrift *Tsushtayer*, deren Mitherausgeberin Dvoyra Fogel war.[19] Über tausend jüdische

---

[16] In Wien wurde Jiddisch erst während der Ersten Republik anerkannt. Soxberger, *Literatur und Politik*, 67-68.

[17] Soxberger, *Literatur und Politik*, 52-53.

[18] Dieter Hecht, „Die Stimme in Wahrheit der jüdischen Welt: Jüdisches Pressewesen 1918-1938," in: Frank Stern und Barbara Eichinger (ed.), *Wien und die jüdische Erfahrung 1900-1938: Akkulturation-Antisemitismus-Zionismus.* (Böhlau Verlag: Wien, Köln und Weimar 2009), 99-114, hier 108.

[19] Kohlbauer-Fritz, *In a Schtodt woss starbt*, 133-134. Анастасия Люобас [Anastasia Lubas, Übers.], „Debora Fogel, ‚vayse verter' in der dikhtung" [„Білі слова" в поезії] in: Tsush-tayer 3 (1931), 42-48 (https://prostory.net.ua/ua/krytyka/374-bili-slova-v-poezii, 9 November 2020).

Frauen studierten damals an der Wiener Universität. Viele von ihnen kamen nach dem Ausbruch des Krieges aus Galizien in Wien an.[20]

Dvoyra Fogel[21] in Lviv (Lemberg) zwischen zwei Weltkriegen

„Mir scheint, dass das von zwei Weltkriegen eingerahmte Lviv zur Hälfte aus den Erinnerungen an den ersten Krieg bestand, die jedoch der Vorahnung des nächsten Krieges ähnelten." So schreibt Dana Pinchewska (Богдана Пінчевська) in ihrer Rezension über das Prosawerk von Dvoyra Fogel (Debora Vogel).[22] Damit erklärt Pinchewska die innere Unruhe der Prosa von Fogel, die dem die Stimmung von Lemberg charakterisierenden Kummer entsprungen sein soll – als wären die Einwohner der Stadt die Helden im Schlussakt eines Dramas gewesen.[23] Nach dem Ersten Weltkrieg wurde Lemberg zum Zufluchtsort für jüdische Schriftsteller und Maler, die den surrealistischen und avantgardistischen Richtungen folgten. Unter ihnen waren Anhänger des künstlerischen Kreises von Fernand Leger wie Mark Wlodarski, Ludwig Lille, Emil Kunke und Bruno Schulz, die zusammen mit Dvoyra Fogel eine moderne künstlerische Atmosphäre in Lemberg schufen.

Nach Anna Kaszuba-Debska begann Dvoyra Fogel erst nach der Rückkehr nach Lemberg auf Jiddisch zu schreiben.[24] Doch kann der Wiener Aufschwung der jiddischen Kultursprache und das Werk der Künstler von „Jung-Galizien"[25] einen bedeutenden Einfluss auf Fogel gehabt haben. Dafür spricht auch, dass Dvoyra Fogel mindestens drei von diesen Künstlern, Schmuel Jakob Imber, Mendel Nejgreschl und Melech Ravich, persönlich kannte.

Dvoyra Fogel ist in Bursztyn (Galizien) in einer Familie der *Maskilim* geboren. Um 1910 zog die Familie nach Lemberg, der Heimatstadt von Dvoyras Eltern. Ihr Vater Anschel Fogel war Hebraist und Schuldirektor. Nach dem Ersten Weltkrieg arbeitete er in der jüdischen Gemeinde und führte ein jüdisches

---

[20] Herriet Pass Freidenreich, „Gender and Identity: Jewish University Women in Vienna," in: Frank Stern und Barbara Eichinger (ed.), *Wien und die jüdische Erfahrung 1900-1938: Akkulturation-Antisemitismus-Zionismus.* (Böhlau Verlag: Wien, Köln und Weimar 2009), 297-305, hier 298.

[21] Der Name der Dichterin sowie ihre Gedichte werden nach YIVO-Regeln transkribiert.

[22] Дана Пинчевская, „*И вновь цветёт акация…*": *О прозе Деборы Фогель* [Dana Pinchewska, „*Die Akazien blühen wieder…*": *Über die Prosa von Debora Vogel*] (2010), 4 (https://libking.ru/books/nonf-/nonfiction/496204-dana-pinchevskaya-i-vnov-tsvetet-akatsi-ya-o-proze-debory-fogel.html, 5 November 2020) (Übersetzung L. H.).

[23] Пинчевская, *И вновь цветёт акация* [Pinchewska, *Die Akazien blühen wieder*], 3.

[24] Anna Kaszuba-Debska, „Дебора Фогель – Дозя" (Debora Fogel) in: *Projekt Szpilki* 2012 (https://projektszpilki.pl/biografie.php?i=36&lang=ru#googtrans(pl|ru, 11 November 2020).

[25] Soxberger, *Literatur und Politik*, 69.

Waisenhaus in Lemberg. Die Mutter, Lea Ehrenpreis, führte vor dem Umzug nach Lemberg eine Handwerk-Schule für Mädchen. Dvoyras Onkel mütterlicherseits, der Publizist und Zionist Marcus Ehrenpreis, war Oberrabbiner Schwedens von 1914 bis 1948. Die Sprache der Familie war Polnisch, aber Dvoyra konnte schon als Kind gut Deutsch. Jiddisch hielt der Vater für die Sprache der Provinz, die Mutter lehnte es wegen der zionistischen Tradition ihrer Familie ab.

1914 floh die Familie nach Wien, wo Dvoyra am Gymnasium lernte. Das Abitur machte sie allerdings erst in Lemberg, als die Fogels 1919 nach Galizien zurückkehrten.[26] Nach Kohlbauer-Fritz war Dyoyra Fogel schon am Wiener Gymnasium in der linken zionistischen Bewegung *HaSchomer haZa'ir* aktiv.[27] Laut der *Anthology of Jiddish Poetry of Poland* und der Arbeit von Anna Kaszuba-Debska geschah dies jedoch erst nach der Rückkehr nach Lemberg.[28] Nach dem Gymnasium studierte Dvoyra an den Universitäten in Lemberg und Krakau. 1926 promovierte sie über den Einfluss der Hegelschen Ästhetik auf Jozef Kremer an der Krakauer Universität.[29] 1927 reiste Fogel nach Berlin, Paris und Stockholm, wo sie Onkel Ehrenpreis besuchte. 1928 unterrichtete sie an der Lemberger Universität. Zur gleichen Zeit lernte Fogel Rachel Auerbach (Rokhl Oyerbakh) kennen und schloss sich der Jüdischen Volksuniversität sowie der Gesellschaft jüdischer Philosophie-Studenten und Union der polnischen Künstler an. Seit 1928 schrieb Fogel Rezensionen zur Kunstgeschichte, besondere Aufmerksamkeit schenkte sie dabei der Avantgarde und zeigte tiefe Kenntnisse des Kubismus und Surrealismus. Dank Fogels Arbeiten konnten heutige Forscherinnen neue Informationen über das kulturelle und künstlerische Leben des Judentums von Lemberg gewinnen.[30]

---

[26] Anthology of Yiddish Poetry of Poland between the two World Wars (http://www.yiddishpoetry.org/Anthology/poets/fogel/indexfogel.html, 11 November 2020).

[27] Kohlbauer-Fritz, *In a Schtodt woss schtarbt*, 131-132.

[28] Anthology of Yiddish Poetry of Poland.

[29] Пинчевская, *И вновь цветёт акация* [Pinchewska, *Die Akazien blühen wieder*], 4.

[30] Zu den Rezensionen von Fogel und ihrer Bedeutung für die Geschichte jüdischer Gemeinschaft Galiziens vgl. Богдана Пінчевська, „Світське єврейське мистецтво Східної Галичини першої третини XX століття: Людвік Лілле й Дебора Фогель" [Bogdana Pynczewska, „Jüdische Kunst in Nordgalizien im ersten Drittel des zwanzigsten Jahrhunderts: Ludwig Lille und Deborah Forel"], in: *Judaica Ukrainica* 3 (2014), 128-139, hier: 135-137 (http://judaicaukrainica.ukma.edu.ua/ckfinder/userfiles/files/JU_3_2014_Pinchewska.pdf, 20 November 2020).

1929 erschien Fogels erster Essay über „Themen und Formen in der Kunst von Chagall" in der Zeitschrift *Cusztajer* (*Tsushtayer*), die sie zusammen mit Rachel Auerbach herausgab.[31] 1929 hielt Fogel auch Vorlesungen über polnische Literatur und Psychologie in Zakopane. 1930 wurde der zweite Essay von Dvoyra Fogel in der zweiten Ausgabe von *Tsushtayer* veröffentlicht. Dem folgte die Erscheinung ihres ersten Gedichtbandes *tog-figurn*. 1931 erschien die dritte Ausgabe von *Tsushtayer* mit Fogels neuen Publikationen. In demselben Jahr heiratete sie den Bauingenieur Schulim Barenbluth. 1934 wurde Fogels zweiter Gedichtband *manekinen* veröffentlicht und ein Jahr später erschien das Prosawerk *akacjes blien (Akacje kwitna)* auf Jiddisch und Polnisch.

Seit 1935 war Fogel Mitglied in der Gruppe jiddischer Avantgardisten von New York, mit denen sie bis zum Ausbruch des Zweiten Weltkrieges zusammenarbeitete. In der New Yorker Zeitschrift *Inzich* erschienen Fogels Prosawerke und Essays. 1936 kam Dvoyras Sohn Ascher-Anselm zur Welt. Die Ausgabe des für Herbst 1939 geplanten vierten Gedicht- und Prosabandes von Fogel blieb aus, da Polen 1939 von den deutschen Truppen besetzt wurde. Seitdem setzte sich Fogel für die bedürftigen jüdischen Künstler ein, die von der westlichen Grenze nach Lemberg geflohen waren.[32] Im Juni 1941 wurde auch Lemberg okkupiert. Im August 1942 wurde Dvoyra Fogel zusammen mit ihrem Mann und ihrem fünfjährigen Sohn im Lemberger Ghetto von den Nazis getötet.

Heute kennen vor allem die polnischen Leserinnen Dvoyra Fogels Werke. Viel weniger ist Fogel in der Ukraine oder in Russland bekannt, obwohl sie den Geschmack des kulturellen Lebens von Lemberg (Lviv) in den Dreißigern des letzten Jahrhunderts diktierte.[33] Die wenigen, die den Namen von Dvoyra Fogel schon gehört haben, kennen sie eher als Muse von Bruno Schulz.[34]

Die Monotonie der Wiederholungen

Dvoyra Fogel war sehr engagiert und tat auch viel dafür, dass ihre Werke verstanden werden. Sie suchte Kontakte, reiste viel und traf Leute. Trotzdem schrieb sie in einem Brief von 1938 an Bruno Schulz, wie gut es ist, ganz allein zu sein. „Da kann man gut sehen", fügte sie hinzu.[35] Die literarische Einsamkeit wählte Fogel bewusst, indem sie ihre Gedichte in jiddischer Sprache schrieb, die

---

[31] Kaszuba-Debska, „Дебора Фогель" [Debora Fogel].
[32] Kaszuba-Debska, „Дебора Фогель" [Debora Fogel].
[33] Пінчевська, „Світське єврейське" [Pynczewska, „Jüdische Kunst,"], 134-135.
[34] Пінчевська, „Світське єврейське" [Pynczewska, „Jüdische Kunst,"], 134-135.
[35] Kaszuba-Debska, „Дебора Фогель" [Debora Fogel].

für wenige Leserinnen und Literaturkennerinnen zugänglich war, und modernistische Richtungen vertrat, die am Rande des kulturellen Hauptstroms standen. Fogel suchte nämlich nach neuen künstlerischen Mitteln und einer Sprache, die die Lyrik mit bildender Kunst verbindet. Die Innovationen und Sprachversuche waren für den Kubismus vom Anfang des 20. Jahrhunderts typisch, jedoch bildete sich der künstlerische Weg Dvoyra Fogels aus ihren individuellen Reflexionen. Auch Bogdana (Dana) Pinchewska bezweifelte, „dass Debora von ihrer künstlerischen Umgebung gebildet wurde".[36]

Auf Grund von Fogels Essays und Briefen ist anzunehmen, dass ihre künstlerische Tätigkeit mit den theoretischen Studien verbunden war. Das zeigt sich zum Beispiel in Fogels Auffassung der sinnbildenden Funktion der Sprache.[37] In einem Brief an den Dichter Elieser Blum, der unter dem Pseudonym B. Alkvit ihr Rezensent bei der New Yorker jüdischen Zeitschrift *Inzich* war, schrieb Fogel zum Beispiel über die Rolle der Vergleichspartikel „wie" in ihren Collagen. Im Unterschied zur Metapher, so Fogel, sei der Vergleich ruhiger. Die Metapher lasse zwei Dinge verschwinden, indem sie sie zusammenschmelze. Der Vergleich würde die Dinge nur trennen, sodass beide trotzdem einander nah bleiben. Deshalb wählte Fogel den Vergleich und nicht die Metapher für ihre „Aufgaben".[38] Über das Verhältnis zu den kubistischen und surrealistischen Kunstrichtungen schrieb Fogel in demselben Brief folgendes:

> Ich bitte Sie, sich den Außenpuls und die Gedankenfolge meiner Collagen nochmal anzuhören. Dann werden Sie den Unterschied zwischen ihnen und den surrealistischen Montagen verstehen. Die Collagen-Methode kann verbinden. Jedoch genauso, wie sich die kubistischen Collagen von den surrealistischen unterscheiden, unterscheiden sich – vielleicht nicht so ausdrücklich – die Letzteren von den post-surrealistischen Collagen, wie ich mir meine Montagen zu bezeichnen erlaube. Ich halte diese Versuche für eine Übergangsform auf dem Weg zu den realistischen Montagen.[39]

---

[36] Пинчевская, *И вновь цветёт акация* [Pinchewska, *Die Akazien blühen wieder*], 2 (Übersetzung L. H.).

[37] Vgl. Kazimierz Ajdukiewich, „Sprache und Sinn," in: *Erkenntnis* IV (Leipzig 1934), 100-138. Ajdukiewich war einer der Philosophieprofessoren von Fogel.

[38] Пинчевская, *И вновь цветёт акация* [Pinchewska, *Die Akazien blühen wieder*], 2.

[39] Пинчевская, *И вновь цветёт акация* [Pinchewska, *Die Akazien blühen wieder*], 1-2 (Übersetzung L. H.).

Eigene Gedichte nannte Fogel Collagen, ihre Prosawerke, zum Beispiel *akacjes blien*, Montagen. In die Collagen brachte Fogel verschiedene Elemente der realen Welt wie Autoräder und Stein, Glas und Textilien ein, um die Texte so lebenstreu zu gestalten, wie es mit Hilfe einer Sprache möglich war. Aus diesem Grund griff sie auch zum Gebrauch unterschiedlicher Rhythmen innerhalb eines Gedichtes und verzichtete auf Reime. Und doch charakterisierte Fogels Gedichte eine dichterische Form, die mit Hilfe von lexikalen, grammatischen und phonetischen Parallelismen beziehungsweise Wiederholungen und einer alogisch erscheinenden, jedoch präzisen räumlichen Gestaltung von Strophen erreicht wurde.

Die Parallelismen sind nicht nur die uralten Mittel der Metrik. Jurij Lotman beschrieb sie als „binäre Kombinationen", in denen ein Element durch das analoge andere verstanden wird.[40] Er betonte auch, dass der Klang des Wortes eine besondere Rolle in der poetischen Rede spiele. Während es der Sprache eigentlich egal sei, wie der Inhalt lautet, habe die phonetische Form der Lyrik immer einen semantischen Wert, was bedeutet, dass die Wörter phonetisch zusammenhängen. Sowohl phonetisch als auch semantisch sei die poetische Struktur viel intensiver als die alltägliche Rede.[41]

Die Intensität charakterisiert die Lyrik von Fogel. Schon die ersten Worte ihrer Gedichte können die Leserschaft anziehen, überraschen und in die Welt ihrer Collagen versetzen. Fogel selbst nannte die Wiederholungen in ihren Werken „vayse verter" (weiße Wörter),[42] die keine eigentliche Bedeutung hätten und allein dem poetischen Ziel des ganzen Werkes dienten. Dieses Ziel kann auf Grund Fogels Äußerung über den dichterischen Stil als Streben nach der Trennung der Statik-Lyrik von der Lyrik der Dynamik erklärt werden.[43]

Das Gedicht „zontik fun farstot-hayzer" (*Sonntag der vorstädtischen Häuser*)[44] aus dem Band *tog-figurn* von Dvoyra Fogel fällt zum Beispiel vor allem durch den Gebrauch der sich wiederholenden Elemente wie Wagen, Räder, „Reparaturwerkstatt", „Reparaturladen" und „Garagenhaus" auf, die in der Lyrik sonst nicht oft vorkommen. Die Maschinen, darunter die Automobile,

---

[40] Ю. М. Лотман, *Структура художественного текста: Анализ поэтического текста* [Juri M. Lotman, Die Struktur des künstlerischen Textes: Analyse des poetischen Textes] (Просвещение: Ленинград 1972), 90-91.

[41] Лотман, *Структура* [Lotman, Struktur], 90-91.

[42] „Weiße Wörter". Любас [Lubas], „Debora Fogel, ‚vayse verter'".

[43] Любас [Lubas], „Debora Fogel, ‚vayse verter'".

[44] „Sunday of the Suburban Houses": Anastasiya Lyubas (Übers.), in PaknTreger Magazine of the Yiddish Book Center (https://www.yiddishbookcenter.org/language-literature-culture/pakn-treger/2018-pakn-treger-translation-issue/sunday-suburban-houses, 5 November 2020).

faszinierten die Futuristen, sie wurden sogar zum Anlass der Veröffentlichung ihres Manifestes.[45] Doch war „a geler vogn" (der gelbe Wagen) für Fogel ein Element der modernen Banalität. Sie verband alle Elemente in einem Bild, um die Monotonie des siebten Tages im Leben einer Vorstadt darzustellen.

zontik fun farstot-hayzer

far der kalekhgrine vogn-reparatur-verkstot
ligt 1 royt rod
un a geler vogn mit 3 royte reder.

far a geln hoyz, far dem erstn und tsveytn groen hoyz
sitsn dem gantsn sibetn tog long:
drey, vir, finef klumpn fun geln teyg mit glos-oygn,
reder vos hobn nisht wuhin tsu gayn.

un kayn vogn fart nisht aroyn, kayner aroys
in dem roytn garozsh-hoyz on fenster

ober montik 6 a zayger fri
geyen wayter in der vaytkayt fun etlekhen meter:
der griner reparotur-lodn, der royter garozsh,
groe hayzer, vogn mit 4 reder un klumpn mit fis.

vider is groys di חלל-koyl:
kon oyfnemen hayser, vogen, layber.

Sonntag der vorstädtischen Häuser [46]

Vor der mattgrünen Wagenreparatur-Werkstatt
Liegen 1 rotes Rad
Und ein gelber Wagen mit 3 roten Rädern.

Vor dem gelben Haus, dem ersten, und dem zweiten, dem grauen
Sitzen den ganzen siebten Tag lang
Drei, vier, fünf Klumpen aus gelbem Teig mit glasigen Augen,
Räder, die nirgendwohin zu gehen haben.

Und kein Wagen fährt darein, und keiner daraus
In dem roten fensterlosen Garage-Haus

---

[45] Albrecht Koschorke, „Die Männer und die Moderne," in: Wolfgang Asholt und Walter Fähnders (ed.), *Der Blick vom Wolkenkratzer: Avantgarde, Avantgardekritik, Avantgardeforschung* (Editions Rodopi B.V.: Amsterdam und Atlanta 2000), 141-162, hier: 144.

[46] Übersetzung L. H.

Aber am Montag, um 6 Uhr früh
Gehen alle um etliche Meter weiter:
Der grüne Reparatur-Laden, die rote Garage,
Die grauen Häuser, der Wagen mit 4 Rädern und die Klumpen mit Füßen.

Der kuglige Raum ist wieder groß:
Er kann wieder Häuser, Wagen und Leiber einnehmen.

Schon die einführende dreizeilige Strophe schafft ein Bild der Erstarrung, welches in der zweiten Strophe noch eindeutiger wird. Der dritte Teil des Gedichtes betont die Monotonie und stärkt das Gefühl der Ausweglosigkeit durch Anhäufung von Negationsmitteln.

Einerseits generieren die sich wiederholenden Präpositionen, Ziffern und Zahlen, Farben und Dinge die Monotonie des Textes. Andererseits erzeugt die regelmäßige Rekursivität im Text auch das Gefühl der Bewegung.[47] Als würden die Laute (darunter der gleichpositionierte Konsonant „g" im dritten Teil) über die Zeilen rollen. Wenn die Wiederholungen mit geringen Änderungen ergänzt werden, wird die Wahrnehmung der „statischen Bewegung"[48] noch deutlicher:

Der Wagen hat in der vierten Strophe schon „4 Räder", der Uhrzeiger steht auf „6" im Vergleich zu den Ziffern „1" und „3" im ersten Teil. Das Verb „gehen" wird im vierten Teil mit dem Wort der Fortbewegung „weiter" kombiniert, die Klumpen, die bisher den ganzen Tag dasaßen, bekommen Füße. Alles spricht für eine Bewegung, die sich am Ende doch als monoton – oder periodisch – erweist. Denn alles wiederholt sich.[49]

Der Wortschatz des Gedichtes scheint karg und viel zu banal für ein lyrisches Werk zu sein. Hinter der Banalität versteckt sich jedoch sorgfältige Erwägung der Verhältnisse zwischen den geometrischen Formen und Farben, der Dynamik und der Statik.[50] Die Darstellung der langweiligen Vorstadt wirkt am Ende grotesk, parodiemäßig und irritierend. Die Wiederholung eines Wortes (oder einer Wortgruppe) mit kleinen Änderungen ist übrigens für die biblischen Texte typisch. Der ungarische Sprachwissenschaftler und Psychoanalytiker Iván Fónagy nannte solche Art der Wiederholung den „Gedankenrhythmus", der die

---

[47] Fónagy Iván, „A költőmű ritmusairól" in: *Magyar Műhely* 27 (Juni 1968), 59-75.
[48] Fónagy, „A költőmű", 70.
[49] Das hebräische Wort („Raum") wurde in der jiddischen Variante nicht transkribiert, um auf den Hebraismus aufmerksam zu machen.
[50] Любас [Lubas], „Debora Fogel, ‚vayse verter'".

Züge eines Themas über mehrere Verse hindurch verbindet.[51] Bei Fogel sind sogar synonyme Wiederholungen zu finden, in denen semantisch analoge Wörter einander phonetisch ähneln. Zum Beispiel wurde das Wort „kugelförmig" in einer Zeile des Gedichtes „papir-figurn-panoram" des Bandes *manekinen* zweimal wiederholt: „di kugelike panoram mit papir-lalkes, di koylike panoram!"[52] Einmal klingt es als „kugelike", das zweite Mal als „koylike". Das Wort „koyl" ist ein Synonym für „kugel" (Kugel), nur kommt es aus der ukrainischen oder weißrussischen Sprache ins Jiddische und ist für die Ostjüdinnen verständlich.

Bemerkenswert ist auch, dass Fogel gleiche Worte in mehreren Gedichten wiederholt. Das Wort „garnisht" (gar nichts) in Verbindung mit dem unbestimmten Zahlwort „mer" (mehr) wiederholte sie in mindestens drei Gedichten aus dem Zyklus „trinklider" (1930-1932) des Bandes *manekinen* und jedes Mal war es das Schlusswort des Textes. Im Gedicht „trinklid" wiederholt sich „un mer garnisht" als Konklusion der Statik des Dargestellten im letzten dreizeiligen Teil: „un mer garnisht/un mer garnisht tun/vorum voszhe kon men mer noch tun."[53]

Die traurige Statik spürt man auch im Gedicht „a lid vegn oygn" (Ein Lied über Augen), dessen Schlusszeile das Element „garnisht" enthält: „fun velkhe s'kon garnisht mer kumen".[54] Das dritte Mal findet man „garnisht" im Gedicht „farbn-lid in zummer" (Farbenlied im Sommer): „mer kumt garnisht far."[55] Wie in den ersten beiden Fällen steht „garnisht" hier am Ende des Textes. Dass Fogel so oft zu diesem Schlusswort griff, könnte auf ein persönliches Trauma zurückgeführt werden. Freud erklärte die Wiederholungen in der Redeweise einiger Patienten mit dem Kriegstrauma. Unbewusst würden die Menschen nach der Wiederherstellung des früheren Zustandes streben, was sich in dem Wiederholungszwang äußere.[56] Bei Fogel könnte der Wiederholungszwang mit

---

[51] Iván Fónagy, „A halálösztön és a nyelv dinamikája," in: Thalassa 2-3 (August 1997) 33-41, hier: 35

[52] „[...] das kugelförmige Panorama mit Papierpuppen, das kugelige Panorama!" (Übersetzung: Anna Maja Misiak) Anna Maja Misiak, „lider/Gedichte. dvoyra fogel/Debora Vogel" in: *Variations* 15 (2007) 213-222, hier 218 (https://www.ingentaconnect.com/content/plg/var/2007/00002007/00000015/art00016?crawler=true, 11 November 2020).

[53] „Und weiter nichts/und weiter nichts tun/was kann man denn noch mehr tun." Kohlbauer-Fritz, *In a Schtodt woss schtarbt,* 138-139.

[54] Misiak, „lider/Gedichte," 214.

[55] Misiak, „lider/Gedichte," 216.

[56] Fónagy, „A halálösztön," 36.

der damaligen Verarbeitung der Trauer über den Tod ihres Vaters erklärt werden. Vielleicht versuchte sie sich selbst zu überzeugen, dass gegen Tod gar nichts zu tun war.

Dvoyra Fogels Kampf um die Identität und Gleichberechtigung

Alle Facetten des Lebens und der literarischen Tätigkeit von Dvoyra Fogel können in einem kurzen Artikel nicht erschlossen werden. Die Geometrie der Körper, der eigenartige Gebrauch von Satzzeichen sowie der Farben in der verdinglichten Welt ihrer Gedichte wurden von anderen Autorinnen, zum Beispiel Katrin Hillgruber und Bogdana (Dana) Pinchewska,[57] mehr oder weniger ausführlich besprochen.

Man hätte noch über die eventuelle Weiblichkeit[58] von Fogels Poesie sprechen können, doch fand ich keine weibliche Narration in ihren Gedichten.[59] Das narrative Element war in Fogels Gedichten überhaupt kaum vorhanden, denn Fogel sprach nicht zu einem bestimmten Thema, sondern sie schuf eine neue Sprache im Prozess der Dichtung, die eher als geschlechtsneutral bezeichnet werden könnte. Das Einzige, was den damaligen gesellschaftlichen Stereotypien der Weiblichkeit hätte entsprechen können, ist die Statik von Fogels Lyrik im Unterschied zur angeblichen Dynamik der Männlichkeit. Die literarischen Geschlechter dürfte Fogel selten konstruiert haben, ich fand nur einen solchen Versuch im „trinklid" (Trinklied) aus dem Band von Kohlbauer-Fritz.[60] Die Frauen wurden in diesem Gedicht durch ihre Samtkleider, passiv und unpersönlich dargestellt, als wären sie nur dekorative und weiche Figuren neben den tatkräftigen Männern mit „streichelnden, traurigen Händen".[61]

Zur Kongruenz zwischen Fogels Auftreten als Frau und ihrer Dichtung ist nicht viel zu sagen, denn es fehlt an zeitgenössischen Berichten. Nach der

---

[57] Katrin Hillgruber, „Die synästhetische Poetin," in: *Der Tagesspiegel* vom 08.03.2017 (https://www.tagesspiegel.de/kultur/geometrie-des-verzichts-von-debora-vogel-die-synaesthetische-poetin/19472968.html, 11 November 2020); Пинчевская, *И вновь цветёт акация* [Pinchewska, *Die Akazien blühen wieder*].

[58] Im Sinne der Zugehörigkeit zu einem biologischen Geschlecht.

[59] Anja Utler, *,Weibliche Antworten' auf ,menschliche Fragen'? Zur Kategorie Geschlecht in der russischen Lyrik (Z. Gippius, E. Guro, A. Achmatova, M. Cvetaeva)* (Diss., Regensburg 2003), unveröffentlichtes Manuskript, 29-30 (https://epub.uni-regensburg.de/10231/1/Utler_Weiblich%20Antworten.pdf, 22 November 2020).

[60] Kohlbauer-Fritz, *In a Schtodt woss schtarbt*, 138-139.

[61] Ebenda (Übersetzung L. H.).

Erinnerung von Melech Ravitch wirkte Fogel als eine sehr begabte, gebildete und lebendige junge Frau „aus guter Familie" auf die Gesellschaft, die sie mit ihrem Intellekt begeisterte.[62] Fogels Philosophie-Doktorat dürfte Ravich imponiert haben, da er dieses Detail mit gewisser Bewunderung betonte.[63] Er erwähnte auch Fogels angenehme, zärtliche Stimme und dass sie Jiddisch, das nicht ihre Muttersprache, besonders liebte und sorgfältig pflegte. Über skandalöse Beziehungen von Fogel gibt es keine Berichte, zu ihrem biologischen Geschlecht stand sie im Unterschied zu einigen anderen Avantgardistinnen eindeutig.[64]

Fogel lebte wie eine Jüdin aus einer traditionellen bürgerlichen Familie, aber dieses Leben befriedigte ihre intellektuellen Ansprüche anscheinend nicht. Sie hätte mehr freien Raum für künstlerische und wissenschaftliche Entfaltung gebraucht, worüber sie auch ihrem Freund A. Lyels schrieb:

> Solche Menschen wie Sie braucht die jiddische Literatur besonders […] ich bewundere Ihre ständige Bereitschaft und Verantwortlichkeit. Dieses Gefühl kommt teilweise davon, dass ich diese Begabung auch habe, nur kann sie nicht so sehr zum Ausdruck kommen deshalb, weil […] ich würde mir meine Meinung erlauben: wegen unglücklichen Glückes, welches das Dasein einer Frau bedeutet. Die „metaphysische" Rolle der Frau ist im Strom der erschöpfenden Kleinigkeiten hinzuschwimmen.[65]

Ihren Platz als Dichterin und Wissenschaftlerin wollte Fogel in der Avantgarde finden, die eine revolutionäre Wahrnehmung der Realität spiegelte. In allen Richtungen dieser Bewegung wirkten viele Frauen mit, dennoch war die Avantgarde keine Ausnahme von den damaligen Versuchen der modernen Rhetorik der „Vermännlichung" der Literatur. Diese Rhetorik lautete: „Einfach, klar und mannhaft".[66] Die Stimmung in der europäischen Literatur war frauenfeindlich. Als Beispiel könnte das Pamphlet des Kunsthistorikers Wilhelm Worringer angeführt werden, der sogar über einen literarischen Gender-Krieg schrieb: „Dieser Krieg ist über alle Gegensätze der Rassen und Nationen hinaus zu etwas viel Schlimmeren [sic] geworden: zu einer Art von

---

[62] Kaszuba-Debska, „Дебора Фогель" [Debora Fogel].
[63] Kaszuba-Debska, „Дебора Фогель" [Debora Fogel].
[64] Zum Beispiel Zinaida Gippiues. Utler, „Weibliche Antworten," 43.
[65] Kaszuba-Debska, „Дебора Фогель" [Debora Fogel].
[66] Koschorke, „Die Männer," 149.

Kampf zwischen zwei verschiedenen Geschlechtern."[67] Die Frauenstimme in der Literatur wurde als „Hysterie unserer Feinde" bezeichnet.[68] Mit Verbitterung äußerte sich Dvoyra Fogel über die Benachteiligung von Frauen in der künstlerischen Tätigkeit:

> Und noch die berufliche Tätigkeit mit der so miserablen Entlohnung, die man sich bei zwei Artikeln pro Monat nur vorstellen kann, beansprucht mich völlig, während die männliche Konkurrenz bei uns es nicht erlaubt, dass eine Frau die Position ergreift. In einigen Zeitungen hat sich zum Beispiel eingebürgert, dass Männer, sogar die geistlosen und graphomanen, honoriert, die Frauen dagegen mit Honneurs anerkannt werden.[69]

Als jiddisch-schaffende Dichterin und Schriftstellerin blieb Fogel am Rand der avantgardistischen Welt. Als Dichterin des städtischen Alltags, den Fogel ohne besondere Tragik fast sachlich und kühl schilderte, stand sie allein unter den damaligen jiddischen Lyrikerinnen. Doch gab Fogel den Kampf um ihren individuellen Weg in der jiddischen Kultur nie auf und arbeitete hart weiter, auch wenn sie so oft über Ausweglosigkeit und Verzicht schrieb.[70]

Larissza Hrotkó, PhD, zurzeit pensioniert, davor: Unterricht an der Jüdischen Universität-Rabbinerinstitut (ORZSE) in Budapest, Arbeit in der wissenschaftlichen Forschungsgruppe. Eine der letzten Publikationen von ihr war „Streit und Sorge um die Identität einer jüdischen Gemeinschaft" in: Judith Gruber, Sebastian Pittl, Stefan Silber, Christian Tauchner (ed.), „Identitäre Versuchungen" (Verlagsgruppe Mainz in Aachen: 2019). Eine der letzten Arbeiten war der Beitrag „Jüdische Gemeinschaften im Kontext des ungarischen Rechtspopulismus und Ethnonationalismus. Einblicke in die politische Instrumentalisierung des Glaubens von rechts außen" im bald erscheinenden Symposion-Band „Widerstand erforderlich? Identitäts- und Geschlechterkämpfe im Horizont von Rechtspopulismus und christlichem Fundamentalismus in Europa heute" der Grazer Universität von Oktober 2020.

---

[67] Koschorke, „Die Männer," 147.

[68] Koschorke, „Die Männer," 147.

[69] Kaszuba-Debska, „Дебора Фогель" [Debora Fogel]. Die Übersetzung ist teilweise aus dem Artikel von Katrin Hillgruber, „Die synästhetische Poetin," in: *Der Tagesspiegel* vom 08.03.2017 (https://www.tagesspiegel.de/kultur/geometrie-des-verzichts-von-debora-vogel-die-synaesthetische-poetin/19472968.html, 11 November 2020).

[70] Wie zum Beispiel im Gedicht „Das Lied über Augen": Misiak, „lider/Gedichte," 214-215.

Journal of the European Society of Women in Theological Research 29 (2021) 151-155.
doi: 10.2143/ESWTR.29.0.3289665

BOOK REVIEW

Julie Hopkins, *'The Wings of the Spirit:' Exploring Feminine Symbolism in Early Pneumatology: A Reassessment of a Key Metaphor in the Spiritual Teachings of the* Macarian Homilies *in the Light of Early Syriac Christian Tradition* (Peeters: Leuven 2020).

Hopkins could have drawn bold conclusions from her meticulous investigation, published as the first book in a new ESWTR publication series *Studies in Religion*. But she abstains, which seems very prudent from an academic point of view, especially because her study inscribes itself into a well-researched area, namely the Fathers of the Church. This does not mean, however, that other feminists may not be tempted to work out new hypotheses on the basis of the solid work of Hopkins.

Julie Hopkins holds a Ph.D. from the University of Bristol (1989) and a postdoctoral degree from the University of Wales in Lampeter (D.D.Lic., 2010). She describes her own journey as springing from a life-long interest in early Christian religious experiences and Women's Studies, beginning with research projects on the Celtic hermit saints of the 4th-6th centuries, going to the desert fathers and mothers of Egypt, and finally to the Syrian Orient (2020: IX). From 1988 till 1999 Hopkins held the first post as lecturer and researcher in Feminist Theology at the Faculty of Divinity at the Free University of Amsterdam, and is a Baptist pastor. Living in Canterbury, she is now also engaged in spiritual counseling in Roman Catholic, Orthodox as well as Protestant churches in GB.

Hopkins' first book *Towards a Feminist Christology: Jesus of Nazareth, European Women and the Christological Crisis* (1994) is not just a feminist Christology, drawing upon extensive reading into the feminist theology of the 1970s, 1980s, and the beginning of the 1990s, as the title suggests. Hopkins also raised some of the points developed in her present work: notably how did the intellectual climate of the councils of Nicaea and Chalcedon, informed as it was by Neo- and Middle Platonic thought, still succeed in affirming the incarnation of God in the flesh? Through stressing the sex of Jesus, *homoousios* (1994: 91f)!

The main scholarly debate in which Hopkins engages in this book is about pneumatology. The question is: Were the Cappadocian Fathers only inspired by platonic philosophy or did early Syrian theology also play a role? This is of course important because the Cappadocian Fathers were the main actors in the ecumenical councils of Nicaea and Constantinople, which also inform present day Christianity. When the Nicene Creed in 325 was negotiated in order to reach religious consensus in the Roman Empire, the Holy Spirit was included "almost as an afterthought", as Hopkins puts it (p. 55). "We believe in the Holy Spirit." The main battle in Nicaea was to defeat Arianism and to reach a consensus about the full divinity of Jesus Christ and his consubstantiality with the Father, *homoousios*. The Cappadocian Fathers, however, became gradually convinced that God was One and was to be seen as a Trinity of Persons. The Spirit, *Constantinopolitanum* said following Gregory of Nyssa, is "the Lord, the Giver of Life, who proceeds from the Father; who with the Father and the Son together is worshipped and glorified. Who has spoken through the prophets." The Holy Spirit was affirmed as fully divine, – divinely patriarchal, one may add.

A different story could be read if the influence of Syriac, and more specifically Macarian, writing on the Spirit would be taken into account. Hopkins' claim is that, contrary to the main scholarly debate since Jaeger (1954), Gregory of Nyssa may not have been influenced mainly by Platonic thought but also by the "Mesopotamians". Actually, Hopkins tends to agree with Plested (2004), that the influence – at least in the later years of Gregory's life – may have gone the other way round: that Gregory had read Macarius. And Macarius, now believed to be Symeon of (the Greek speaking) Mesopotamia, was deeply informed by Eastern Syrian tradition in his *Epistola Magna* and his Homilies, *Macriana*.

By the end of the 4th century, a pneuma-eschatology had developed in the Syrian tradition as can be seen in the anonymous "Book of Steps" and in (the writings of) Aphrahat. Because the Spirit is gendered in the feminine in Syriac and Aramaic and verbs are conjugated according to gender, the Holy Spirit and Her actions informed the theological imagination: the "hovering" wings of the Spirit in the theology of Ephrem the Syrian were associated with virtually every aspect of the sacramental life of the Church.

Macarius has been considered one of the leaders of the Messalianism, a charismatic movement condemned in 390 at the synod in Side. Hopkins, however, follows Maloney (1992), who describes the monastic life regulated in Macarius' *Epistola Magna,* as "a very loose monastic organization with the prime accent on the development of interior humility and purity of heart to gain incessant prayer" (p. 25, note 6). And she agrees with Plested (2004), who understands *Epistola Magna* as "a kind of manifesto", with a vision for a monasticism based upon inward religious experiences (p. 25). But Macarius wrote in Greek and probably came from the Greek speaking part of Syria, west of Euphrates. As a teacher of religious experiences, he developed a new theological language in order to grasp the interior processes known in Syriac theology, and translated it for the Greek speaking parts of the Roman Empire.

Hopkins traces how Macarius understands the maternal functions of the Holy Spirit: "The maternal Spirit is described comforting her newborn baby, suckling it with milk from her breast. She cuddles her infant and when it falls over and cries, with loving pity she picks it up and nurses it. She teaches it to talk in her own mother-tongue and gradually weans it from milk to solid food." (p. 31) Just like the mother-bird teaches her fledglings until they are able to fly, the Holy Spirit is raising the heart of the Christian, finally making him able to fly away to the world above, the heavenly church.

In Macarius' teaching the Spirit is seen as the divine principle of action. The Christian does not "fashion wings for himself" (Origen). Nor is the Christian's moral worthiness a prerequisite for the reception of the Holy Spirit (Basil). Moral empowerment comes by divine grace. The protective wings of the spirit aid the struggling Christian in keeping the commandments of Christ to do good works, the wings of the Spirit will offer protection and escape from enemies, as well as "single mindedness" and illumination in prayer. The Wings of the Spirit may work in the "intellectual spirit" and on the day of resurrection the Holy Spirit may rise from within "covering and warming the bodies of the saints". This resurrection experience may even be anticipated in the present life of the perfect (p. 43).

Plato in *Phaedrus* 245c-249d claimed that the philosopher could re-grow the immortal wings he once possessed in pre-existence by rational detachment from the material world and contemplation of the eternal Forms, while Macarius stressed that if the Christian does not have wings given to him by divine grace, he cannot "fly into the divine air and enjoy the liberty of the Holy Spirit [...] Let us pray to God to give us 'the wings of the dove'." (p. 42).

The question is, then, how the Syriac and Greek wings metaphors were synthesized? According to Gregory's younger brother Basil, the Greek LXX translation of Gen 1:2b lacked the Hebrew metaphorical meanings connected with the Spirit of God "who broods like a bird over its young". And through Basil the Syriac tradition of the Holy Spirit as a mother bird hovering over the waters of creation entered into the Christian traditions. Basil did not grant consubstantiality to the Spirit. But after the death of Basil, Gregory, the older brother, became a leading proponent of Trinitarian theology in Constantinople 381 where he underlined the fully creative activity of the Spirit and therefore also vindicated the Spirit's title to full divinity.

Gregory in Constantinople praised the Mesopotamians: "they do not study rhetoric; but they have such power over the spirits [...] that they expel demons not through syllogistic arts but through the power of faith" (p. 62). Hopkins therefore agrees with Staats (1967) and Plested (2004) that this could indicate that Gregory became increasingly influenced by Macarian writing in the latter part of his life. Perhaps this was also the reason why he did not participate at the council of Side (390) where Messalianism was condemned. Gregory might have read Macarius in the meantime.

Hopkins, following Meredith (1999: 85) does see a "Platonic theorem" at the centre of Gregory's spiritual writings: "the upward march of the created spirit to knowledge and enjoyment of God occasioned by the loveliness of God and demanding moral perfection as well as mental abstraction." (p. 65f) In Plato, however, the "wings of the soul" are pre-existent and immortal while the Cappadocians saw these inborn wings as a metaphor for the image and likeness of God lost by Adam. Awakened to rationality and spiritual insight, "the wings of the soul" may aid the person toward virtue and moral perfection.

If Macarius' "wings of the Spirit" had been borrowed from Gregory's "neo-Platonic" usage of the "wings of the soul", however, one could have expected Gregory's "Platonic theorem" to shine through. But it does not. This, according to Hopkins, "calls for a reassessment of the perceived wisdom that Macarian wings language was simply an appropriation of Gregorian usage" (p. 67).

A "cross-fertilization" between the Gregory and Macarius' teaching may have taken place. We know that Gregory read Macarius' *Epistola Magna* and conversely Macarius may have read Gregory's *Commentary on the Song of Songs*. Hopkins therefore concludes that the "very fluidity of the Syriac metaphor of the 'wings of the Spirit' as interpreted by the wordsmith Macarius made it a flexible spiritual symbol which could function as a bridge between Greek and Syriac cultural and religious traditions" (p. 74).

Hopkins' book is an impressive scholarly work. I would recommend that it – including the texts used by the author in her work as a spiritual counselor – be published and addressed to the general public. On a more feminist scholarly note, I would like to hear presentations by and conversations between Julie Hopkins and prof. Silvia Schroer whose work on pneumatology in her *Wisdom Has Built Her House* (2000) may supply the work of Julie Hopkins with interesting historical perspectives on early Syrian theology.

In her preface Hopkins states that "The feminine name and functions of the Spirit helped to shift my theology from a critical feminist deconstruction of patriarchal and androcentric God-language towards a reclaiming of my Christian heritage as a spiritual resource for today. However, it still continues to raise the whole question of how to deal with the issue of gender in translation and how to integrate the feminine divine into church liturgy, hymnody and preaching" (ix). Hopkins' book worked exactly like this for me: it rekindled my love for theology – complicated and exciting as it is. But I would have liked to see a feminist evaluation of the – Mary Daly would have called it "stolen mythic power" – which this investigation into the Syriac versus the Platonic inspired theology of the Spirit also calls for. Is this not our prophetic task today? Is this not what She wants from us?

Lene Sjørup, pastor, Ph.D.

Hopkins, Julie M., *Towards a Feminist Christology. Jesus of Nazareth, European Women and the Christological Crisis* (Kok Pharos: Kampen 1994; and William B. Eerdmans 1995).

Jaeger, Werner, *Two Rediscovered Works of Ancient Christian Literature: Gregory of Nyssa and Macarius* (Brill: Leiden 1954).

Maloney, George, *Pseudo-Macarius: The Fifty Spiritual Homilies and the Great Letter* (Paulist Press: Mahwah 1992), Classics of Western Spirituality.

Meredith, Anthony, *Gregory of Nyssa* (Routledge: London, 1999).

Plested, Marcus, *The Macarian Legacy: The Place of Macarius-Symeon in the Eastern Christian Tradition* (OUP: Oxford 2004), Oxford Theological Monographs.

Schroer, Sylvia, *Wisdom Has Built Her House: Studies on the Figure of Sophia in the Bible* (The Liturgical Press: Collegeville, MN 2000).

Staats, R. "Die Asketen aus Mesopotamien in der Rede des Gregor von Nyssa, *In suam ordinationem*," in: *Vigiliae Christianae* 21 (1967), 165-179.

ESWTR Journal – editorial board members